The eBay Business Answer Book

The eBay Business Answer Book

THE 350 MOST FREQUENTLY ASKED QUESTIONS ABOUT MAKING BIG MONEY ON eBAY

Cliff Ennico

AMACOM
American Management Association
New York • Atlanta • Brussels • Chicago • Mexico City • San Francisco
Shanghai • Tokyo • Toronto • Washington, D.C.

Special discounts on bulk quantities of AMACOM books are available to corporations, professional associations, and other organizations. For details, contact Special Sales Department, AMACOM, a division of American Management Association, 1601 Broadway, New York, NY 10019.
Tel.: 212-903-8316. Fax: 212-903-8083.
Website: www. amacombooks.org

Library of Congress Cataloging-in-Publication Data

Ennico, Clifford R.
The eBay business answer book : the 350 most frequently asked questions about making big money on eBay / Cliff Ennico.
p. cm.
Includes index.
ISBN-13: 978-0-8144-0045-6
ISBN-10: 0-8144-0045-0
1. eBay (Firm) 2. Internet auctions. 3. Internet auctions—Law and legislation—United States. 4. Electronic commerce. 5. Electronic commerce—Taxation—United States. I. Title.

HF5478.E5757 2008
658.8′7—dc22 2008007006

Printed in the United States of America.

Printing number

10 9 8 7 6 5 4 3 2 1

To the hundreds of wonderful eBayers around the world who take precious time away from their businesses and lives every day, without compensation or reward, to help out the confused, the struggling, and the just plain inexperienced by patiently answering their questions on eBay's chat rooms, discussion boards, and online Answer Center. You are the unsung saints of the eBay community and are among the most beautiful human beings in cyberspace. Even when you're wrong . . . ☺.

Contents

Acknowledgments

Any book is a team effort, and *The eBay Business Answer Book* would not have been possible without the support, friendship, inspiration, love, and occasional "noodging" of these individuals, among others. My many thanks to:

- Janelle Elms, noted eBay author and my "partner in crime" on the eBay University tour, for being such a great resource on all things eBay (www.janelleelms.com)
- Catherine Seda, Internet marketing guru extreme (www.catherineseda.com), for teaching me how to seduce spiders (the online variety . . . I think)
- The eBay Certified Education Specialists around the country who shared with me their answers to the toughest eBay questions, but particularly my airplane buddy Jack Waddick of Chicago, Illinois (www.oakviewtraining.com), "ghost leg video queen" Cindy Shebley of Everett, Washington (www.clovercitysells.com), and my adopted stepparents Marcia Cooper and Harvey Levine, of Fort Lee, New Jersey (www.generalenterprises.net)
- Robin Cowie, Chris Malta, and Colette Marshall of Worldwide Brands, Inc. (www.worldwidebrands.com), and Peter Zapf of Global Sources (www.globalsources.com), for becoming the virtual coauthors of Chapter 3 of this book, on product sourcing (and a special thank-you to Rob for offering to cast me as an extra in his next killer-aliens-from-outer-space movie)

- Jacquie Flynn, my editor at AMACOM Books, for believing that a lawyer can actually write about things other than law and taxes

and

- Most important, my wife, Dolores, for letting me keep most of the stuff I buy on eBay

• • • Introduction

Not too long ago, it would have been considered a contradiction in terms—or oxymoron—to refer to an "eBay business."

When eBay first got off the ground in the mid-1990s, it was considered a fun thing: "Oh, look, Irma, we can sell stuff from the attic and actually make a few bucks without all of the hassle of doing a garage sale!"

But then people got hooked: "Gee, Irma, there's somebody in Timbuktu who's actually willing to pay us five bucks plus shipping for that old, broken chair we thought was worthless. . . . Is there any more stuff around here we need to get rid of?"

Then people realized they could make serious money selling stuff on eBay:"Irma, we've made $30,000 in six months selling on eBay, so I'm quitting my day job. By the way, have you seen Junior around lately? Oh . . . well, okay, but you did get the buyer's PayPal payment before you shipped him, didn't you? I would hate to have to eat the return postage . . ."

And so you have it. Today there are about 1 million people in the United States alone making a full-time or part-time living selling things on eBay, the world's largest online retailer, to eBay's more than 233 million unique registered users worldwide.

But making the transition from an eBay selling hobby to a real online e-commerce business isn't easy. You will have questions, and *The eBay Business Answer Book* is here to help you answer them.

Questions? You Have Questions?

Any professional speaker knows that the scariest part of any talk, panel, or presentation is the question-and-answer period at the end, because this is the only part of the program you cannot control—anything can happen here, from the sublime to the ridiculous. One of the key performance skills of any speaker lies in how he or she handles questions from the audience, because it's being done in real time without a safety net.

As a faculty member of eBay University for the past several years, I have had the privilege of teaching an "eBay for Business" class to thousands of eBayers around the United States. I have been asked literally hundreds of questions, and after a while, like any speaker, I noticed that the same questions keep coming up over and over again, especially from newbie, or inexperienced, sellers.

I have spoken to other eBay University instructors as well as many of eBay's Certified Education Specialists around the country (see Appendix A for more information about these folks), and they have shared similar experiences and confirmed my suspicion that eBay entrepreneurs keep asking the same questions over and over again.

This book is a collection of FAQs—frequently asked questions—that many newbie and experienced eBay sellers are getting stuck on and that aren't always answered in other eBay books or on the eBay website.

The Questions You Should Be Asking When Running an eBay Business

The questions you should, and sooner or later will, ask when you start taking your eBay selling seriously as a real business fall into a number of common categories:

- Choosing the right stuff to sell on eBay and finding the right sources for your eBay inventory
- Registering your business for federal, state, and local taxes

- Knowing what you can't legally sell on eBay
- Making sure your eBay listings don't create problems for buyers or eBay
- Making sure all your eBay listings (or as many as possible) sell through to buyers so you don't have to relist the items
- Dealing with difficult, or downright crazy, buyers
- Understanding and complying with eBay's policies and User Agreement
- Knowing when you can (and can't) back out of a deal if you've made a mistake (or get a better offer)
- Knowing what taxes you have to pay, how much, and to whom
- Knowing how to report your eBay selling income and expenses for tax purposes
- Knowing when to charge your buyers sales taxes
- Knowing what you can (and cannot) deduct for tax purposes
- Understanding how to set up and market an eBay Store
- Using search engine optimization and search engine advertising (they are two different things, did you know that?) to drive traffic to your eBay listings and eBay Store
- Keeping accurate and thorough books and records that track your eBay selling profits and losses and other key financial data
- Selling to buyers overseas on eBay
- Dealing with partners, employees, and independent contractors
- Coping with multiple businesses, when selling on eBay isn't the only thing you do to make money

The questions in *The eBay Business Answer Book* are organized along these lines, so you can find the answers you need as quickly as possible.

Why a Book, When I Can Get All the Answers I Need on the eBay Site?

When you come right down to it, eBay is really two things:

1. It is a Fortune 100 corporation based in San Jose, California.
2. It is a community of buyers and sellers worldwide who engage in commerce on eBay.

One of the amazing things about eBay is that if you get stuck on something and can't find the answer anywhere else on the eBay website (see Appendix B for a step-by-step guide on how to do this), you can ask the entire eBay community for help, and you will actually get answers from them. Furthermore, some of the answers (actually, most of them) are right!

The Community section of eBay's website contains several important resources for eBay sellers. There are discussion boards, where eBay members exchange views on just about every aspect of eBay selling and buying. There is an Answer Center, where sellers and buyers can ask questions of other eBay members and (most of the time) get the right answers. There are Groups, where eBay sellers in a particular country or region of the United States, or with a particular common interest (such as eBayers working from their homes, eBayers who want to share their favorite recipes, or eBay sellers who have received negative feedback from Buyer X and are banding together to torch his house and family), can share advice, support, and viewpoints. There is also a listing of free webinars, or workshops, offered by eBay members (including me) on specific topics of interest to the eBay community.

If that isn't enough, there are Blog and Wiki sections in the Community space, where eBay members volunteer information on just about every topic you can imagine.

I guarantee that the answer to just about any question you may have about doing business on eBay can be found on the eBay website somewhere, if you just take the time to look for it.

Then why this book? Simple—you don't have the time to look for the information!

The amount of information on the eBay website is often overwhelming. Just as an example, go to the Answer Center in eBay's Community section, click on PayPal, and you will see 608 pages—*pages!*—of discussion threads (about fifteen threads to a page) dealing with just about every topic under the sun relating to PayPal alone. A *discussion thread* consists of an eBayer's question, followed by multiple (and often redundant) answers from other eBay community members. These threads are arranged in reverse chronological order (the most recent ones first), and there is no index by subject matter to help you quickly find the information you need. Do the math: If you have a PayPal question, it's probably been addressed in the Answer Center, but you will have to search through over nine thousand individual questions to find your answer. Your time is much more valuable than that.

One of the reasons you find the same questions being asked over and over again—especially in the Answer Center, but really everywhere in the Community section—is that eBay sellers (like all entrepreneurs, let's face it) are under incredible time pressure. They need answers, and they need them *now*! They don't have time to wade through hundreds of discussion threads looking for the one piece of advice they need. So they post their question without doing any research whatsoever, in the hope of getting a quick, simple answer.

This book is not an attempt to reinvent the wheel. It is simply an attempt to get you the answers you need to your most pressing eBay business questions—right here and now!—so you can get on with the business of selling stuff and making money on eBay.

Where the Questions (and Answers) in This Book Came From

The eBay Business Answer Book is an attempt to provide real-world answers to the most common questions eBay sellers ask about starting and running a business on eBay. Each question in this book is an actual question that has been asked (many, many times) by eBay sellers in a seminar, in a workshop, or on one of the eBay community resources described here.

In deciding which questions should appear in this book, I relied first of all on my own experience as an eBay University instructor teaching the popular course "eBay for Business." I polled other eBay University instructors and eBay Certified Education Specialists (see Appendix A) around the country and asked for a list of their most frequently asked questions. Where the same question came up multiple times, I made sure to include it in this book. Where my expert friends seemed to differ slightly in their answers (or where my answer was different from theirs), I tried to include all relevant viewpoints so readers would know we are all as confused as they are.

Finally, I spent hundreds of hours doing what most eBay sellers don't have the time to do: combing through the thousands of discussion threads in eBay's Answer Center, discussion boards, and chat rooms looking for those business-related questions that come up over and over again.

You will note that occasionally the same or a very similar question appears twice in some of the chapters. There are two reasons for that:

1. Attendees at eBay University seminars and other live presentations tend to ask the same question in different ways. So, for example, "When do I have a real business on eBay?" and "When do I have to start paying taxes when I sell on eBay?" are fundamentally the same question, but they appear separately in this book because I want to make sure I am answering exactly the question a reader wants to ask, using the language the person would actually use to ask me a question in one of my presentations.

2. Some of the eBay experts I interviewed for this book had slightly different takes on the answers to particular questions. For example, a Web designer almost certainly has a different perspective on what you should do with an eBay Store than a marketing expert does—and where it was not possible to combine them into a single answer, I thought readers should see all expert opinions to get a more thorough, comprehensive answer to their questions.

How to Use This Book

Each chapter is devoted to a specific topic (such as product sourcing or setting up an eBay Store), and there is occasional redundancy where the same question falls into more than one category.

Questions in each chapter are arranged in general-to-specific order. So, for example, Chapter 3, on product sourcing, begins with the basic question "Where do I find stuff to sell on eBay?" As the chapter continues, the questions become more and more specific until you get to the last question, "Where are three places I can score containerloads of bobble-head dolls from Korea?" (Just kidding about that one.)

If you get to the end of a chapter and your question still hasn't been answered, it means one of two things: Either your question was too specific to be included in this book or it isn't a common question that's being asked by lots of other eBayers. Go now to the appendixes at the end of this book, where you will find:

- A list of resources where (perhaps) you can get the answer to your unique question (Appendix A).
- A step-by-step guide for finding the answer you need on the eBay website (Appendix B).
- If you believe that you really, truly must submit your question to the entire eBay community in the eBay Community Answer Center or a discussion board, a list of Ten Things to Do Before You Post Your Question on eBay (Appendix C) to make sure you don't make a fool of yourself. (Whenever I meet an eBayer I don't like—a very rare occurrence—I say to them, "May you someday find yourself the subject of a discussion thread in the eBay Community section.")

If all else fails and you still don't have your answer, and your question is (in my humble opinion) truly unique, novel, state-of-the-art, and envelope-pushing, please feel free to contact me at crennico@gmail.com, and I will either answer your question or refer you to an eBay expert who can help you. Be warned, however: Your question (and answer) may appear in my nationally syndicated newspaper column and will almost certainly appear in the next edition of this book.

A Word About Legal and Tax Information

A lot of questions in this book deal with legal and tax issues affecting eBay sellers and the eBay community generally. I have discussed most of these at greater length in *The eBay Seller's Tax and Legal Answer Book* (AMACOM Books, 2007,

$19.95), and I suggest readers look there for more detailed and thorough answers than are possible in an FAQ book like this one.

Any legal and tax information in this book is strictly for educational purposes and is not to be relied on as legal or tax advice, which can be given only by a lawyer or tax professional who is licensed to practice in your state.

A Final Word Before We Launch

This is a book about selling on eBay; this is not a book by eBay. I am not an eBay employee, I speak for eBay University as an independent consultant. Neither eBay, PayPal (an eBay company), nor any of their employees has reviewed, vetted, approved, or authorized anything in this book. While many of the questions addressed in *The eBay Business Answer Book* have cropped up (many, many times) in eBay's Community section, I have rephrased them in my own words (to avoid invading anyone's privacy or infringing on anyone's copyright) and have either provided my own best answer to the question or asked a leading eBay expert to give his or her best answer to the question. The names of these experts appear throughout this book and in the Acknowledgments, and I'm grateful to all of them for their help and support.

"Subject to the foregoing," as we lawyers say, *The eBay Business Answer Book* is entirely my doing, and I am solely responsible for its contents.

1 Do I Really Have a Business Here?

Are You Really in Business When You Sell on eBay? Business Versus Hobby

Q: ***"I started selling on eBay last year and have made about $50,000 so far. At what point do I have a real business on eBay?"***

A: You would be amazed—amazed!—how many times this question crops up in eBay University programs around the country. A lot of people have made a lot of money on eBay without realizing they have to do something about paying taxes, filing tax returns, keeping accurate books and records, and so forth. Selling on eBay is one of the greatest ways to back yourself into a successful business, because usually you're having so much fun that you're not even aware you *are* an entrepreneur until it's too late!

This is really two questions that need to be answered separately.

The first question is: At what point do I have to start paying taxes on the money I made selling on eBay? The answer to this one is easy: If you have made so much as $1 of profit (your total income from eBay selling, less whatever you paid for the goods, less the eBay and PayPal fees), you have to report it as income on your tax return and pay income taxes on it. The Internal Revenue Service (IRS) doesn't care whether your eBay selling is a business or a hobby as long as you are making money; income from both businesses and hobbies is taxable.

The second question is a bit tougher to answer: Should I be treating my eBay selling as a business or a hobby? The answer depends on whether or not you are making money selling on eBay.

If you are making money selling on eBay, you have to pay taxes on your profits whether you treat it as a business or a hobby. If you treat your eBay selling as a business, you can deduct a lot of business expenses you incurred in order to sell on eBay. So why not treat it as a business?

If you incurred a loss (you made less in eBay profits than what you paid for the goods you sold) and your eBay selling is a business, you can apply that loss to reduce the income you made from other sources (such as the salary from your day job). If you can't use all of the loss this year because you didn't have enough income from other sources to soak it up, the IRS allows you to carry it forward into future years—up to twenty years in the future—to reduce your taxable income.

If you incurred a loss and your eBay selling is a hobby, you can apply the loss only to reduce income you might have earned from other hobbies. So, for example, if you made a $100,000 profit selling your rare coin collection at Sotheby's and lost $10,000 selling bobble-head dolls on eBay, you can apply the $10,000 loss against the $100,000 gain to report only $90,000 of taxable income.

You cannot, however, apply a hobby loss against income you earned from other sources (such as the salary from your day job). Nor can you carry it forward the way you can a business loss—if you can't use it this year, you lose it forever. Many people who have hobby losses don't even bother reporting them on their tax returns because they're pretty much useless.

All things considered, if you are willing to take your eBay selling seriously and be disciplined about things like record keeping and documenting your business transactions, you should not hesitate to treat your eBay selling as a business for tax purposes. Just try not to look as if you're having too much fun!

Q: ***"At what point will the IRS consider me as having a business when I'm selling on eBay?"***

A: The decision whether or not to treat your eBay selling as a business is pretty much up to you. As you can see from the answer to the previous question, I'm pretty much biased in favor of treating it as a business unless there's a compelling reason to do otherwise. Still, there's always the risk that the IRS will treat your eBay selling as a hobby even though you declare it a business on your tax return. If the thought of a tax audit keeps you awake nights, it may be better to treat your eBay selling as a hobby until you're 100 percent sure you will meet the IRS requirements.

The IRS treats an activity as a business if it makes money (i.e., a profit) in three consecutive tax years, including the present one. For businesses younger than that or businesses that make money in some years but lose money in others (a typical pattern for early-stage eBay sellers), the IRS uses what it calls a "facts and circumstances" test to determine whether treatment as a business is appropriate. It looks at such factors as:

- How disciplined you are in keeping good business records and accounts
- Whether you have formed a corporation or a limited liability company (LLC) for your business and are complying with the laws that apply to those legal entities
- Whether you keep regular hours working in the business
- (Believe it or not) whether the activity is, by its nature, overly pleasurable or fun

A more complete discussion of this topic appears in Chapter 1 of my book *The eBay Seller's Tax and Legal Answer Book.*

Q: ***"Who decides whether my selling on eBay is a business or a hobby—me or the IRS?"***

A: Basically, you decide whether to treat your eBay selling as a business or a hobby for tax purposes by filling out the appropriate lines on your tax return (see the answer to the next question for details). But the IRS has the final word here—if you treat your eBay selling as a business and the IRS disagrees during an audit, they can reclassify your eBay selling as a hobby and disallow any business-related deductions or losses you may have claimed. To my knowledge, the IRS has never challenged a taxpayer's claim that his or her eBay selling was a hobby and forced the person to reclassify it as a business.

Q: ***"Even if I made money selling on eBay last year, can I still treat my eBay selling as a hobby?"***

A: Yes, although there is absolutely no tax advantage to doing so. You would report your income (profit) from selling on eBay on the Other Income line of Form 1040.

Q: ***"Do I have to pay taxes on the money I make on eBay if it's just a hobby?"***

A: Yes, if you made money (profit) selling on eBay this year and have no hobby-related losses to offset the profit (or don't have enough hobby-related losses to offset your income entirely), you would report your income (profit) from selling on eBay on the Other Income line of Form 1040.

Do You Need a Legal Entity to Be in Business on eBay?

Q: ***"Do I have to have a corporation or legal entity to be a business on eBay?"***

A: No. The vast majority of eBay sellers are either sole proprietors or informal partnerships of family members or friends.

A *sole proprietor* is simply a human being over the age of twenty-one with a pulse who is engaged in a trade or business. You don't need any legal paperwork to designate yourself as one (other than a birth certificate that hasn't been revoked), although most states require you to file a document called a *trade name certificate* or *DBA certificate* (for "doing business as . . .") with your town or county clerk's office if you are doing business using a name other than the one appearing on your birth certificate. So, for example, "Clifford R. Ennico, Attorney at Law" is not a trade name, but "Cliff's Antiques" *is* a trade name.

A *partnership* is two or more human beings engaged in a trade or business and sharing in the profits and losses of that business. Believe it or not, you don't need any legal paperwork to form one—you can become partners with just a handshake. Sometimes you can even form partnerships by accident, as we'll discuss in Chapter 2. When you're in a partnership, you are required to file IRS Form 1065 (partnership tax return) by April 15 each year. Each partner reports as income his or her *percentage share* of the partnership income and pays taxes on it. So, for example, if you and I are fifty-fifty partners and our partnership made $100,000 in eBay profits last year, you report $50,000 as income on your tax return and I report $50,000 as income on mine.

By forming a corporation or limited liability company (LLC), however, three very good things happen:

1. You qualify for all sorts of tax deductions and other benefits that sole proprietors and partnerships can't take (see Chapter 12).

2. If (heaven forbid) you are ever sued because of something you did on eBay, your personal liability is limited to whatever money you have put into the corporation or LLC; your household and other personal assets are not at risk.

3. If you are ever audited by the IRS or your state tax authority, they are much more likely to view your eBay selling as a business rather than a hobby.

The trade-off is that when you form a corporation or LLC you will have to do lots of legal paperwork to keep your legal entity alive. If you fail to keep current, the government strips away your entity and your personal assets are now at risk, as if you had never formed the entity in the first place. Corporations and LLCs require diligence and discipline; if the thought of doing legal paperwork is unappealing to you, do not form a corporation or LLC.

For a thorough discussion of the pros and cons of corporations, LLCs, and other legal entities, see Appendix G.

Reporting Your eBay Income and Paying Taxes

Q: ***"Is there a certain amount of money I have to make on eBay before I have to start paying income taxes on it?"***

A: No. If you make even one penny of profit selling on eBay, you are required to report it as income on your tax return and pay income taxes on it. Contrary to some urban legends circulating in the eBay community, there is no minimum amount of income below which you have to pay income taxes. There are, however, minimum threshold amounts for paying self-employment taxes and estimated taxes, which are discussed in Chapter 12.

Q: ***"Where do I report the income from my eBay selling?"***

A: It depends entirely on whether you treat your eBay selling as a business or as a hobby.

If you are pursuing a hobby and making money selling on eBay, you report your income (profit) from eBay selling on the Other Income line of your Form 1040.

If you are selling as a hobby, you lose money selling on eBay, and you do not have income from any other hobby to offset it, you do not report your loss at all on your tax return—it's a *personal loss* or a *hobby loss*, and you just suck it up.

If you are selling as a hobby, you lose money selling on eBay, and you do have income from another hobby to offset it, you report the loss as a *capital loss* on your tax return.

If you are a business, whether you make money or lose money selling on eBay, you fill out Schedule C (Income or Loss from a Trade or Business) and slap it onto your Form 1040.

Q: ***"If I have different product lines and am willing to take the time to set them up as different businesses with different tax IDs, can I deduct the ones that didn't make money and report the ones that did, rather than have my successful lines have to pay for my failures?"***

A: If I understand your question correctly, you are asking if you can create separate tax IDs for the businesses that make money, report the income from each business on a Schedule C, then treat the businesses that lose money as hobbies and lump the losses together with your Form 1040 personal filing.

If that's correct, the short answer is, "Sure, why not?" Just remember that losses from a hobby cannot be deducted from your day job income; if the items you sold at a loss on eBay qualify as *capital assets*—virtually all antiques and collectibles will qualify—you may be able to deduct those losses against other capital gains (say, from your stock portfolio).

Q: ***"How do you start being a business after having operated as a hobby for several years? How does inventory already in-house get reflected?"***

A: Start filing a Schedule C this year. You can deduct the *cost of goods sold* of any inventory you sold on eBay this year, but the cost of goods sold of any inventory you have at the close of business on December 31 cannot be deducted on this year's return. You can deduct it only when the inventory actually sells, presumably sometime next year.

Q: ***"I am fairly new to eBay and just started selling used items from around the house. I am making good money—nothing in comparison to what I paid retail for these items, of course, but still good. Do I claim my earnings next***

year as income for selling these used items? What part of the 1040 form do I use? I don't consider this activity a business. Do I claim it as a hobby, then?"

A: It depends on whether you made money. It sounds to me as if you sold these used items for less than what you paid for them at retail. If that's correct (and you can document that), then you will have a loss for tax purposes this year. If you file Schedule C on your Form 1040 this year and treat your eBay selling as a business, you will be able to deduct your loss against other income you made this year—including the wages from your day job.

If you prefer to continue treating your eBay selling as a hobby, you should determine whether the items you sold qualify as a *capital asset* (your accountant can help you with that). If they do, you can take the loss as a capital loss on your Form 1040 and deduct the loss against other capital gains you may have, such as income from a stock portfolio, but *not* against ordinary income (such as wages from your day job).

Taxes Due from Prior Years

Q: ***"I've been selling on eBay for a couple of years and just recently realized I should have paid taxes on the money I made. I will report the income I made this year on Schedule C when I file my tax return next April 15. But how should I report the money I made in previous years?"***

A: You have choices here. You can file *amendments* to your prior years' tax returns, report the income from your eBay selling each year on the amendments, and pay the taxes you owed each year, along with interest and penalties imposed by the IRS for late payment. This is the way the IRS would prefer that you report your mistake. The downside, of course, is that you may be waking a sleeping dog at the local IRS office and opening the door to a thorough audit of *all* of your recent tax returns to uncover what other innocent mistakes you might have made.

The second choice is what most people in your situation would do. Figure out the income (profit) you made from your eBay selling in past years, add it onto the income you report from your eBay selling this year, and report the total on Schedule C when you file next April 15, as if you made everything this year.

It is unlikely that the IRS will discover that you were actually in business for prior years. Even if they do discover your prior activity, by reporting the past income and paying taxes on it this year you will stop the accruing of interest and penalties on the overdue taxes—you will have to pay these only for the prior years for which you did not report income.

If you choose to "forget" the income from prior years and make believe it didn't happen, the *interest and penalties* on the overdue taxes will continue to accrue until the IRS discovers you failed to report them—maybe years from now (there is no statute of limitations for underreporting income if the IRS believes you did so fraudulently).

2 How Do I Start Selling Professionally on eBay?

Your eBay User ID

Q: ***"I have been buying on eBay for some time and now want to start selling. Should I use the same eBay registered ID I have been using for some time, or should I have a separate user ID for my eBay selling?"***

A: Steve Lindhorst (www.genuineseller.com), an eBay University instructor, strongly recommends having different eBay user IDs for your selling and buying activities on eBay. "It just isn't a good idea for buyers to see exactly how much you paid for the merchandise you are selling on eBay," says Lindhorst, who adds that you should not disclose the user ID you use for buying to anyone other than people you are sourcing product from.

Another reason for buyers, especially, to have multiple user IDs is the problem of *eBay stalkers,* who follow your bidding activity to see what you are bidding on, then "snipe" it out from under you by bidding during the last few seconds of the auction. Once you become known for knowledge or expertise in a certain type of merchandise, people will follow you to see what you are bidding on because you know where the really good stuff is. Having a separate user ID to cloak your identity may make sense, although in time the new user ID gets the same reputation the old one did.

You may set up multiple user IDs on eBay as long as they are tied to different e-mail addresses. Lindhorst also recommends having them tied to separate bank accounts and credit card numbers, just to be safe.

I do not know for a fact, but I am told by several eBay community members who have asked to remain anonymous, that a number of prominent eBay sellers have separate user IDs that they use exclusively when participating in eBay's community chat rooms, discussion boards, and the Answer Center. That way, they can risk asking silly or basic questions without other members knowing who they are and spreading the word that "So-and-So has a feedback score of 10,000 and he *still* doesn't know . . ." Because these user IDs are seldom if ever used in selling or buying transactions, they tend to have zero or extremely low feedback, giving the impression that the users asking the questions are newbies, when, in fact, they are not.

Q: ***"I have a brick-and-mortar store that sells a lot of new, high-quality merchandise. I want to sell on eBay to help get rid of some of my lesser-quality inventory, but I don't want to get the reputation of being a liquidator. Should I list my eBay user ID under my real store name, or should I use a fake name or pseudonym to keep my store's reputation?"***

A: First of all, eBay isn't just about junk or flea-market items. A lot of top-of-the-line merchandise sells on eBay. You might find that some of your high-quality inventory sells for more on eBay than it does in your brick-and-mortar retail store!

Having said that, eBay University instructor Steve Lindhorst (www.genuineseller.com) says, "It doesn't really matter if the store is listed under its real name, because you can always explain to folks what you are doing," adding that this is a special problem for car dealerships selling on eBay Motors. "I tell car dealers all the time to list cars on eBay Motors they would never put in the front row of their lot," says Lindhorst, explaining that "if a buyer feels they're getting a good deal after you've told them in great detail why this vehicle is a 'project car' (that is, one that 'needs some work'), they won't have a bad impression of you just because you also sell higher quality vehicles. Additionally, other shoppers will see you are honest about the project vehicles and conclude you're also honest about the higher quality vehicles you list."

Q: ***"Can I use a brand name as part of my eBay user ID—for example, 'bestBarbiedollsoneBay123'?"***

A: You cannot use a registered trademark as part of an eBay user ID. If you do and the trademark owner catches you, they can force you to cease using the user ID because it infringes on their trademark—after you have built up an impressive feedback score!

You are also prohibited by eBay rules from using the name "eBay" or "-Bay" as part of your user ID.

Q: ***"If I have a user ID with built-up feedback and I want to change it because I've found a much better name that will help me 'brand' it, can I change the name without losing my feedback score?"***

A: Yes, eBay allows you to do this. The only caveat is that for thirty days after making the change, your user ID will have the dreaded "sunglasses" designation next to it, warning potential buyers that you changed your name recently so something fishy might be going on. Consider not listing anything during this thirty-day period until the sunglasses go away.

Q: ***"Can I use my website URL as my eBay user ID?"***

A: A user ID on eBay may not contain any of the URL suffixes, such as ".com," ".net," or ".org." If your website has a cool and distinctive name, however, consider using the name without the ".com" as your user ID; most eBay buyers are savvy enough to know that if your user ID is "flibbertigibbet," your Website URL is probably "flibbertigibbet.com." Also, be sure to create an About Me page with a link to your website URL—this is the only place eBay will allow you to do that.

Naming Your Business

Q: ***"Are there any rules for naming your business when you sell on eBay?"***

A: Yes. Generally, there are five steps you should follow when choosing a name for your business:

1. Sooner or later you are going to want to have a website for your business, so make sure you can get a cool, easy-to-remember URL from Network Solutions (www.networksolutions.com). Always try to get a URL for the top-level ".com" domain, because people tend not to remember ".net," ".biz," or ".us." Also, never choose a ".org" domain name unless you are a bona fide nonprofit organization.

2. Go to the U.S. Patent and Trademark Office (www.uspto.org) and make sure that no one else has registered as a federal trademark or service mark the name you want. If someone else has registered the name as a federal trademark, you cannot use it for the same or a similar line of products or services. (Frankly, if the trademark owner is a lot bigger than you, I wouldn't use the name for anything!)

3. Go to your state secretary of state's office (to find their website, go to http://www.iaca.org/node/62 and click on 2007 Directory—virtually all state secretary of state offices are members of this organization) and see whether someone has formed a corporation or limited liability company (LLC) in your state with the same name. If they have, you cannot use the name for your business.

4. Go to your county or town clerk's office (you will probably have to do this in person, as few clerk's offices will allow you to search their databases electronically) and see whether someone has filed a trade name or "doing business as" (DBA) certificate for the same name. If they have, you cannot use the name for your business.

5. Finally, do an Internet search of the name and see if there are any other businesses using it. If a small mom-and-pop store on the other side of the country is using the same or a similar name, you needn't be too worried about using it, but if you see that a giant Fortune 500 corporation is planning to use the name for one of its new products, back off.

I always recommend that small business clients use good judgment and common sense when picking a name. You don't want to build a successful brand on eBay, only to receive a cease and desist letter from a giant company, ordering you to stop using your name because of a legal conflict.

Here's a trademark tip: Sometimes the best business names have nothing to do with the stuff you're selling on eBay. Think about it. What does "Monster" have to do with looking for jobs online? What does "Arm and Hammer" have to do with baking soda? When in doubt, consider picking a name that's colorful and easy to remember, and for which the ".com" domain name is available. You can always (and should) give a more detailed description of your merchandise when optimizing your eBay listings and eBay Store for search engines later on.

Q: ***"What type of name should I give my eBay Store?"***

A: Your eBay Store does not have to have the same name as your legal business entity. In fact, it's best that you not use your company name as the name of your eBay Store. Why? Because you want this name to be optimized for search engines.

If your company name is "Flibbertigibbet Fantasies LLC," but you sell antique mechanical banks and toys from the 1800s, calling your eBay Store "Flibbertigibbet Fantasies" won't get you any traffic from the search engines because people searching for antique toys and mechanical banks won't be typing in "fantasies" as their keyword.

For best results, you should name your eBay Store "Flibbertigibbet Antique Toys, Mechanical Banks, and Cast Iron Antiques." By describing specifically the type of merchandise you sell using the most common keywords your buyers use when searching for these items, you dramatically increase the odds of getting search engine traffic—the whole reason you are setting up an eBay Store in the first place.

Frankly, I would lose the "Flibbertigibbet" altogether, because it takes up too much space, and call my eBay Store simply "Antique Toys, Mechanical Banks, Cast Iron Antiques." Not the prettiest name, I admit, but beautifully optimized for search engines. Then, when people click on my store page, I would welcome them to "Flibbertigibbet Fantasies LLC, your place for antique mechanical banks and cast iron toys from America's past!"

Building Credibility as a New Seller

Q: ***"I have just started selling on eBay, but no one will buy from me because my feedback score is zero. How can I get my feedback score up to 20 so that people will begin buying from me?"***

A: This is probably one of the biggest challenges for newbie eBay sellers. Most buyers will be hesitant to buy from a seller with a low or zero feedback score. To sell fixed-price items using eBay's popular Buy It Now! feature, a seller has to have a feedback score of at least 20. So how can an eBay seller reach that number?

Here are some tips from leading eBay experts:

- Begin by selling inexpensive items on eBay, on the theory that buyers are more likely to take a risk on a newbie seller if it's only a $5 item, whereas people will not take the risk of buying a $100 item from a newbie seller.
- If that doesn't work, buy ten or fifteen low-priced items on eBay and pay for them promptly so you generate positive feedback.The feedback system on eBay distinguishes between a user's selling and buying activity,

but many buyers (regrettably) will look only at the overall feedback score without digging into the details. Once the desired feedback score has been reached, stop buying and use the user ID exclusively for selling, so the buying feedback fades into the background.

- Do everything possible to give buyers the "warm fuzzies"—the sense that you're okay to deal with—such as qualifying for PayPal's Buyer's Protection Policy, ID Verifying your eBay user ID, creating a detailed About Me page, posting a blog describing the merchandise you are selling, and using only a verified address and a confirmed account on PayPal.
- Last but not least, do everything you can to avoid negative or neutral feedback on eBay. People generally won't buy from people with a feedback score less than 50 unless their positive eBay rating is 100 percent. Bend over backward to give your buyers the best service you can, and prepare yourself for the possibility that you may have to let a bad buyer win every once in a while to preserve your precious 100 percent positive rating.

Q: ***"How can I quickly establish credibility as an eBay seller?"***

A: Building up your feedback score as an eBay buyer and seller is the most obvious way to quickly establish credibility on eBay. Here are several other tips, courtesy of eBay Certified Education Specialist and PowerSeller Jack Waddick of Chicago, Illinois (www.oakviewtraining.com):

- *Create a free eBay About Me page.* Tell a little about who you are, what you sell, your level of interest in the products you sell, and maybe even a little about why you are selling the things you are selling. ("Grandma just passed away at 98 after 73 wonderful years of collecting Hummels . . .")
- *Write eBay Reviews and Guides.* If you have experience (good or bad) with a particular product (that you are selling or not) write an eBay Review and share that experience with others. If you have expertise in a certain area (e.g., coins, golf equipment, computers), write an eBay Guide and share that particular expertise with other eBayers. Reviews and Guides help you establish credibility and build trust with the eBay community, which could help convince some people that you are the best person from whom to be buying these items.

- *Use a short video.* Including a short video on your eBay About Me page can be a great icebreaker and a nice way to warm up the online experience by adding a smiling face to that eBay user ID. For items that typically lend themselves to a demonstration, including a short video in your eBay listing (for free) is like stepping right into that buyer's home with your product. If a picture is worth a thousand words, what is a one-minute demonstration video worth? For guidance on how to shoot effective videos for eBay, check out *Adding Video to Your eBay Listings*, a one-hour video (of course) by eBay Certified Education Specialist Cindy Shebley (www.ghostlegproductions.com).

Getting Business Licenses

Q: ***"Do I need a retail business license to sell on eBay?"***

A: Generally, you don't need a license to sell on eBay unless you are dealing with merchandise (such as motor vehicles) that can be sold only by licensed dealers in your state. Virtually all states, however, require retailers (both online and brick-and-mortar) to obtain a certificate or permit authorizing them to charge and pay sales taxes on the items they sell to in-state buyers and to claim exemption from state sales taxes for the items they source for resale on eBay (see Chapter 13). This certificate or permit goes by several names, most commonly *sales and use tax permit*. Some states, however, refer to their sales tax certificate or permit as a *business license*. If this is the business license you are referring to, then, yes, you will need one of these to sell legally on eBay.

Let me put it this way: If you are going into business, you are going to have to take care of some paperwork with the state and the federal government first—notably, registering for state and local sales taxes and getting a state and federal tax ID number. Declaring "I am now in business!" isn't good enough.

Q: ***"Do I need any sort of license to sell stuff on eBay?"***

A: Here is Cliff's Rule when it comes to licenses: Your state probably will require you to obtain a license to sell something on eBay if that something has the potential to injure someone if it is abused. For example, since motor vehicles might injure their drivers and passengers if they are not maintained properly, virtually every state requires dealers in motor vehicles to be licensed. Same with alcohol and tobacco products (although, of course, these cannot be sold on eBay).

How can you find out whether you need a license to sell something on eBay? Virtually every state in the United States has created a licensing center—a website on which all of the state government agencies that issue licenses have banded together and created a master list of information and links describing all state and local government licenses. So, for example, the Connecticut state licensing center can be found at http://www.ct-clic.com.

To find the licensing center website in your state, go to http://www.sbaonline.sba.gov/hotlist/license.html, a directory of the licensing centers in all fifty states and U.S. possessions.

Q: ***"Do I need a motor vehicle dealer's license to sell cars, boats, and other vehicles on eBay?"***

A: Generally, the vast majority of people selling cars and other motor vehicles on eBay fall into one of four categories:

1. Automobile dealers
2. People selling their own cars (known on eBay Motors as *Fisbos,* short for "for sale by owner," or FSBO)
3. People setting up eBay listings and eBay Stores for a local dealer and receiving a flat fee for their services
4. People selling other people's cars on eBay, whether or not they receive a commission or fee for their services

According to eBay University instructor and eBay Motors expert Steve Lindhorst (www.genuineseller.com), automobile dealers are covered by their existing state licenses, while people setting up eBay listings and eBay Stores for licensed dealers are not required to obtain a license as long as they do not take part in the sales process (i.e., the auto dealership has its own eBay user ID that is listed as the seller, answers all e-mail questions from buyers, and conveys title to the vehicle) and they receive a flat fee for their services. Lindhorst cautions, however, that "if you even so much as answer an e-mail in the process of selling a car for someone else, you are now inserted into the sale process and may need a dealer's license."

According to Lindhorst, anyone else selling a vehicle may be required to obtain a dealer's license, including:

- Anyone who sells a car for someone else, whether or not they receive compensation for doing so.
- "Fisbos" who sell a certain number of vehicles or hit a certain monetary level determined by their state dealer laws. ("For example, "says Lindhorst, "a state may require a dealer license of an individual who sells either five motor vehicles or has motor vehicle sales reaching $100,000.")
- Someone who sells cars for a local dealership and receives a percentage of the winning bid amount as his or her compensation. ("Such people might be treated the same for licensing purposes as the dealer's own salespeople," says Lindhorst.)

Even if no state dealer's license is required, people who sell more than five used cars per year are subject to the Federal Trade Commission's "used car rule" requiring them to make certain specific disclosures to buyers before each sale (for information about the FTC rule, see http://www.ftc.gov/bcp/conline/pubs/buspubs/usedcarc.shtm).

Because state dealer licensing laws are "all over the place," Lindhorst advises that you talk to a lawyer before selling someone else's car on eBay, even if you are not being compensated for doing so. "The fines and penalties are extremely heavy for violating these rules," says Lindhorst, adding that anyone planning to sell motor vehicles on eBay should first review eBay's Dealer License policy at http://pages.ebay.com/help/sell/dealerlicense.html.

Forming a Legal Entity

Q: ***"Do I need to form a legal entity, such as a corporation or limited liability company (LLC), to sell on eBay?"***

A: It depends. The vast majority of eBay sellers are sole proprietorships and informal partnerships of friends or family members, who have never felt the need to incorporate their business on eBay.

A *sole proprietor* is simply a human being over the age of twenty-one with a pulse who is engaged in a trade or business. You don't need any legal paperwork to form one (other than a birth certificate that hasn't been revoked), although most states require you to file a document called a *trade name certificate* or *DBA certificate* (for "doing business as . . .") with your town or county clerk's office if you are doing business using a name other than the one appearing on your birth certificate. So, for example, "Clifford R. Ennico, Attorney at Law" is not a trade name; "Cliff's Antiques" *is* a trade name.

A *partnership* is two or more human beings engaged in a trade or business and sharing in the profits and losses of that business. Believe it or not, you don't need any legal paperwork to form one—you can become partners with just a handshake. Sometimes you can even form partnerships by accident, as we'll discuss in Chapter 2. When you're in a partnership, you are required to file IRS Form 1065 (partnership tax return) by April 15 each year—unless the sole partners are a husband and wife, in which case you would file Schedule C on Form 1040 each year. Each partner reports as income his or her percentage share of the partnership income and pays taxes on it. So, for example, if you and I are fifty-fifty partners and our partnership made $100,000 in eBay profits last year, you report $50,000 as income on your tax return and I report $50,000 as income on mine.

Generally, there are three reasons for forming a legal entity such as a corporation or LLC:

- You need protection from liability in the event you are sued because of something you did or didn't do on eBay.
- You are looking to raise outside capital from investors, and they will only invest in a legal entity.
- Because a corporation's income is taxed at a lower rate than an individual's name, you are trying to shelter some of your eBay income from taxes.

Q: ***"How do I pick the right legal entity for my eBay selling business?"***

A: Appendix G to this book is a multipage outline, called "Demystifying the Business Organization," that I have been handing out at my legal and tax seminars for over fifteen years. Sit down tonight with a pot of strong coffee (or a V.S.O.P. brandy) and read Appendix G from start to finish. I guarantee you will come away knowing as much as most attorneys do about partnerships, corporations, Subchapter S corporations, limited liability companies, and the differences between them.

Should you ever lose your copy of this book, the outline is also available as a free download from my website at www.cliffennico.com.

Q: *"Should I incorporate in Delaware or Nevada? I've heard you can save money on taxes there."*

A: Unless your business on eBay is physically located in Delaware or Nevada, there is absolutely no advantage in incorporating there. A lot of people think they can avoid paying their state's business taxes by incorporating in one of these states. Not true. If you form a corporation in Delaware or Nevada, but are actually doing business in State X (you have an office or mailing address there, for example), you have to qualify your entity as a foreign corporation or foreign LLC in State X and register for State X's business taxes. Fail to do this, and you are operating an illegal, unregistered business in State X—if State X's tax authority catches you several years down the road, you will have to pay all back taxes you owe to State X, along with interest and penalties for late payment, and a possible referral of your business to your state attorney general's office for criminal prosecution.

I don't want to scare you, dear reader, but there are a lot of evil people out there on the Internet selling you the idea that you can form a corporation in Nevada for only $100 and (this is never stated explicitly, only suggested, to avoid outright fraud) avoid paying business taxes anywhere else. It simply isn't true. If your eBay selling business is located in State X and you want to form a corporation, LLC, or other legal entity, the only place to incorporate is in State X. Period. End of story. World without end. Amen.

Registering for Federal and State Taxes, and Tax ID Numbers

Q: *"Do I need a federal tax ID number to sell on eBay?"*

A: If you have a partnership, corporation, or limited liability company (LLC) for your business selling on eBay, you are required to obtain a federal tax ID number. You can't use one of the partners' Social Security numbers as a tax ID.

If you are a sole proprietor, or an LLC with only one owner (called a *member*), the IRS allows you to use your Social Security number as a federal tax ID number. But I think it's a lousy idea—get a federal tax ID number anyway. Why? Because when you're in business, you have to give this number out to many, many people. For example, if you take consignments of goods for sale on eBay, you have to send IRS Form 1099 to each one of your *consignors* (the people who consign goods to you) at the end of each calendar year. Each of those forms will have your tax ID number on it. Do you really want all of those people to know your Social Security number? Enough said.

To get a federal tax ID number, fill out IRS Form SS-4, available as a free download from www.irs.gov. You can fill out the form online or print it out and call the IRS's toll-free telephone number (1–800–829–4933) to get a tax ID number over the phone. Even better, have your accountant fill out the form for you—that way, you know there won't be any mistakes, and most accountants I know won't even charge you for this service. They want your tax return business, and filling out this form properly makes their lives a lot easier down the road.

Q: ***"What's the biggest mistake eBay sellers make when they set up their businesses?"***

A: Failing to register for state and local sales taxes, and getting a state tax ID number (often called a *resale number*).

When you set up a business in just about every state in the United States, you are required to fill out and file a *business tax registration form* with your state tax authority. At the very least, every eBay seller needs to register for state sales and use taxes.

The easiest way to register for sales and use taxes is to have your accountant fill out the form for you. Most accountants will do this without charge because they want to get your tax return business, and filing this form properly makes their lives a lot easier down the road.

If you want to do this yourself, you first have to find the website for your state tax authority. Go to http://www.taxsites.com/state.html for a directory of state tax websites, and click on your state. Once you have found your state tax authority's website, click on the Forms and Publications link, and look for your state's business tax registration form.

Q: ***"Are there any other state and local taxes eBay sellers have to worry about?"***

A: In some states, municipalities have the power to levy their own income taxes on corporations, limited liability companies (LLCs), and other business entities. So, for example, in New York City, corporations and LLCs have to pay income taxes to both the state and city governments.

Many states also levy a minimum tax on corporations and LLCs, regardless of the amount of income earned. So, for example, Connecticut imposes a minimum yearly tax of $250 on domestic corporations and LLCs, even if they didn't make a penny of income during the year.

Some states impose a personal property tax on business equipment and inventory. This is calculated the same way as your real estate property tax—you determine the value of your taxable property, then apply the mill rate ($XXX for each $1,000 of property value) to determine the tax owed.

A few states (dwindling in number) impose inventory taxes or floor taxes on a retailer's year-end inventory. To determine the tax owed, you conduct a physical inventory on December 31, determine your inventory value on that date, and apply the state's tax rate to the value. Usually, there is an exemption from tax for goods sold in interstate commerce, which should apply to most inventory sold by eBay sellers. Hint: If you live in a state with a floor tax, put everything up for sale on eBay during the month of December with a $0.01 starting bid and no reserve.

3 Where Do I Find Stuff to Sell on eBay?

Finding the "Right Stuff" to Sell and Identifying Niches

Q: *What should I be selling on eBay?*

A: This is probably the most frequently asked question in the eBay community. Once you've cleaned out your attic, as well as your friends' and relatives' attics, you will need to find stuff from somewhere if you want to continue selling on eBay and making money at it.

There really is no one right, "perfect" answer to this question, but eBay experts consistently point out six rules you should consider when deciding what to sell on eBay:

1. *Sell what sells.* Marcia Cooper and her partner, Harvey Levine, an eBay PowerSeller couple and Certified Education Specialist team based in Fort Lee, New Jersey (www.generalenterprises.net), say that this is the key to success on eBay: "You don't sell what you want to sell; you sell what people are actually buying on eBay." Do research on eBay to find niches where there are lots of buyers and a high sell-through rate (ratio of successful listings to total listings). If something is not selling on eBay, ask yourself if eBay is an appropriate venue for that type of merchandise.

2. *Sell merchandise for which you can find reliable sources.* One of the disadvantages of selling antiques and collectibles on eBay, according to eBay University instructor Steve Lindhorst (www.genuineseller.com), is that "it's tough to get a good, steady source for product in those categories—everything's unique, and you tend to get estate sale lots that are all over the place." It's hard to build a reputation or "brand" on eBay when you're selling books, Hummel figurines,

antique clothing, estate jewelry, and 78-rpm records at the same time. You will also wear yourself out creating unique listings for each of those items.

3. *Sell merchandise that delivers consistently decent profit margins.* You can sell a lot of bobble-head dolls on eBay, but if you're making only a $2 profit on each sale it will take you a long time to make enough to earn a decent living. Look at the profitability of the things you sell on eBay and source only those products that will give you a reasonable return on your investment. A useful tool for this is ProfitBuilderSoftware, a profitability analysis program developed by eBay PowerSeller Corey Kossack specifically for eBay sellers (www.profitbuilder software.com).

4. *Sell merchandise you can list repetitively and quickly.* If it takes an hour for you to list something on eBay and you make only a $2 profit on each listing, you are working for only $2 an hour—well below minimum wage! Try to find products that can be listed repetitively, using the same listing template and photographs, and very, very quickly (using software tools such as eBay's Turbo Lister 2).

This is one of the main reasons it's so hard to make a decent living on eBay when you sell only antiques and collectibles, according to Marcia Cooper, because "each item is unique. It has to be described separately and photographed separately, and that takes time." If you are only an occasional or part-time seller on eBay, or if you are selling antiques and collectibles, focus on high-margin merchandise for which each listing brings you a profit in the hundreds-of-dollars or thousands-of-dollars range.

5. *Sell what you know, not necessarily what you love.* Most eBay experts agree that it's difficult to sell successfully on eBay if you don't know anything about the merchandise you are selling. Buyers are looking for sellers they can trust and depend on, and they are not going to get "warm fuzzies" about a seller who says, "I don't know nuthin' about this stuff, I just found it in the back of my closet, and I ain't takin' it back" in every one of his listings (especially if there are misspelled words in the item description as well).

"A lot of people say you should sell what you're passionate about, but I think you're better off selling what you know," says eBay University instructor Steve Lindhorst (www.genuineseller.com), who explains that "if I'm selling serpentine belts on eBay Motors, I can tell you why one brand of serpentine belt is better than another. Now, I'm not passionate about serpentine belts—I really don't know if anyone can be passionate about serpentine belts—but it gives my buyers a lot of confidence that I know what I'm doing and that they should buy from me rather than someone else."

Another danger of "selling what you love," says Lindhorst, is "because you're a collector you're going to want to keep some of the stuff you source for sale on eBay."

Those eBay sellers who know their merchandise have three major advantages over those who don't:

- They can source product more easily, because they know where the best deals are.
- They can market their auction listings and eBay Store more effectively, by making themselves experts on certain merchandise and displaying that expertise on eBay's blog pages, Reviews and Guides, and other content-rich pages that attract search engine spiders.
- It's easier for them to stay out of legal, eBay policy, and "bad seller" hassles on eBay—if they have specialized knowledge about Gucci handbags, such as the different styles and models and how they're made, it's much more likely they'll be able to spot fakes and knockoffs and keep them out of their eBay listings.

6. *Sell stuff that other sellers aren't selling.* Most eBay experts agree that the site is saturated with sellers and that it's getting tougher and tougher to find profitable niches. "When I first started selling on eBay more than a decade ago, there were only about a dozen people doing what I'm doing on eBay," says Marcia Cooper, "but today there are more than 1,000 people selling stuff similar to mine." Look for niches on eBay where there are a relatively large number of buyers, a high sell-through rate (the ratio of successful auctions to total auctions), and a relatively low number of competitors.

Researching Your Market

Q: ***A lot of the categories on eBay are saturated with sellers right now. What's a good way to find profitable niches where there isn't as much competition?***

A: In a word, *research.* You have absolutely no idea what to sell on eBay unless you do your homework and find out where the selling opportunities are.

According to Matthew Hedges, CEO of SimpleMarketResearch.com, "Gone are the days of randomly picking products to sell online without doing any research. The internet is now full of professional online sellers whose sole source of income is from their eBay Stores and auction listings. They don't risk their livelihoods on guesswork. They perform market research, in many cases very simple market research steps, to ensure the products they sell are products that will fit their budget and turn a tidy profit . . . and any serious seller must learn how to do this too if they really want to compete in today's internet marketplace."

Market research is the key factor in deciding what to sell and how to find a niche. A seller who is going to struggle selling on eBay will pick products without researching first to see if that item is something consumers are buying and whether they (the seller) can compete successfully with other eBay sellers. Research what keywords people are typing into eBay and general search engines such as Google and sell only those products relating to keywords that generate a high demand and have low competition.

For example, let's say you are a collector of antique mechanical banks and are thinking about selling these on eBay. These classic children's toys were made in the United States and the United Kingdom from about 1870 to 1930 and were designed to teach children the value of saving money by making it fun. A typical mechanical bank is made of painted metal and depicts a highly interesting and colorful scene (such as William Tell with his crossbow getting ready to shoot an apple off his son's head). The child places a coin somewhere on the bank (in William Tell's crossbow) and by pushing a lever causes the bank to do something entertaining while it's depositing the coin (William Tell shoots the coin into a slot behind his son's head, which causes a bell to ring).

By searching the active listings on eBay for "mechanical banks," you would find anywhere from three hundred to five hundred listings at any given time. Good news: There are lots of mechanical banks for sale on eBay, and people are buying them.

By clicking on Advanced Search and searching under Completed Listings for "mechanical banks" (you will have to log on to eBay before you will be allowed to do this), you will see about twice as many listings, with their closing prices (if the item actually sold on eBay). A quick review of these completed listings and closing prices will tell you there are three separate markets on eBay for antique mechanical banks, as follows:

- Original mechanical banks from the golden age (1870 to 1930) that are in poor overall condition or have had numerous repairs, replacement of parts, and other tinkering done to them over the years, selling for anywhere from $300 to $3,000
- Reproduction mechanical banks made in China or Taiwan within the last few years, selling below $25
- So-called Book of Knowledge mechanical banks (reproductions made during the 1950s and early 1960s by John Wright's Book of Knowledge company using the same casting process and models as the original banks), selling for $100 to $500

Looking at these listings, you will note that the vast majority of mechanical banks sold on eBay are one-offs—the seller does not specialize in mechanical banks but merely has one or two in his inventory, probably the result of an estate sale purchase. This means there is little competition for an eBay seller or eBay Store specializing in mechanical banks and knowing the merchandise well. So far, so good.

You will also note that while the vast majority of mechanical banks offered for sale on eBay are recent Chinese reproductions, most of these listings fail to attract any bidders at all—the banks fail to sell through to an actual buyer—while the majority of mechanical banks that actually sell on eBay are in the medium to high end of the market (original banks and Book of Knowledge reproductions). This is also good; the demand for medium- to high-end mechanical banks is strong, meaning consistent sell-throughs at decent profit margins.

Now search under "eBay Stores" for "mechanical banks" and look at the names of the stores listing these items to see if there are any eBay Stores that specialize in mechanical banks. You will probably find that there are only one or two stores specializing in mechanical banks and that they focus (not surprisingly, given the aforementioned data) at the medium to high end of the market—original banks and "Book of Knowledge" reproductions.

Armed with this information, you now have several things to think about:

- Is the market for mechanical banks big enough to support another eBay Store at the high to medium end of the market (original banks and Book of Knowledge reproductions)?
- Since there are hardly any mechanical banks for sale on eBay at the extremely high end of the market (original banks selling for more than $3,000), is this a market opportunity for an eBay seller who really knows the merchandise well and can answer tough questions about condition, paint loss, and so forth, that less experienced sellers can't handle, or is this because buyers of extremely high-end original mechanical banks in "pristine" condition do not trust banks that are for sale on eBay?
- Since there are no eBay Stores specializing in modern mechanical banks (banks with original designs and high-quality reproductions made after, say, 1970), would an eBay Store specializing in these items attract a sufficiently large following of collectors to make up for the low profit margin on each bank and the currently low sell-through rate for cheap Chinese reproduction banks on eBay? (In other words, is there a possible new market category for mechanical banks that's being overlooked on eBay?)

The answers to these questions depend on your knowledge of mechanical banks and their collectors, your comfort level in dealing with highly complex antiques that have to be researched and examined individually, your ability to source low-end reproduction banks at prices that enable you to make a decent profit on each sale, and other considerations beyond the scope of this book.

There are resources that can help you with your market research. For eBay research, tools like HammerTap.com's Deep Analysis, Terapeak.com, and the OneSource Market Research Tool (www.worldwidebrands.com) are well worth considering. In addition, eBay has a market research tool available for free at http://pages.ebay.com/marketplace_research/index.html.

To see an interesting article comparing the HammerTap and Terapeak products, check out http://www.allbusiness.com/specialty-businesses/home-based-businesses/4057735-1.html.

Q: ***I'm selling antiques and collectibles on eBay. While HammerTap and Terapeak are great, they only provide data for eBay listings that have closed in the last thirty to ninety days. That's great for people selling laptops that are***

always available on eBay, but for some of the stuff I'm selling, I would have to go back years to find eBay listings for the same item. Are there any online databases that go back that far?

A: For a subscription fee of $9.95 a month, the PriceMiner database at www.goantiques.com can give you access to auction results going back a long time. A number of collectors' associations also keep tabs on auction results and give their members access to that data on their websites. For example, collectors of antique mechanical banks who join the Mechanical Bank Collectors of America (www.mbca.com) can access auction results for specific banks in all condition ranges going back fifteen years.

Q: ***What if I do my research on eBay, and there's nobody selling the same stuff I'm selling?***

A: This can mean one of two things: Either you have a gold mine on your hands or (more likely) people don't want the stuff or won't buy it on eBay. It's always a lot easier to sell on eBay where there are other people selling similar stuff—people already know to visit that category frequently to see what's new. If your products don't fall within any of eBay's established categories, people won't know where to look for them. Find the category that most closely resembles the items you're selling, list a couple of items there (to test the market), then place some duplicate listings in Really Weird Stuff (there is such a category—it's at the end of the "Everything Else" section) and any other category that remotely relates to your items, and see where your bidders are coming from.

Buying from Wholesalers

Q: ***If I'm selling on eBay, will real wholesalers work with me? When should I tell a supplier that I sell on eBay? Should I tell them at all?***

A: Not all wholesalers will work with eBay sellers for various reasons. Some manufacturers fear their items will be devalued in the market, and others have strict guidelines (especially expensive brand names) for where their products can be sold. As an eBay seller, you don't want to waste time setting up accounts, only to discover a supplier won't allow you to sell their products there. Before you set up an account with a supplier, you will want to ask the supplier if they allow their products to be sold on eBay. It is better to make sure in advance rather than having your account frozen or shipments not delivered.

However, there are many wholesalers (especially in niche markets) that understand the power of the eBay market and are very willing to work with you. Worldwide Brands (www.worldwidebrands.com) researches wholesalers daily specifically looking for wholesalers that will work with eBay sellers and online retailers. The majority of the suppliers listed in their OneSource database will work with eBay sellers.

Q: ***What are the differences between the various methods of product sourcing (drop ship, light bulk, large-volume wholesale, liquidation, and importing)?***

A: "No single sourcing method will make you truly successful. Using only one method is like driving a car with only one wheel; four wheels works much better. Every online seller, especially an eBay seller, needs to develop a product sourcing strategy," according to Robin Cowie, President of Worldwide Brands Inc. (www.worldwidebrands.com).

Most eBay sellers source their product from one of six sources:

1. *Local sourcing:* The seller finds products from local sources such as the attic, the basement, the garage, garage sales, flea markets, local thrift shops, and outlet stores.

2. *Drop ship:* A product-sourcing method whereby you sell on eBay as a retailer of a supplier's product line; however, the supplier ships products one at a time directly to your customer from the supplier's warehouse. Even though you are the seller of drop-shipped goods, you do not have to maintain an inventory or handle shipping. You do, however, handle the collection of the money from the customer and pay the supplier the wholesale cost for the product purchased. Drop shipping is considered an ideal way for elderly and disabled people to make an income selling on eBay (to learn more about a nonprofit organization dedicated to helping disabled people drop ship on eBay, check out the Disabled Online Users Association at www.doua.org). Drop shipping can also be used for testing product ideas on the market, testing the supplier process, and carrying larger, heavier items in your store selection for which you would not normally want to handle the shipping.

3. *Light bulk:* A product-sourcing method whereby the seller purchases from a wholesaler in minimum quantities for less than $500—ideal for storing in a garage, basement, or a storage unit. The seller manages all interactions with the customer and the product, from collecting the payment to handling the inventory to shipping to the customer. The profit margins increase with this product-sourcing method because wholesalers can offer larger wholesale discounts on product.

4. *General wholesale/large volume:* This is similar to the light bulk method; however, the quantity of product is much higher. The larger the quantity purchased directly from the wholesaler, the higher the discounts received by the seller. When a retailer buys in really large volumes, the supplier will add *volume discounts,* depending on how much money the retailer is willing to spend. The more money you are willing to spend on inventory, the bigger your volume discount; the bigger your volume discount, the cheaper you can sell the product and the larger the profit margins that are obtainable!

5. *Liquidation:* A product-sourcing method whereby a seller can source commercial surplus inventory and *closeout* products through wholesalers.

6. *Importing:* This means sourcing products from foreign countries. Importing can be done individually, through wholesalers that handle the importing process, or through *customs brokers* you pay to handle importing paperwork.

To learn more about product-sourcing basics, check out Worldwide Brands' free educational video course available at www.worldwidebrands.com/productsourcingvideo.

Q: ***What do I need in order to work with a wholesaler? How do I get them to give me an account? What can I do to increase my odds that a wholesaler will work with me? What can I do to make them take me seriously?***

A: To be a reseller of products from a wholesaler, you need a sales tax permit and a state tax identification number (commonly called a *resale number*) from your state tax authority. For information on how to get one of these, see the related questions in Chapter 2. Some wholesalers as well will require proof that you have registered your business name with a local or state government agency (for a limited liability company or corporation, you would get a *certificate of good standing* from your state secretary of state's office; for most sole proprietorships and partnerships, you would get a filed copy of a *trade name certificate* or *fictitious name certificate* from your town clerk's or county clerk's office).

To import certain goods from overseas, you may also need an *import license* or permit from a federal government agency (see related questions in Chapter 18).

Wholesalers (depending on the state) are required by law to have your resale number on file. If you are working with a wholesaler that does not require a resale number, then it is very likely that they are not a genuine wholesaler! If you are an *international retailer* (an eBay seller residing outside the United States that does not have a U.S. registered business), you are not required to provide suppliers with a resale number. Always confirm with a supplier that they will work with an international retailer. Some suppliers won't work with international retailers because of trade and export agreements that they have with their manufacturers regarding selling outside the United States.

To increase your odds that a wholesaler will work with you, make sure to present a highly professional image. Using a business address instead of a home address and posting official business hours are examples of presenting a professional image. Consider a private mailbox with your local UPS Store rather than a post office box, because a UPS Store will give you an actual street address, such as "123 Main Street, #456." A supplier needs to know the best times to contact you. In addition, they want to know that you are a real business. Use a business landline for communications with your suppliers. It doesn't sound very professional when your cell phone drops the call. When you're working from home, you need to keep in mind that the distracting noises in the background (such has your pet dog barking) can give you an unprofessional image. A professional business would not have these distracting noises in the background (see related questions in Chapter 19).

Q: ***What exactly is a middleman, and what are the pros and cons of doing business with one?***

A: Unfortunately, when eBay sellers decide to start purchasing wholesale products to resell, they often get caught in the "evil middleman scenario." In order to understand this scenario, you have to be somewhat familiar with the *product supply chain,* which is how a product gets from the manufacturer to the end consumer, your customer. When it's working the way it should, it goes like this:

Manufacturer sells to Wholesaler sells to
Retailer sells to Consumer

Many people have the mistaken impression that the second link in the chain, the wholesaler, is a middleman, because the wholesaler is in the middle, between the manufacturer and the retailer (that's you).

That's not true, according to Worldwide Brands business development manager Colette Marshall (www.worldwidebrands.com). The wholesaler is there for a very important reason: Manufacturers don't always have the infrastructure to actually manufacture, sell, and deliver small numbers of their products directly to retailers. Wholesalers provide the infrastructure for selling and delivering the manufactured goods to retailers. This infrastructure includes warehouses, order systems, delivery trucks, account representatives, and so on. So the wholesaler is a legitimate wholesale supplier, not a middleman.

When an illegitimate middleman inserts itself into the product supply chain, it looks like this:

Manufacturer sells to Wholesaler sells to MIDDLEMAN
sells to Retailer sells to Consumer

A middleman, according to Marshall, is someone who takes your rightful place in the product supply chain and bumps you down a link: "They try to make you believe they are Link Two in the chain (a wholesaler), when they are really Link Three (a retailer). Sometimes, it's worse than that, with multiple layers of 'middlemen' between the legitimate wholesaler and you." The trouble with "evil middlemen," explains Marshall, is that they take away from your profit margins by increasing the wholesale price (they buy from the manufacturer at the same price as the other sellers but mark up the wholesale price when they resell to you), making it difficult for you to compete on any online platform, especially eBay.

Q: ***Why are my wholesale prices for an item higher than what I see other sellers retailing that same item for? How are they making a profit?***

A: Because the other sellers are buying in much higher quantities than you are, they are getting a volume discount much lower than yours on a per-item basis. Or you might be buying goods from an "evil middleman" (see previous question).

Q: ***Other suppliers are beating my prices. Do I have to drop my prices to compete?***

A: You can, but watch out for your profit margins. Use a software tool such as Corey Kossack's ProfitBuilderSoftware (www.profitbuildersoftware.com) to calculate your eBay fees and other costs of doing business to make sure you can still make a decent profit at the lower price. If you can't, then perhaps these other sellers have a better source of product than you do, and you should look into sourcing product from another wholesaler or supplier that will give you more aggressive discounts.

Sourcing Product from China and Importing

Q: ***I would love to be able to order products directly from the overseas manufacturers, especially in China, but I'm afraid I don't have the skills to handle the negotiations myself. Is there any place that can help me make contact with manufacturers and help put the deals together?***

A: If you are new to importing and don't have any import experience, your best resource for sourcing product from China or elsewhere in Asia is Worldwide Brands Inc., based in Orlando, Florida (www.worldwidebrands.com). Worldwide Brands offers you the ability through their OneSource database to purchase through direct import buyers. These are companies that set up warehouses within the United States to have the product imported from manufacturers in countries such as China. These companies handle all the importing arrangements, and you purchase directly from the distributor within the United States. This way, you don't have to be concerned about handling the import logistics or the manufacturer negotiations. For an excellent overview of the issues involved in importing from China, check out http://www.chinasuccessstories.com/2007/07/25/import-from-china-getting-started.

According to Peter Zapf, vice president of community development for Global Sources (www.globalsources.com), which helps global buyers find suppliers in China and works with Worldwide Brands, eBay sellers looking to source product directly from Asia should consider three services:

1. *Global Sources Direct (GlobalSourcesDirect.com):* This is an online wholesale site offering product directly from China. That is, you go to the site,

select the products you want, put them in your shopping cart, and they are shipped to you via air courier from China so you receive them within ten days. Minimum order quantity is relatively small, at one carton. Global Sources Direct is also listed in the Worldwide Brands database. According to Zapf, it's the easiest way to access China-manufactured products, because you don't deal with suppliers, quality control, or logistics. Global Sources Direct handles all that for you.

2. *Global Sources (www.GlobalSources.com):* This website provides a directory of suppliers. Verified suppliers have been physically visited three times or more by Global Sources. You can search for products and suppliers and also work with them directly. The verified suppliers list hundreds of thousands of products in a wide range of categories. Examples of just some of the products are digital photo frames, all-terrain vehicles (ATVs), handbags, and vacuum cleaners. According to Zapf, this site is great for folks who either have experience or want to build experience with the import process. Similar to their U.S. counterparts, Chinese manufacturers have varying minimum order quantity requirements, and you will need to contact suppliers to check on their minimum order quantities.

3. *China Sourcing Fairs (www.ChinaSourcingFairs.com):* Hosted by Global Sources, these trade shows have thousands of Chinese suppliers exhibiting their products. Everyone from big box retailers to eBay PowerSellers attend these shows in order to find and meet suppliers. The biggest shows are in Hong Kong and include:

   - *Electronics and components* such as consumer electronics, digital entertainment, in-car electronics, computer and networking supplies, WiFi and VoIP products, health and personal care electronics, security and safety, electronic components, power supplies, and much more
   - *Fashion accessories* such as handbags, jewelry, belts, hats, footwear, and sunglasses
   - *Underwear and swimwear,* including related accessories
   - *Gifts and home products* such as premiums, kitchen and household products, home décor, glassware, basketware, garden and outdoor products, stationery, sporting equipment, and leisure items

All you need to do is get on a plane and show up. There is no entry fee. According to Zapf, this is a great opportunity to network with other international buyers. In addition, Global Sources hosts a seminar at the show called "Buying from China: What New Buyers Need to Know." So if you are new to importing, you can learn about buying from China and also meet thousands of suppliers. Hey, it's tax deductible!

Many eBay sellers buy in small volumes (one hundred pieces or fewer). For these volumes, Zapf advises that eBay sellers may want to consider working with trading companies rather than buying direct from China. The advantage of a trading company is that it can act as an intermediary on your behalf and can often handle smaller minimum order quantities. However, Zapf points out, since the trading company hasn't actually manufactured the product, there is a longer chain to go through when getting information about the products.

Q: ***What if I want to get a product manufactured for me, rather than buying already manufactured products?***

A: If you have product you'd like to get manufactured, there are a fair number of buyer agents that can help on your behalf, according to Zapf. There is a cost associated to working with them. They charge either a fixed fee, a percentage of the order, or a combination of both. Generally, order volumes need to reach US$20,000 or higher for their added cost to offset the savings of having goods manufactured in China, although this figure varies from product category to product category.

Many eBayers ask about purchasing products from China with Western trademarks or brands. The owners of these trademarks and brands control their distribution channels closely and don't try to create pricing structures that support cross-border sales. When buying goods from China with Western trademarks or brands, eBay sellers must be careful to ensure that the goods are not knockoffs or illegal overruns (the Chinese manufacturer received an order for ten thousand copies but actually made twenty thousand and didn't tell the Western company about it).

Another issue for eBay sellers sourcing their inventory from overseas is the so-called gray-market sale. Unlike fakes and knockoffs, gray-market goods are authentic products being sold by unauthorized resellers and/or authorized business partners of the manufacturer in violation of their distribution agreements—for example, by selling to unauthorized resellers or selling outside their authorized territories.

As a result, a fair number of the opportunities you see to purchase such products are, in fact, offering counterfeit products. Selling these will almost certainly get you kicked off eBay, as well as sued by the manufacturers of these products if they can prove you knowingly imported counterfeit or knockoff goods.

To avoid liability, Zapf says you can ask the seller for proof that they are an authorized distributor and you can check with the brand owner whether the seller is an authorized distributor. "When looking to buy from China, instead of looking for Western branded products, you should be looking either for a new and innovative product, for a well-priced unbranded product, or to have a product manufactured which you can put your own brand on," Zapf advises. Zapf also advises staying away from services that list or promote counterfeit products. Large volumes of these types of listings indicate a low-quality service—probably not the place you want to find your next trusted supplier.

Drop Shipping

Q: ***What exactly is drop shipping and how does it work?***

A: *Drop shipping* is a method of sourcing products for your retail business that eBay Store owners, especially, may want to consider. Drop shippers are simply wholesalers that are willing to send products directly from their wholesale warehouse to your customers' front doors one at a time. With a special type of drop shipping, known as *blind drop shipping,* a supplier will not only ship your product directly to your customer but also includes labels printed with your company branding so that the product appears to have been shipped directly from your company's location. Not all suppliers will blind drop ship, but there are many that will definitely offer standard drop shipping as a method for delivering your product to customers. According to eBay Store designer and consultant Rebecca Shapiro, of Oasis Connect (www.oasisconnect.com), here's how it works:

- You find a company that drop ships a product you want to sell and set up a retail account with them.
- The drop shipper provides you with images and descriptions for your Internet store and auction listings.

- You sell the product to a happy customer and collect their money.
- You place the order with your drop shipper, providing them with the customer's name and address.
- Bona fide drop shippers pack products for you and ship them directly to your customer for you.
- A good-quality drop shipper will send the product directly to your customer with *your* store name on the package (otherwise known as blind drop shipping). Not all drop shippers do this, but they still may be good resources.
- Your customer is satisfied with the product and service and shops with you again.
- The drop shipper charges you their drop-shipping wholesale price (there can be a difference between wholesale purchase and wholesale drop-shipping prices).
- You make a profit on the difference between the wholesale price and the retail price.

Among the benefits of drop shipping are:

- You don't have to warehouse inventory.
- You don't pay for merchandise up front and have it sit on your shelves while you wait for it to sell.
- You don't have to ship orders and make arrangements with shippers.
- You don't have to pay for packing supplies, boxes, and someone to ship orders.
- You can identify products that sell well for you without having to spend a lot of money up front.

Shapiro says drop shipping can be a cost-effective way to do business, especially when you are growing your business and investment in inventory is limited by your cash flow: "Drop shipping is a real business and can significantly enhance your existing product line so treat it like one. More online businesses are finding that a healthy blend of purchased, on-site inventory mixed with drop shipped inventory makes for a more robust store selection. And everyone knows that a full online store keeps customers on site and buying."

Shapiro advises being professional with your drop shippers by organizing yourself and staying on top of orders, and communicating clearly with your customers that their items are being drop shipped.

Q: ***Can I really make money with drop shipping?***

A: For online sellers, the drop-shipping product-sourcing method offers numerous advantages: no inventory investment, no storage or shipping issues, and the ability to offer a much broader product selection. It's also an excellent model to test new products and identify hot sellers (so you can source them in bulk for even greater profits).

But for a wholesaler, according to Worldwide Brands business development manager Colette Marshall (www.worldwidebrands.com), the operating costs are higher for offering drop shipping: "For example, extra manpower is needed to take one item out of a bulk lot and repack it and label into a smaller box; hence, there will usually be a fee associated with drop shipping orders."

In addition, wholesale discounts are limited on one item. For the convenience of the advantages of drop shipping, the sacrifice is taken in the profit margins associated with each product. Drop shipping can be profitable, but it depends on the product and sales volume.

Q: ***How can you tell if you're dealing with a good drop shipper?***

A: Unfortunately, locating real wholesale drop shippers isn't all that easy. Most new Internet retailers start by looking in the search engines. However, this is actually the *worst place possible* to look for legitimate wholesalers and drop shippers. Janelle Elms, eBay expert and author of *The Seven Essential Steps to Successful eBay Marketing*, estimates that 95 percent of the companies listed from a Google search for the keywords *drop shippers* are incompetent or worse. Robin Cowie, president of WorldwideBrands.com, also emphasizes that "you'll almost never find legitimate wholesale suppliers advertising in the search engines. The suppliers that advertise there are, with few exceptions, middlemen and scammers, trying very hard to convince you they're true wholesalers."

So how can you find drop shippers that are reputable? Elms offers three tips:

1. Go to Google, type in the drop-shipping company's name with the word *reviews* after it. This will bring up a list of blogs, discussion boards, and other places where people drop shipping from these companies post positive or negative feedback about them.

2. Go to the Better Business Bureau online (www.bbbonline.org) and check for a record on the company. (Elms cautions that you be wary of drop shippers listed as "certified" on the eBay site, because "many eBay certified companies have the world's worst record at the BBB").

3. Go through Worldwide Brands' exclusive product-sourcing directory service. "They have grilled every company listed in that directory beforehand, and if they see evidence of service problems, they will not hesitate to pull a drop shipper's listing," Elms says.

Q: ***I'm doing business with a drop shipper. What happens if I sell something for them on eBay and they no longer have the item in stock?***

A: This is one of the biggest risks in dealing with drop shippers, says Elms, "because they don't care about your feedback on eBay; if they ship several weeks late because of a stocking problem they still get their money. But you now have negative feedback—and rightly so—because you promised to ship within 7 days after the auction ended."

Always ask a drop shipper if they will give you notice when their inventory of a particular item is running low. Also, have a friend buy an item from the drop shipper to see how the drop shipper processes transactions and how it will look from an eBay buyer's perspective. (Elms recommends that you don't do it yourself—you don't want the drop shipper to know that you're checking them out because then they will go out of their way to give you a "perfect" experience.)

Finally, Elms advises that you always keep one or two of your best-selling drop-shipped items in your own inventory, just in case. "During the holiday crunch even some of the best drop shippers have a slowdown in turnaround time," says Elms, adding, "I always want to make sure I have a couple of inventory items in my own stock so I can give prompt service to a buyer who really needs the item quickly." Robin Cowie at Worldwide Brands also recommends having a backup supplier who can provide similar product in case a supplier runs out of inventory or there is a natural disaster that impacts the shipping of the product from a particular supplier. This also gives you the benefit of price comparing between suppliers.

Q: ***What things should you include in a drop-shipping contract?***

A: In order of importance:

- A provision requiring that they give you notice when their inventory of a particular item is running low
- A provision requiring them to deal with sales taxes in the states where they are doing business (or at least telling you where you must charge sales tax so you can collect these taxes from your buyers—see related questions in Chapter 13)
- A provision requiring them to use your mailing labels when shipping to your buyers ("because otherwise when the drop shipper ships they will include copies of their own catalogues and brochures so the buyer will deal directly with them in the future," says Elms)
- A provision allowing you to become an actual wholesaler for the drop shipper for high-volume items and getting the volume discounts you wouldn't ordinarily qualify for

A sample drop-shipping agreement form for eBay sellers appears as an appendix in my book *The eBay Seller's Tax and Legal Answer Book.*

Consignment Sales, Taking Consignments, and eBay Trading Assistants

Q: ***Is there any real difference between drop shipping and taking consignments of inventory?***

A: When you sell consignments on eBay, you are acting as an agent for someone else. You collect a commission (usually a percentage of the winning bid or retail price on eBay) and remit the balance to the person you're selling for. You handle all aspects of shipping the product to the winning bidder. As an online retailer using drop shipping, you are a business purchasing wholesale products from a licensed distributor or manufacturer and reselling those products. The wholesaler handles the shipment to the consumer for you, but you handle all other interaction with the consumer on the auction. The relationship you have with a wholesaler is long term and a renewable source of the product, whereas your relationship with a consignor (the legal term for the person for whom you are handling the consignment sale) is usually a one-time transaction.

Q: ***Do you have to be an eBay Consignment Shop or an eBay Trading Assistant to take consignments of inventory to sell on eBay?***

A: No, although there are some advantages to being an eBay Trading Assistant (see questions that follow). Any eBay seller can take consignments—in fact, I think you're crazy not to do so, especially if you are selling antiques and collectibles on eBay, as consignments are an excellent source of quality inventory.

You do not need a license to take consignments on eBay, although a handful of states are rumbling about requiring eBay sellers who take consignments to obtain auctioneer's licenses.

Just take out an advertisement in your local newspaper along the following lines: "Want to sell on eBay but don't have the time or patience to do it yourself? We take consignments! Call [your toll-free telephone number]."

Q: ***What are the biggest mistakes people make when taking consignments from people to sell on eBay?***

A: When taking consignments, always keep in mind that the people consigning stuff to you are not professional retailers or wholesalers. Often their decisions are based on emotion, and they have a nasty tendency to change their minds in the middle of your eBay listing. Never, *ever* take consignments without a *written* consignment agreement that includes the following important provisions:

- A statement that the consignor has the legal authority to sell the goods. (If you're dealing with an estate, ask for a copy of the consignor's *letters testamentary* appointing him or her the executor of the estate.)
- If the consignor is an individual or estate, the person's Social Security number or Employer Identification Number (EIN). This is important, as

you will have to send the person IRS Form 1099 at the end of the year if you handled more than $600 in consigned merchandise during the calendar year.

- A provision ensuring that once you take delivery and possession of the goods, the consignment is irrevocable and the consignor cannot back out of the deal without your express written permission. It is *essential* that you take possession of consigned goods; otherwise, you have no protection if the consignor changes his or her mind, the goods are lost or stolen, and so forth.

A sample consignment agreement for an eBay seller appears as an appendix in my book *The eBay Seller's Tax and Legal Answer Book.*

Q: ***If I'm already taking consignments from people to sell on eBay, what are the advantages of becoming an eBay Trading Assistant?***

A: An eBay Trading Assistant is someone—usually an experienced eBay seller—whom eBay has certified and lists in its Trading Assistant directory as a reliable person to take consignments. Generally, an eBay Trading Assistant must have completed at least one hundred successful selling transactions (not necessarily consignment sales) and have an excellent overall feedback rating.

The biggest advantage of being an eBay Trading Assistant, according to Marcia Cooper (www.generalenterprises.net), is that you are listed in eBay's directory, which is often the first place consignors look when they are seeking a local or regional consignment solution. Says Cooper, "We have gotten many, many, many calls from the Trading Assistant directory on eBay, and it's gotten us a ton of business."

For a great book on building a successful eBay Trading Assistant business, see *The eBay Entrepreneur: The Definitive Guide for Starting Your Own eBay Trading Assistant Business,* by Christopher M. Spencer (Kaplan Business, 2006).

4 Is It Okay to Sell This Stuff on eBay?

Animal Pelts, Skins, and Furs

Q: ***"I have a leather and fur vest that I bought at a high-end designer boutique in New York City last fall. The tag says that it's Lippi fur (sometimes spelled 'Lipi,' also known as the Chinese leopard cat). From what I've researched about it, it's not an endangered species, or illegal, which I originally assumed anyway because it's widely used in the fashion industry, and the brand is well known. I want to sell it on eBay, but there's an eBay policy that states 'No sales of any item that contains cat or dog fur will be allowed.' Why is that, and will this policy prevent me from selling the vest on eBay?"***

A: The first step is to check with the U.S. Fish and Wildlife Service (http://www.fws.gov/endangered/wildlife.html) to find out if the particular animal species appears on an Endangered Species List. If it does, you can't sell items with that animal's fur on eBay. Period.

Animal pelts and skins from nonendangered species may generally be listed on eBay if not in violation of the seller's specific state laws. For example, sales of bearskin rugs are prohibited by California law because the bear is California's state animal. However, because it is prohibited by federal law, no sales of any item that contains cat or dog fur are allowed.

While it's okay to sell items made of Lippi fur, it is prudent not to use the words *cat* or *dog* in your eBay listing for the item. Because eBay's search engines aren't always the most sophisticated, your listing may be pulled if they determine (however incorrectly) that you have stuffed Fluffy and put her up for sale to pay the vet's bills.

Antiquities, Historical Artifacts, and Native American Items

Q: ***"On a recent field trip to a Civil War battlefield with my kids, I found an old musket ball. Can I sell this on eBay?"***

A: Generally, historical artifacts may be sold on eBay, but not if they are illegally taken from a public park or historical site owned by the federal or state government. If the battlefield you visited was a public park (and it sounds like it was), you cannot sell this item on eBay. You should report your find to the organization or entity that runs the battlefield park, as you probably are in violation of state laws regulating archaeological finds on public property. For more information about eBay's artifacts policy, go to http://pages.ebay.com/help/policies/artifacts.html.

Q: ***"I have an old Native American ceramic jug that was handed down to me by my grandfather, who lived in the southwestern United States. I would like to sell this item on eBay but am concerned that it may have been illegally looted from a Native American grave site. My grandfather died long ago, so I can't ask him how he came across this object. Is there any reliable way to find out if this item is legal?"***

A: Yes. The National Museum of the American Indian, in Washington, D.C. (www.nmai.si.edu) operates a repatriation office where you can send objects such as this to be evaluated. To find this, click on the Outreach tab on the museum's home page, then click on Repatriation.

When you submit an item to the museum for evaluation, they will consult with the tribal authorities in the area where your grandfather lived in an effort to determine if it was an item normally buried with deceased tribal members or is otherwise of significant historical importance. Be advised that if the museum's repatriation office determines that the item was "grave goods," the item will probably be seized, as federal statutes give Native American tribes broad authority to reclaim items illegally looted from tribal lands. If, however, they conclude that the item is of no particular historical value and does not constitute grave goods, they will send you a certificate to that effect, which is a wonderful thing to include in your listing description!

A lot of people groan when I talk about repatriation in my eBay seminars and workshops, but keep this in mind: Grave robbing is illegal in virtually all countries on earth. How would you feel if someone on eBay was auctioning a pocket watch engraved as a gift to your grandfather, when you know the item was buried with him decades ago? There are much better, legal ways to source your product when you sell on eBay.

Brand-Name Merchandise, Trademarks, Copyrights, and Selling Knockoffs

Q: ***"What are the rules when it comes to selling trademarked or branded items, such as Gucci handbags or Tiffany jewelry, on eBay?"***

A: The rules about selling trademarked items on eBay are simple to state but difficult to apply in practice. Even experienced eBay sellers make mistakes in this area. The rules are basically these:

- You cannot sell knockoff or counterfeit items on eBay—never, ever, world without end, amen.
- It's up to you to determine whether an item is genuine or not; eBay won't help you.
- If the manufacturer or owner of the brand or trademark participates in eBay's Verified Rights Owner (VeRO) program and wants your listing terminated because they think you are not selling genuine merchandise, even if you are, eBay will shut down your listing and, for repeated violations, kick you off eBay.
- If you have questions about whether an item is genuine or not, eBay wants you to talk directly to the rights owner or manufacturer about it.
- Many leading manufacturers have posted About Me pages as part of their participation in the VeRO program, but these pages offer no guidance whatsoever to eBay sellers in determining whether an item is genuine or not—most simply repeat eBay's rules about not selling counterfeit or knockoff items and warn you of the perils of doing so.
- You cannot hold yourself out as an authorized reseller of a manufacturer unless you truly are one.

Really helpful, huh?

Participants in the VeRO program are required by eBay to give you an e-mail address where you can ask questions about their merchandise, but don't hold your breath waiting for your e-mail messages to be answered. There are some very good business reasons why manufacturers and brand owners won't go out of their way to help you sell their merchandise on eBay, among them the following:

- Many luxury goods makers view eBay as a liquidation or "flea market" venue and do not want their brands sold there under any circumstances for fear of tainting their brands' marketing image.
- Many manufacturers want to protect their distribution channels from low-cost competition from eBay sellers.
- Many manufacturers, especially of luxury goods, want to discourage the sale of used (but genuine) merchandise competing with their new high-margin offerings.
- Many manufacturers want to avoid lawsuits and negative publicity from buyers who are angry about their eBay purchases (because of irresponsible or inexperienced sellers) and claim that the manufacturers have aided and abetted the eBay seller's actions by encouraging sales on eBay.

There are also some very good business reasons why eBay won't do more to help you sell branded merchandise on the site:

- It views itself as a marketplace or platform on which transactions take place; eBay is legitimately concerned about jeopardizing its neutral status by taking sides between sellers and trademark owners.
- Let's face it, eBay isn't too worried about being sued by one or two sellers who feel their listings were arbitrarily removed. However, it is *petrified* (and rightly so) at the prospect of being sued by powerful Fortune 500 corporations (such as the parent corporations of Gucci and Tiffany) with deep pockets and big-name law firms behind them, and will go a long way to avoid offending these companies.

To begin your education on eBay's brand-name merchandise policies, take a look at their Guidelines for Creating Legally Compliant Listings (http://pages

.ebay.com/help/tp/compliant-listings.html). Then take eBay's tutorial "Intellectual Property Policies and VeRO" (there's a link to that on the above page, but you will have to sign in using your eBay user ID and password to take the tutorial). Finally, review eBay's VeRO page and read the frequently asked questions that are posted there: http://pages.ebay.com/help/policies/questions/vero-ended-item.html. You now know as much as anyone does about selling brand-name merchandise on eBay.

The bottom line is that when you sell brand-name merchandise on eBay without the manufacturer's permission or authorization, you are taking a risk and have to expect that occasionally eBay will terminate one of your listings. If you plan to sell these items more than occasionally (for example, as part of estate consignments), you should make an effort to become an authorized distributor of the manufacturer's merchandise and state that clearly in each of your eBay listings.

Q: ***"I sell mostly golf clothes, most of them Nike. I have recently started more auctions than I used to, and I just received the following notice as I tried to list: 'Attention Seller: In order to maintain a safe trading environment, selling limits are occasionally placed on accounts listing items that are reportedly favored by counterfeiters. At this time, you are limited in the number of items you can list (or revise) in any 7 day period. If you have any additional questions about this subject, email us at Customer Support. We sincerely value you as a member of our trading community and look forward to a continued successful relationship.' What's this all about? I'm a seller in good standing, with a terrific feedback score and rating."***

A: In an effort to reduce the marketing of counterfeit name-brand and designer items, eBay has established certain policies. Here are some links that may help explain what they have done and why they did it:

- http://auctionbytes.com/cab/abn/y06/m11/i29/s01
- http://pages.ebay.com/help/announcement/25.html#question6

Q: ***"As part of an estate consignment, I received several brand-name apparel items. The estate was extremely well-to-do, and I can't imagine these people would have purchased knockoffs. Should I list these items as genuine and describe the circumstances under which I acquired them? If not, where***

can I get information that would tell me whether these items are genuine or not?"

A: Never underestimate the rich when it comes to saving a buck. Just because someone can afford to buy an original Gucci handbag doesn't mean they won't buy knockoffs from a street vendor if it will help them save their pennies for that original Monet in Sotheby's annual Impressionist sale. A few of my well-heeled clients tell me they often buy knockoff jewelry and accessories for every-day wear because "if it gets lost or stolen, I won't lose too much sleep about it."

Do not list anything as genuine on eBay if you have doubts about it or if you simply don't know whether it is genuine or not. This applies especially to trade-marked or branded items. Contact the manufacturer or the nearest authorized distributor, and have them look at the item to help you determine whether it's genuine.

If that's not practical (for example, because you have too many items from the consignment that you have to list on eBay), list the item as "a used [what-ever]," describe the circumstances under which you acquired the item, take lots of detailed photos (including a close-up of any markings), and scrupulously avoid using the brand name or trademark in your listing title and description. Knowledgeable buyers who think your item is genuine will bid the item up without your having made any misrepresentations about its status. If they ask questions, answer them to the best of your ability and post your answers on the listing page, where other potential bidders will see them. And if even a single buyer e-mails you saying the item is "almost certainly" a fake or knockoff, take your listing down before eBay does.

Q: ***"We have genuine Prada and Carlo Mancini handbags that we want to sell on eBay. They are 100 percent authentic. They have original tags, and we have the receipts from the purchase. My concern is that someone might purchase one of the bags, then switch it for a knockoff and claim that we sent them a phony bag. Any suggestions as to how to protect against this happening?"***

A: Once an item has been shipped, it's almost impossible to control what the buyer does with it. Nothing is absolutely foolproof, but here are some tips:

- Always take detailed photos of the items you sell on eBay before shipping them.

- Never sell items like these to buyers with low feedback scores or buyers in countries that are notorious for online fraud activities.
- Consider using an ultraviolet pen or other invisible marking device to tag the item before you ship, and make a notation of the tag so that if the buyer complains, you can describe it in your report to eBay.

Q: ***"While cleaning out my house, I found an empty Tiffany box from when I bought my ex-wife her engagement ring. I was going to throw it out, but then I thought, 'Hey, why don't I sell it on eBay?' There may be somebody out there who bought something from Tiffany's but lost the box." Will I get in trouble if I sell this on eBay?"***

A: You almost certainly will. While there might be someone out there who needs a genuine Tiffany box for a legitimate reason, I'll bet there is more than one guy out there who bought a cheap engagement ring for his girlfriend and would just *love* an original Tiffany box to put it in, for reasons that should require no explanation.

The very explicit policy that eBay has established against "encouraging others to infringe trademarks, copyrights and other intellectual property" can be found at http://pages.ebay.com/help/policies/encouraging.html. Read it, then throw the box away.

If that doesn't scare you enough, think about what will happen to the buyer when his girlfriend finds out the engagement ring isn't really from Tiffany and the cops haul you in as an accessory to murder!

Items Incorporating Celebrity Likenesses or Images

Q: ***"I took some great photos of a famous celebrity during this year's eBay Live! show. Because I'm such a fan of this guy, and I know a lot of people in the eBay community are, I've made up key chains and other body jewelry items featuring these photos. I know he won't mind—he's crazy about eBay, I understand—but will eBay pull my listings if I put these up for sale there?"***

A: I'm flattered, I really am . . . ☺. But, unfortunately, you can't sell these items on eBay. Under eBay's Faces, Names, and Signatures Policy (http://pages.ebay.com/help/policies/signatures.html), "sellers are not permitted to list an item containing the image, likeness, name, or signature of another person unless the product was made or authorized by that person."

You should e-mail this celebrity, send him photos of these items (or better yet, ask where you can overnight some samples), and ask his permission to use this photo on the items. If he grants it, then you can sell the items on eBay, but be sure to put some language in each item description saying specifically something like this: "I have written authorization from [celebrity's name] to offer these items." Knowing the way many celebrities operate, however, don't hold your breath waiting for his response—celebrities are notoriously difficult when it comes to protecting their image and their legal right to publicity, and I strongly doubt that any famous person, no matter how eBay-friendly, will let this happen without getting a significant piece of the action.

Drug Paraphernalia

Q: ***"On a recent visit to China, I visited an old antiques store and picked up what appears to be an authentic 1800s pipe for smoking opium. It's made of ivory, is carved with all sorts of figures, and is absolutely gorgeous. Is there any problem selling something like this on eBay?"***

A: Unfortunately, yes—eBay's policy on drugs and drug paraphernalia (http://pages.ebay.com/help/policies/drugs-drug-paraphernalia.html) permits the sale of some tobacco-related pipes and other antiques, even if they might have been used to smoke illegal substances, but the sale of any product that was specifically designed for the consumption of an illegal drug is prohibited on eBay. The policy specifically refers to "pipes used to smoke peyote or opium, whether new or antique," so you're out of luck. This also applies to that bong you can prove was actually used by Jimi Hendrix during the Monterey Pop music festival in 1967.

You should also check with a good import/export lawyer. China recently passed a law prohibiting the export of "art items" over one hundred years old without a government export permit. Your pipe might fall within the definition of "art items." If it does, you may have to send it back to China. Good luck getting a refund.

Event Tickets

Q: ***"I live in Connecticut and bought some tickets to a Broadway show in New York City a while back. Because of a family emergency, I will not be able to attend the show. I don't have time to find a buyer for these tickets in my neighborhood. Can I put these up for sale on eBay?"***

A: You may sell event tickets on eBay as long as there's compliance with state law. For a summary of eBay's requirements, go to http://pages.ebay.com/help/policies/event-tickets.html.

In this case, the event is in New York, and you (the seller) are located in Connecticut. Under eBay's policy, you can sell these tickets on eBay without limit, because New York (where the event will take place) is a "non-regulated location." If you were selling tickets to an event scheduled to take place in Connecticut (such as a home game of the minor league baseball team the Bridgeport Bluefish), you could sell the tickets, but for not more than $3 over their face value, even if the bidder was from another state.

Information Products

Q: ***"I am self-publishing an e-book on how to get better results when bidding on eBay and beat the snipers. Is this something I could sell on eBay?"***

A: Self-published material has something of a schizophrenic life on eBay. An actual printed book, self-published or otherwise, can be listed in the Books section on eBay. Your e-book, however, is likely to be considered an information product subject to eBay's Compilation and Information Sales Policy (http://pages.ebay.com/help/policies/compilation.html). Under this policy, your e-book must:

- Not contain any cross-category information (for example, an e-book on "How to Detect Forgeries in Ancient Roman Coins" might be problematic if people searching in the "ancient coins" category are likely to stumble on it)
- Be listed only in the Everything Else > Information Products category

- Not be combined as a bonus item with any other listing
- Not contain any specific brand names or keywords unless the listing is offering the item in question
- Not contain excessive use of keywords to describe the contents of the compilation or informational media
- Not offer information on how to either purchase specific items or receive them for free, outside of eBay
- Not provide listings of URLs that offer buyers the opportunity to purchase items outside of eBay

Offensive Materials

Q: ***"In searching randomly on eBay, I find lots of neo-Nazi and Aryan Nation items. Why is it that these items do not violate eBay's Offensive Items Policy?"***

A: Technically, they do, but it's often difficult to distinguish between an item of genuine historical value and an item whose sole purpose and object is to promote racist, sexist, or religious propaganda. There is also the question of permitting freedom of expression. In the spirit of a famous U.S. Supreme Court decision, the First Amendment was expressly designed to allow full and free debate of all possible viewpoints and provide "freedom for the thought we hate." The proper way to deal with speech you find improper or offensive is not to suppress it but to debate, challenge, and refute it.

eBay has an Offensive Materials Policy that should be consulted in situations like these; the complete text can be found at http://pages.ebay.com/help/policies/offensive.html. The portion of this policy that deals with Black Americana is particularly astute and deserves to be quoted in its entirety:

> Occasionally, there may be listings of antiques or historical pieces (often referred to as "Black Americana") that, while unacceptable in today's society, are relics of an era where racially inappropriate and insensitive products were widely available. While these items are offensive to eBay and its community, eBay recognizes that such his-

> torical items find their way into museums and private collections, and serve as important tools for education about the past. eBay permits such listings of historical pieces, but at the request of community members, **eBay will not permit listings of racial or ethnically inappropriate reproductions.** [Emphasis in original.]

Less astute (and actually quite confusing) is the portion of eBay's Offensive Materials Policy that deals with Nazi, Ku Klux Klan, and other "hate group" memorabilia. That portion expressly prohibits sales of (among other things):

- Items that bear symbols of the Nazis, the SS, or the KKK, including authentic German World War II memorabilia such as Olympic medals that bear such marks
- Items that were owned by or affiliated with Nazi leaders
- Music or films that promote hatred and racial supremacy
- Holocaust denial books

But the policy expressly permits sales of (among other things):

- German coins and postage stamps (cancelled or otherwise) from the World War II era, regardless of markings
- World War II memorabilia that does not bear the Nazi or SS markings
- Books and movies about World War II or Nazi Germany that do not contain propaganda, even if the Nazi symbol appears on the item.

I have a lot of trouble making sense of these rules. If I am reading them correctly, then:

- A gold medal from the 1936 Berlin Olympics awarded to U.S. track and field star Jessie Owens—an African-American athlete and one of the greatest sports heroes of all time—would be barred from sale on eBay because it has swastikas on it and is therefore "Nazi propaganda" (if you have one of these, not to worry—the Smithsonian Institute in Washington and other major American museums will probably pay you a fortune for it) but

- An envelope from 1936 with a German stamp postmarked "Death to All Non-Aryans!" (in German, of course) is okay to sell on eBay because it isn't "Nazi propaganda."

It will take a better lawyer than I am to reconcile those two examples, and I sincerely hope eBay will revisit and revise its "hate group memorabilia" rules in the near future, so sellers will have better guidance in this area.

The best advice is to contact eBay and get a ruling if you're selling a Nazi-related item that is not clearly identified one way or the other in eBay's policy, and do not use a specific reference to "Nazi" or "KKK" in the item listing to avoid having the listing pulled by eBay's listing filters.

Q: ***"Does antique artwork that depicts rooster fighting (commonly known as 'cock fighting') violate eBay's policy against listing items that actively promote and/or glorify violent crime?"***

A: The Offensive Materials Policy that eBay has established is written fairly broadly and does not specifically refer to rooster-fighting items.

The items referred to in eBay's policy are not all-inclusive; eBay specifically reserves the right "in its discretion, [to] remove items when the item or description graphically portrays violence or victims of violence, and lacks substantial social, artistic or political value." Gory photos of automobile accidents and murder scenes (except, of course, for historical photos such as those of the St. Valentine's Day Massacre in Chicago) are clearly included in the sweep of this policy.

Our ancestors were not always politically correct when it came to the games and sports they indulged in—in ancient Rome, people stood in line for hours to watch condemned criminals being torn to pieces by wild animals in the Colosseum, and an ancient Roman fresco depicting such a scene could almost certainly be sold on eBay. In Shakespeare's England, a common entertainment was to watch captured bears fighting for their survival against a pack of rabid dogs. A set of Elizabethan engravings depicting scenes of bear baiting could almost certainly be sold on eBay (and actually would be worth a bloody fortune).

In the United States, rooster fighting was once quite legal, and it still is in certain foreign countries. The prohibition on rooster fighting in many states today is often driven not so much by animal rights or antiviolence concerns as it is the state's desire to control illegal gambling. For gambling of any kind to be legal in just about all states, it must be operated or regulated by the state government (or by a Native American tribal government, which is independent of state authority). Accordingly, an argument can be made that rooster fighting is not a violent crime at all, because human beings are not the intended victims of the activity (if that sounds silly, keep in mind that in every state of which I'm aware, the intentional shooting of someone's dog or cat is not legally considered murder but rather "trespass to personal property"—you can sue the shooter for damages, but you can't put him or her in jail).

The best advice is to contact eBay and get a ruling if you're selling an item that might offend some people's sensibilities and is not clearly identified one way or the other in eBay's policy. If gladiatorial combat ever comes back into vogue, though . . .

Real Estate

Q: ***"What are the rules about selling real estate on eBay? Must I be a licensed real estate broker?"***

A: The Real Estate section of eBay (pages.ebayrealestate.com) is operated by eBay Real Estate Inc., an affiliate of eBay, in order to limit liability. To find the rules for selling real estate on eBay, go to http://pages.ebay.com/help/policies/real-estate.html. Basically:

- You are permitted to post a classified ad for your property. Potential buyers indicate their interest by means of a contact form and negotiate directly with you.
- You are permitted to post auction-style listings for your property, but the results are not binding; they are merely an offer to purchase, subject to any and all conditions and procedures required by your state law.
- If you own title to your home jointly with your spouse (or anyone else), you cannot sell only your interest in the property on eBay; you have to sell the entire *fee interest* (i.e., both of your interests) on eBay, or nothing at all.

- You cannot sell someone else's property on eBay Real Estate unless you are a licensed real estate broker in the state where the property is located.

Everything Else: Researching Prohibited Items

Q: ***"Where can I get a comprehensive list of items that cannot be sold on eBay?"***

A: Unfortunately, such a list does not exist because it's impossible to put together. The laws of many countries prohibit the sale of items that can be sold perfectly legally in the United States, and vice versa. Nobody knows them all.

The Prohibited and Restricted Items" page of the eBay website contains a list of all restricted and prohibited items for which there is an eBay policy (http://pages.ebay.com/help/policies/items-ov.html). You can also go to the Help section of the eBay site, click on the A–Z Index, click on "P," and then scroll down to the word "Policy," for a complete alphabetical listing of eBay's policies.

Keep in mind, though, that eBay reserves the right to pull listings if it just doesn't feel right about the item you're selling. Be careful to avoid using keywords in your listing titles that might lead eBay's search engine spiders to think (mistakenly, of course) that you are selling a prohibited or restricted item. Put up a listing the wrong way for a nineteenth-century metal sign advertising "drugs, glasses, pipes, and cigarette rolling papers," and you might find your listing pulled because eBay thinks you are selling drug paraphernalia!

5 I'm Trying to Sell Something on eBay, but I'm Not Sure How to Describe It

Fraud, "Buyer Beware," and Disclosing Flaws in Items

Q: ***"I'm selling antiques and collectibles on eBay. Most of the items I'm selling have flaws of some kind—some are obvious when you look at the item, but some aren't. How much information am I supposed to give in my listing description about these flaws? Doesn't the rule of 'buyer beware' apply on eBay as it does everywhere else?"***

A: People who buy antiques on eBay are extremely courageous folks. Even with the best digital photos and the most detailed descriptions, you still don't know what the thing will look like until it shows up at your doorstep and you can look at it up close. I can sympathize with some buyers who want to unwind their purchases and get their money back because the item "looked a lot better in the photographs." People who sell antiques on eBay need to be hypersensitive to this and do as much as they can to manage their buyers' expectations before the listing closes.

There are two ways you can commit fraud in your item descriptions. If you say that something is so when it really isn't, and you know it isn't, that's fraud. But you can also commit fraud by omission. If you know something is flawed, you fail to disclose the flaw in your item description, and the omission is *material*—that is, it would likely cause reasonable buyers to change their minds if they knew the truth—you have committed fraud, even though you kept your mouth shut.

Because buyers on eBay are extremely touchy about sellers who don't tell the full story about their merchandise, don't take the chance. Say everything you know about the item. If an antique has a crack or rust spots, take a close-up photo of these flaws so your buyer can see how material they are to him or her. If you're not sure whether a part has been replaced or an item has been repainted, say you're not sure and offer the buyer thirty days to have the item examined by an expert (really great sellers even recommend experts in the buyer's area) with a full money-back guarantee if the buyer is not satisfied.

Even though "buyer beware" is still the law in many places, a disgruntled buyer will almost certainly give you a black eye by leaving negative feedback for you on eBay and ranting about you in eBay's community forums, and that won't help you build the successful business on eBay that you want to have someday.

Q: ***"Is it possible to be sued for fraud on eBay even though you honestly didn't know about flaws in your merchandise before you listed them?"***

A: First of all, people rarely if ever sue for fraud because of something they bought on eBay: Either the dollar amount is too small or it's too much of a hassle for the buyer to bring a lawsuit against a seller who lives in a faraway state (or another country). What they do instead is leave negative feedback for the seller on eBay, recover their money under PayPal's Buyer Protection Policy (if they used PayPal to pay for the item), and rant and rave about the seller on eBay's community forums in an effort to damage the seller's reputation with other community members.

But to answer the question, in order to prove fraud, a buyer would have to prove in court that you knew, or should have known, that an item was defective or counterfeit before you put it up for sale on eBay. Unless an eBay seller specializes in a certain type of merchandise and holds him- or herself out as an expert, this is extremely hard to prove.

An eBay buyer could, however, sue you for *breach of warranty*. When you put something up for sale on eBay, everything you say in your item description, your photos, and your responses to e-mail inquiries constitutes a legal warranty that potential bidders and buyers are entitled to rely on before making their purchase. If anything you say in your listing is not 100 percent accurate, you have breached that warranty to your buyer and will be required by law to return the buyer's money upon demand, even if you believed everything you said in good faith.

This is one of the main reasons it is so difficult to build a successful business on eBay if you do not understand the merchandise you're selling inside and out. I used to collect antique mechanical banks from the 1800s, and I can tell you with great certainty that a bank from that era that is 100 percent original—with all its original paint and without any repairs, replacements or touch-ups whatever—is an extreme rarity, a one-in-a-million item that could easily sell in the five- to six-figure range if one ever came up for auction. These banks have been played with by six generations of American children, and they often contain delicate mechanisms that freeze up or break down if you so much as look at them cross-eyed. For anything like this to survive 120 years without any sort of damage, repair, part replacement, or paint chipping is almost miraculous.

Yet I see listings of mechanical banks on eBay all the time from sellers who breathlessly hold their banks out to be "100 percent original, in excellent condition"—with an initial bid price of $200! Frankly, these sellers are all breaching their warranties to their buyers and may possibly (if they know of defects in or repairs to the bank they're selling) be committing fraud.

Disclaiming Warranties, Breach of Warranty, Implied Warranties, and "As Is" Sales

Q: ***"I'm selling something that I think is a genuine antique, but I'm not sure because I'm really not an expert in these things. Is it okay to list the item "as is," say that I don't know anything about the item, and ask the buyer to rely on the photos to determine if it's real or not?"***

A: Doing so won't get you into legal trouble on eBay, although it won't do much to build your buyers' confidence. Unless you're very lucky and you've stumbled across a missing Michelangelo that every knowledgeable art buyer who views your listing recognizes instantly, resulting in a feeding frenzy among buyers (don't laugh—something like this happens once in a blue moon on eBay when someone lists an "attic treasure"), you're probably not going to get much for this item. Most sellers who list items this way are, in my humble opinion, simply too lazy to take the time to research the item on eBay or offline to find out what they've got. With just an hour or two of effort, you should be able to learn enough about the item to write at least a basic description that will get you a few reasonable bids.

Also, note that while you can disclaim knowledge about an item, you cannot disclaim the authenticity or legality of an item—for instance, by saying, "I really don't know if this is an original Gucci handbag or not." As an eBay seller, you always warrant that an item you sell on eBay is original and that it may be sold legally. To see eBay's policy on this, go to http://pages.ebay.com/help/policies/authenticity-disclaimers.html.

Q: ***"If I am handling an estate sale and I get a handbag with a Gucci label that doesn't look like a knockoff, how do I describe this item when listing it on eBay?"***

A: Whatever you do, do not list it as a "genuine Gucci handbag" unless you are 100 percent sure it is one. If you don't have the time to get an expert opinion, list it as a used handbag, describe the circumstances under which you acquired it, take lots of detailed photos (including close-ups of any markings), and do not use the word *Gucci* in your listing title or item description. If knowledgeable buyers recognize this as a genuine Gucci handbag, they will bid accordingly and you will get the price you want without risking a misrepresentation of the item. And if even one person e-mails you saying the item is "clearly a knockoff," pull the listing until you can get more information.

Q: ***"I buy a lot of tag sale and estate items in bulk and frequently don't examine them very carefully before I post them on eBay. What I do instead is photograph the box and state clearly in the description that I haven't examined the condition of the item and that the sale is 'as is.' Still, a buyer complained that the box didn't include all the parts. Do I have to give him his money back?"***

A: When you're talking about warranties, you should realize that there are two kinds: express and implied.

An *express* warranty is something you actually say in your listing description. So, for example, if you state in your description that something is "100 percent complete and original," the buyer is entitled to a full refund if he or she can show that even a single part—no matter how small and insignificant—has been replaced, repaired, or gone missing.

An implied warranty is something that you *don't* say outright in your listing but that the buyer has the right to assume, based on what you *do* tell them.

In this case, by photographing the box, you have made an implied warranty that the box contains all the contents it's supposed to have. This buyer was correct in accusing you of a breach of warranty, and you should give him his money back.

Now, you clearly said you had no idea of the condition of what was in the box, so if the box had contained all the required contents but the condition was just so-so, you would have been on stronger ground. But frankly, even in that case I probably would recommend that you return the buyer's money—any seller who's too lazy to open a box and see what's in it before putting it up on eBay is asking for problems. Who knows? There may have been something really great in that old box. Never judge a package by its label!

Q: ***"I sold an antique on eBay last week and the buyer called me to say the thing didn't work. I don't know much about these things, and I didn't say in my description that the item was in 'good working condition.' Do I have to give this buyer his money back?"***

A: Absolutely. Even if you are not an expert in something mechanical, you should at least test it to make sure it works before putting it up for sale on eBay. If you can't do this (because testing it would be too difficult), then you should state clearly that you haven't tested the item and will gladly refund the buyer's money within *x* days of the listing close date if the buyer is not satisfied for any reason.

Q: ***"I recently sold an antique toy from the 1800s on eBay for quite a bit of money. The buyer complained that the toy was painted with lead paint and wanted her money back because she wouldn't allow her child to play with anything that had lead paint on it. Having children of my own, I sympathize completely, but I don't think I should give her money back because this was clearly an antique that children shouldn't be allowed to play with. Scraping off the paint would reduce the value of the toy significantly. Am I in the right here?"***

A: In the answer to the previous question, I said that warranties in eBay listings can be either express or implied. One of the implied warranties that you make in every one of your eBay listings is something lawyers call the "implied warranty of fitness for a particular purpose." This means that if you know an object is normally used for a specific purpose, you warrant that the object can be used for that purpose unless you specifically tell the buyer that it *can't* be used for that purpose.

For example, let's say that I put up for sale on eBay "a genuine 1920s box of Arm & Hammer baking soda." I sell it to a buyer, who e-mails me the following week saying, "I want my money back! I put that box of Arm & Hammer baking soda in my refrigerator and it stinks!" Even though I intended to sell it as an antique and assumed that anyone buying an eighty-year-old box of anything would consider it such, I certainly do know that the biggest reason people buy Arm & Hammer baking soda is to deodorize their refrigerators. Silly as it may sound, I should have warned my buyer that the contents might not still be good.

When you sell toys on eBay—even antique ones—you have to consider the possibility that buyers want something their children can play with. After all, that's what toys are all about. I do know a few people who buy antique mechanical banks in poor to fair condition (which are basically worthless) precisely because they want to teach their children the value of saving money in a fun way and give their child the magic of playing with something over a hundred years old. (Personal note: When I was in fifth grade we studied ancient Rome, and the teacher one day brought in some genuine ancient Roman coins and passed them around. I cannot describe the magic of holding in your hand something that a gladiator, a Christian martyr, or even Julius Caesar himself may have held in his hands at some point. I've been hooked on history ever since. . . . By the way, if any history teachers are reading this, you can buy genuine ancient Roman coins on eBay for about $2 each.)

I would give this buyer her money back, and when you list the item again, state specifically: "This is being sold as an antique; because it contains lead paint, it is not appropriate or healthy for children to play with."

Comparison Listings and Keyword Spamming

Q: ***"I am listing a handbag for sale on eBay that is definitely not a Gucci handbag and definitely not a knockoff, but it does resemble a Gucci handbag in some ways. As long as I clearly state that the item is not a Gucci handbag, can I say in the listing title or description that the item is 'like a Gucci handbag' or 'resembles in some ways a Gucci handbag'?"***

A: One of the surest ways to get into trouble selling on eBay is to use the word *like* or *as* in a listing title or description—eBay does not like it when you compare your item to other, brand-name, goods because there is the risk that people searching on eBay for genuine Gucci handbags will pick up your listing. A lot of unethical sellers will intentionally put into their listings brand names that have nothing to do with their items (for example, "Used Handbag Gucci Hermes Louis Vuitton") in an effort to attract buyers looking for brand-name merchandise. This is called *keyword spamming.*

The keyword spamming policy eBay has established (http://pages.ebay.com/help/policies/keyword-spam.html) deserves to be quoted in its entirety:

> Keyword spamming occurs when members place brand names or other inappropriate keywords in a title or description for the purpose of gaining attention or diverting members to a listing. Keyword spamming in listings is not permitted on eBay. The searchable text sellers place in listings must be directly relevant to the item being sold.

Q: ***"I want to sell an old jewelry box on eBay. It's the same robin's egg blue that Tiffany uses on its boxes, but it is clearly not a Tiffany box—the Tiffany logo doesn't appear anywhere on the thing. To be safe, should I state in my item description that this is 'absolutely, positively not a Tiffany box'?"***

A: Sometimes, trying too hard to do the right thing on eBay can get you into trouble, and this is a good example. Your intentions here are completely honorable, but by even using the word *Tiffany* in your listing, the eBay search bots will include it in the results when buyers search for genuine Tiffany merchandise. Because of that, you are keyword spamming and are in violation of eBay's policy prohibiting that (see the answer to the previous question).

Leave the Tiffany name out of your listing, list the box as an "old robin's egg blue jewelry box," and let people draw their own conclusions.

"New," "Like New," and "Used"

Q: ***"I sell clothing from my own (quite large) closet that has been worn only a couple of times. Can I describe the item in my eBay listing as 'like new' or 'almost new'?"***

A: Use of the words *like new* or *almost new* in listing titles or descriptions is strictly prohibited by eBay's Legally Compliant Listings policy (http://pages.ebay

.com/help/tp/compliant-listings.html#2). If an item has been worn only once or has never been worn but has been removed from its original packaging, it should be described as "used."

Here's a trick my mom uses when she sells stuff at flea markets. Like a lot of moms, she has tons of clothing in her closets that she's had for years but has never worn. Whenever someone at a flea market shows interest in one of these items, Mom says, "It's not new, but I've never worn it; it was given to me as a gift." Consider describing your used clothing this way—you're not violating eBay's policy, yet you aren't mentioning the dreaded word *used*.

Q: ***"I sell children's clothing and underwear on eBay. I sell a lot of clothing, and it is mostly new and always in good condition. Clothing is always washed prior to shipment. Most items have never been worn, and most have tags. There are, on occasion, a few items that have been worn for a few hours or a few times, and that is all. Of course, if there's any chance that it has been worn numerous times, I would definitely say that the item is used. But when it comes to items that have been worn for a few hours or a few times, I usually say these items are new. If they are new with the original tags still on them, I say 'new with tags,' but if not, I just say 'new.' Is this going to get me intro trouble on eBay?"***

A: Oh, yes. A car that you have just purchased and driven off the dealer's lot is a used car. An item of clothing you have worn only once is used clothing. Think how you would feel if you bought an item of clothing on eBay that was listed as new and discovered when it arrived that someone had worn it before? I bet you would be pretty upset! Only items in their original packaging, unopened, and with the original tags should be described as new in an eBay listing. Note also that for used clothing to be sold on eBay it must first be cleaned according to the manufacturer's specifications spelled out on the clothing label (http://pages.ebay.com/help/policies/used-clothing.html)—removal of this label from an item of clothing is a federal offense, believe it or not.

Still, I can understand why you want to avoid using the dreaded word *used* for items that have never been worn and are in pristine condition despite having been removed from their original packaging. See the answer to the previous question about a technique my mom uses in flea markets—it might be helpful.

One more point: The sale of used underwear on eBay is strictly prohibited (http://pages.ebay.com/help/policies/used-clothing.html). Interestingly, eBay permits the sale of used swimwear—buyer beware.

Condition: Grading

Q: ***"I sell rare coins on eBay. Recently I sold a coin and described it as I saw it. I looked at my description and close-up photos and compared them with other, similar coins on eBay. It matched up with Very Fine (VF). Now, I'm not a professional coin grader, but I have been collecting them for ten years, and I believe that my description was correct. Plus, there were pictures showing the coin. The buyer wants a refund because he says the coin is only in Fine Plus (F+) condition, which is slightly below Very Fine. Do I have to give him his money back?"***

A: Describing the condition of an item you are selling on eBay is always tricky, but it's especially so with coins, stamps, and certain antiques that have an established hierarchy of grade levels. For example, ancient Roman and Greek coins are graded using the following scale: Poor, Fair, Good, Very Good, Fine, Very Fine, Extremely Fine, About Mint State, Mint State, and Fleur de Coin (FDC). On this scale, a coin that is listed in Good condition isn't in such great shape after all and may actually look like it went through hell before it made its way onto eBay.

Grades for American coins are even tougher, because within each of these grading categories there is a ranking from 1 to 100, depending on the level of detail that is still visible on the coin—a VF20 coin will look very different from a VF90 coin, even though both are graded Very Fine (VF).

Assigning an object to one of these grading classifications can be very tricky if you are not a recognized expert. There are grading handbooks that tell you in general terms what antiques dealers look for when assigning a grade to an object. In the case of coins, there are classification services (such as the Professional Coin Grading Service in Newport Beach, California, www.pcgs.com) that assign conditions to coins and then slab them in Lucite containers to prevent further deterioration and wear. But there are dealers and professionals who will question even an expert appraisal and evaluation as being either overly conservative or overly generous, depending on their own evaluation of a particular coin.

If you are selling coins on eBay, it's a good idea to:

- Have the coin professionally graded and slabbed (encased in Lucite) by PCGS or one of the other leading third-party appraisal services, if the value of the coin warrants it.
- Have the coin evaluated by a local (reputable) dealer, and state clearly in your listing that "this coin was graded VF20 by a reputable dealer in New York City."
- Grade the coin yourself, and explain in your item description the key factors that led you to grade the coin as you did (for example, "observe specifically that the third tail feather on the Native American's headdress is clearly visible, which I felt merited grading this Indian-head penny as a VF30 rather than a VF20").
- Grade the coin as best you can, and list the coin at the grade immediately below the one you think is appropriate—that way, there is little chance a buyer will think you are inflating the grade, and there is a good chance buyers may think you are overly conservative in your grading and bid the coin up to its true value.

Whenever a buyer questions your grading of an item, as this one did, and you are convinced the buyer knows what he or she is talking about, it's a good idea to post the buyer's e-mail on the eBay listing itself, along with a short note saying, "As we all know, the grading of coins is a highly subjective matter—here are some other opinions of this coin's grade so you can make a more informed decision."

As for giving this buyer his money back, I would do it. In your future listings, don't list a condition at all but rather post several close-up photos of the item and let your buyers draw their own conclusions about condition. In my experience, most buyers will actually give your coins higher grades than a professional grading service would!

Colors

Q: ***"I sell clothing and ladies' fashion accessories on eBay. Recently I sold an orange jersey on eBay, but the buyer wants his money back, claiming that the***

jersey was not the same shade of orange as the photo on my eBay listing depicted. My sales Terms and Conditions state clearly that I do not accept returns on clothing items, for fear they may have been worn by the buyer or removed from their original packaging. Do I have to refund this buyer's money?"

A: This is a tough call. Colors are a particularly sticky subject on eBay, because they are literally all over the spectrum. Often a buyer trying to wiggle out of a bad bargain claims that the color of the item received didn't match the color on your auction photo.

Sometimes it's your fault—for example, if you didn't properly calibrate your digital camera when you took the photo or you didn't light the object properly so the color showed up darker than it actually was.

But a lot of times it's the buyer's fault. Colors often show up slightly different due to the way you set your monitor. If a buyer is using an older monitor and has it calibrated differently than someone using a newer monitor, the color of the object may show up differently on each screen.

There really is nothing you can do about this situation except disclose to potential buyers that you are not responsible for differences in color due to differing monitor settings, and you can be flexible with your return policy if a buyer really makes a stink about it.

For sample language for the Terms and Conditions section of your eBay listing relating to colors, see Appendix B of my book *The eBay Seller's Tax and Legal Answer Book.*

Copying Other Sellers' Descriptions

Q: ***"I sell a lot of different items on eBay, and it takes up way too much time for me to write descriptions of each item from scratch. If I see somebody else selling a similar item on eBay, can I simply cut and paste the person's description into my listing and perhaps edit it a little bit so it describes the exact item I'm selling?"***

A: There's an eBay policy saying you shouldn't use other sellers' descriptions, photos, and other listing content without their permission (http://pages.ebay.com/help/policies/vero-image-text-theft.html), but I don't know that eBay enforces it very aggressively. There's also the need (discussed in Chapter 6) for eBay sellers to do everything possible to minimize the amount of time it takes to list items so they're not reinventing the wheel every time they put up a new listing. Also, there are only so many ways you can describe certain merchandise, such as a particular make and model of laptop computer—put ten monkeys in a room with this item and they will all write the same description, pretty much word for word.

Common sense should rule here. You absolutely should not use someone else's description if the item you're selling is not 100 percent identical to the other item. I also strongly discourage your using anybody else's description word for word unless you are selling generic merchandise that can be described only one way. On the other hand, using several other sellers' descriptions of similar merchandise as templates or guidelines for drafting your own unique item description shouldn't get you into too much trouble on eBay. But . . . if a particular seller is well known on eBay for using certain idiosyncrasies of grammar or syntax in his or her item descriptions, avoid copying them in your own because, although imitation is the sincerest form of flattery, plagiarism can get you kicked off eBay.

Your Selling Terms and Conditions

Q: ***"I would like to put Selling Terms and Conditions on my eBay listings so buyers won't be confused as to when I will and won't accept returns of items. I have looked at the Terms and Conditions on other eBay sellers' listings, and I think they're very forbidding and off-putting, having been obviously drafted by lawyers. Do you know where I can find some more user-friendly forms that will protect me but not scare my buyers off?"***

A: There are three mistakes people make when putting Terms and Conditions on their eBay listing pages.

The first mistake is not to have any Terms and Conditions at all. As long as you are not violating any of eBay's policies or disqualifying your listings for PayPal's Seller Protection Policy (see Chapter 11), eBay allows you wide discretion in setting your return and refund policy, disclaiming warranties, stating clearly how soon after a listing closes you will ship items, and so forth. If you do not clearly state in your listing that you will not accept returns of a particular item, then there's a presumption that you will accept returns under certain conditions, and buyers will be entitled to rely on that assumption if they receive defective or incorrect merchandise.

The second mistake is to go too far in the other direction, posting Terms and Conditions with ten or more pages of legalese that spell out in Byzantine detail how few rights and remedies buyers have when they successfully bid for your items. If it takes more than a minute for people to read your Terms and Conditions, you probably are scaring off some good buyers, because either:

- They are convinced you are an inflexible, bullying nut job who won't even listen to them if they have a legitimate problem with your merchandise.

or

- They don't feel they should have to hire a lawyer every time they bid for something on eBay!

The third mistake is to have a lawyer draft your Terms and Conditions. Your Terms and Conditions should be an extension of your item description. They should be written in the same language, and in plain English. By all means, have a lawyer review your Terms and Conditions before posting them in your listings, but make sure the language and tone of voice are yours.

You can find sample Terms and Conditions for eBay listings in the back of my book *The eBay Seller's Tax and Legal Answer Book.*

Q: ***"What should I include in my listing Terms and Conditions to avoid being cheated by unscrupulous buyers on eBay?"***

A: At the very least, your listing Terms and Conditions should include the following:

- A disclaimer of all warranties that are not expressly and explicitly stated in your item description
- A statement that residents of your state who buy from you will have to pay sales tax in addition to their winning bid amount (unless, of course, your state is one of the few that doesn't have a sales tax)

- A list of people whom you do not want to buy from you or bid on your merchandise (for example, residents of certain countries or people with low feedback scores)
- Your refund and return policy
- If you allow overseas buyers, a statement that their purchase may be subject to customs duties, import restrictions, and value-added taxes, and a recommendation that they consult with their legal or tax advisers before buying anything from you
- Your shipping policy, including an explanation of your shipping and handling charges if you impose these
- A statement of precisely when you will consider the buyer to be in default for failing to pay for an item in a timely fashion

I have included sample Terms and Conditions for eBay listings meeting all of these requirements, and more, at the end of my book *The eBay Seller's Tax and Legal Answer Book.*

6 I'm Listing Stuff on eBay, but I Need to Sell a Lot More to Make a Living

Growing an eBay Selling Business

Q: ***"I'm listing stuff on eBay and I'm making money, but the returns so far aren't exactly spectacular. What are some of the things I can do to grow this business?"***

A: By "growing your business," what you mean is increasing your profit margins. There are three, and only three, ways you can do that. You can:

1. Raise your revenue (your gross merchandise sales on eBay).
2. Lower your costs.
3. Do some combination of the first two approaches.

If your goal is to increase revenue, there are three ways, and only three ways, you can do that. You can:

1. Raise your prices.
2. Sell more inventory on eBay.
3. Sell higher-margin stuff that will yield more revenue for the same cost.

If your goal is to cut costs, well, there are lots of ways you can do that, but be careful—cut your costs too far, and your product and service quality suffer.

Whenever I talk to entrepreneurs about strategies for growing their businesses,

I always refer to the three "ATEs"—so called because each of the three keywords ends with the letters "ate"—as follows:

1. *Automate* your business: Stop listing things one at a time and invest in some bulk listing programs such as eBay's Turbo Lister 2; use templates for your eBay listings so you don't have to create new ones from scratch every time you list something new; use KeepMore.net (a Web-based solution offered by Sagefire, Inc., of Boulder, Colorado, discussed in Chapter 17) or the eBay software tools Selling Manager Pro or Blackthorne, to automate your back-office functions so you're not wasting time printing out eBay sales reports and transferring them by hand to your accounting software; use technology that will automatically update your eBay blogs, eBay Store content pages, and other marketing vehicles whenever you write a new article or create new content.

2. *Delegate:* Hire employees, student interns, or independent contractors (also known as "1099s," and discussed in Chapter 20) to do the grunt work of listing items, packing boxes, dealing with shippers, and responding to buyer e-mails, so you can focus on the activities that are essential to an eBay seller's success—sourcing the right product, finding the right niches, and marketing your eBay presence effectively. Hire a consultant to optimize all your listings and eBay Store pages for search engines so you don't have to do this yourself. Get a good lawyer and have him or her review and negotiate your contracts for you so you don't have to become a legal expert as well as an eBay expert.

3. *Concentrate:* Stop offering goods in too many diverse categories and focus on a handful of manageable niches where (a) you can source quality product easily, (b) there's sufficient buyer demand to keep you selling all year around, (c) there's a high sell-through rate (the ratio of successful listings to total listings), and (d) you get a decent profit margin on each sale.

Ideally, you will find yourself in an environment where your revenue is consistently growing and your costs are gradually diminishing—that's growth in accounting terms, and if you can sustain that over the long term you can't really do much better in business.

Why Stuff Doesn't Sell on eBay

Q: ***"I've put a lot of things up for sale on eBay, and only a few have actually sold to buyers. What am I doing wrong?"***

A: There are lots of reasons this could be happening. For example:

1. Your items might not be listed in the best categories on eBay.
2. Your items are listed solely on eBay's U.S. site when the market for them is primarily overseas.
3. Your items are so unusual that the market for them isn't all that big.
4. There are lots of competitors for the same or similar items, and because they are buying in larger quantities than you possibly can, they're getting better discounts from their suppliers and, accordingly, can offer lower prices to their customers than you can.
5. You are selling antiques and collectibles and each item is unique, so you have difficulty getting multiple sales from the same buyer.
6. You are selling high-priced antiques, but your feedback score is less than 10, so buyers are nervous about buying from you.
7. Your listing photos are fuzzy or raise more questions about the item than they answer.
8. You are listing your items at the wrong time of year (ski parkas in August, swimwear in January), or your listings are closing on the a day of the week that eBay's statistics indicate is not a good day for items of this type.
9. You are pricing your items incorrectly—for example, using an initial bid price so high that you're scaring buyers away.
10. Your Terms and Conditions are so tough and one-sided that they are turning buyers off.
11. Your eBay Store is not optimized properly to generate search engine traffic.

12. Your customer service isn't all it could possibly be—for example, you are too slow to respond to buyer e-mails.

The only way to know for sure what's going wrong is to do *research.* There is no substitute for reviewing other people's closed listings on eBay and taking detailed notes on what worked and what didn't work for those listings. Yes, it takes time, but it pays huge dividends. The two leading eBay auction research services are HammerTap.com and Terapeak.com. Make a deductible investment, subscribe to both of them, and start figuring out what works and what doesn't for the type of merchandise you're selling on eBay.

If all else fails, it's just possible that eBay isn't the right place to sell the type of items you have in stock. That leaves you with a choice: Either you can change your business model to sell more stuff that's saleable on eBay or you can sell elsewhere on the Internet, where your merchandise is more likely to fit. For an excellent book comparing eBay to other online retail venues, see *Selling Beyond EBay: Foolproof Ways to Reach More Customers and Make Big Money on Rival Online Marketplaces,* by Greg Holden (AMACOM, 2006).

Dealing with Competing Sellers

Q: ***"With so many people selling the same item, how do I get people to buy my item?"***

A: In the words of a famous song from the Broadway musical *Gypsy,* "You gotta have a gimmick." It isn't enough to go into a marketplace and say, "Hi, everybody, here I am, and I'm just like all the rest of you with more of the same stuff!" You have to figure out what separates you from the competition—why you're better, faster, cheaper, whatever—and trumpet that so buyers can clearly see your competitive advantage.

Before you even decide to sell an item, doing your *research* is absolutely critical, says eBay Certified Education Specialist and PowerSeller Jack Waddick, of Chicago, Illinois (www.oakviewtraining.com).

By accessing eBay's free research tool (click on Advanced Search from any eBay page, then select Search Completed Items), you can see the last fifteen days of completed listings, both sold and unsold. Sorting that list by highest price first, quickly shows you what the current eBay market price is for that item.

Next, review the top-seller listings for seller feedback, title keywords, description, photos, shipping charges, shipping area, minimum bid, return policy, and so forth.

"Besides the basic listing details, you will also want to pay attention to what merchandising mix worked for the other successful sellers," says Waddick. "Did they offer this item in different quantities (for example, 'two to three pair of jeans'), or perhaps one listing with three or four colors of the same size item (polo golf shirts), or perhaps a core item with several accessories included like a 'kit' that is not commercially available?"

If you spend some time doing your research, you will notice that even successful eBay sellers have weaknesses or errors in their listings that you can turn to your advantage, advises Waddick. Read the positive and negative feedback comments customers have left others.

Next, Waddick advises that you take a good look at the successful sellers' listings: "Maybe the seller isn't using all the good searchable keywords in his title, maybe he doesn't offer the item worldwide, maybe he has bad photos, maybe he is overcharging for shipping, maybe he is sold out of the most popular size or color, maybe he takes too long to ship, maybe he doesn't answer email questions, maybe he has no return policy, maybe he uses threatening language in his listings, maybe his listing descriptions are incomplete and vague, maybe he is not an expert in this item like you, etc." All of these are possible ways you could create a better listing and build a nice roster of repeat customers.

Automating Your eBay Selling Business

Q: ***"What will using Turbo Lister 2 do for me?"***

A: Turbo Lister 2 is a free listing-creation software tool that eBay provides its sellers (www.ebay.com/turbolister).

Many eBay sellers find Turbo Lister 2 to be easier and faster to use than the eBay Sell Your Item (SYI) form, according to eBay Certified Education Specialist and PowerSeller Jack Waddick of Chicago, Illinois (www.oakviewtraining.com).

Waddick lists several distinct advantages of Turbo Lister 2 as a listing creation tool:

- Turbo Lister 2 can be installed on multiple computers, all at no charge.
- You can create and save listings offline and upload them at any time without paying a scheduling fee to eBay.
- You can use a single-page edit panel.
- You don't need multiple screens to create a single listing.
- You can create item templates and duplicate listings for similar items.
- You can choose from among a large selection of colors and fonts for your listings.
- You can create batches of listings for repeat uploading on a regular basis.
- You can use prefilled item information for products that have an ISBN or UPC bar code.
- You can preview each listing and calculate the eBay fees before you post it on eBay.
- You can view an on-screen Help tab if you get stuck on something you can't figure out.
- Your inventory of listings remains on your computer indefinitely, unlike your My eBay page, where they disappear after ninety days.

Q: ***"I'm thinking about using an auction management software tool to help manage my business on eBay. Where can I find good information about the pros and cons of the software that's currently available?"***

A: First, a quick definition: Unlike *listing* software, which helps you create, post, and update auction and fixed-price listings on eBay, *auction management* software actually helps you run your business. A good auction management program not only manages your listings, it also helps you manage your inventory, customer data, consignment plans, shipping with multiple carriers, marketing, the e-commerce functions on your website, accounting, and finances.

Two auction management programs are offered on eBay's website:

- *eBay Selling Manager* is an online tool that helps you manage your listings throughout the sales cycle, providing customizable e-mail templates, relisting tools, and professional label and invoice printing ($4.99 per month, free with an eBay Store subscription; a more advanced version, Selling Manager Pro, is available for $15.99 per month).
- *eBay Blackthorne* allows sellers to list and relist in bulk, track sales, and send bulk e-mail and feedback, and costs $9.99 per month. An advanced version, called *eBay Blackthorne Pro*, adds bulk printing and editing, inventory management, consignment and supplier modules, multiple-user support, and more, for $24.99 per month.

A useful website that compares the various auction management software programs currently on the market, with user reviews and ratings in a *Consumer Reports*–type format, is www.auctionsoftwarereview.com, based in the United Kingdom.

Generally, the following rules apply when selecting an auction management software program:

- *Integration with eBay is key.* Your eBay fees, costs, shipping and handling charges, and other economic data for each eBay listing should be uploaded automatically to the software as each listing closes, so you don't have to track these and manually input them into the program.
- *A specific program is (usually) better than an all-purpose program.* If you are selling only books on eBay and you find an auction management program just for book dealers, you probably should select that one over a more general program, even if it costs a little more or has slightly lower feedback ratings than a comparable all-purpose program.
- *Ease of use is extremely important, especially for smaller sellers.* Many early-stage eBay sellers are not familiar with accounting concepts such as cost of goods sold. Software that takes this into account and simplifies things for less experienced retailers is preferable over software that presumes you've got a master's degree in financial management, a CPA license, and ten years' experience in retail management.

Q: ***"I'm starting to build a serious business on eBay, and I am thinking about buying an auction management software tool to help me keep track of my listings and costs. I know eBay has two products—Selling Manager Pro and Blackthorne Pro—but I can't decide which is right for my business. Do you have any suggestions?"***

A: Before deciding, you certainly should explore the features and benefits of both tools and their potential fit with your specific business needs. I recommend that you take advantage of the thirty-day free trial offered with both products.

Even though Blackthorne Pro is considered an excellent tool for scaling your eBay business, eBay Certified Business Consultant Jack Waddick, of Chicago, Illinois (www.oakviewtraining.com), has found the eBay Selling Manager Pro product to be a better fit for him and several of his eBay business clients.

Waddick says, "Selling Manager Pro is a terrific tool for managing post-sale activities and inventory, but the main reason I started using it is to automate communication. Anyone who has found themselves leaving eBay buyers email or feedback at midnight will love Selling Manager Pro's automatic 'payment reminder email,' 'payment received email,' 'item shipped email,' 'automatic feedback,' and 'feedback reminder email' features."

If, like many eBay sellers, you use the PayPal shipping labels feature to create your USPS and UPS domestic and international shipping labels, you will appreciate the fact that the PayPal system talks to Selling Manager Pro. Since Selling Manager Pro is also integrated in to your My eBay page, you can view your To Dos, Alerts, and Quick Stats on the fly.

Other advantages of Selling Manager Pro, according to Waddick, are that the software tools help you:

- Automatically list and relist items
- Create and schedule listings in bulk
- Create more professional-looking listings using the product's built-in listing designer
- Automatically increase or decrease inventory when listings close
- Schedule listings that you want to automatically recur or relist
- Create monthly profit and loss reports

- Find out your products' success ratio and average selling price
- Export sales data to QuickBooks using eBay's Accounting Assistant software
- Alert you when your inventory of certain items goes below certain prespecified levels

Selling Manager Pro costs $15.99 per month, and eBay offers it free to sellers who purchase an eBay Store in the Featured or Premium category (see Chapter 15). According to Waddick, "It's a small price to pay for the tremendous functionality of this product and, as a bonus, your eBay buyers receive better service, which usually translates into repeat customers as you grow your business."

Hiring Employees, Consultants, and Student Interns

Q: ***"Should I hire a Web designer to create my e-commerce website and my eBay Store, or should I try to do as much of this myself as possible?"***

A: As with any business decision, you have to weigh the costs of hiring a Web designer against the benefits of freeing up your time for more important things, such as sourcing the right products to sell on eBay, researching closed listings to find out what's selling and what isn't, and building your eBay brand through blogs and other content-oriented marketing activities.

The question you should be asking yourself here is "How many more items will I have to sell on eBay each year to cover the fees of my Web designer?" If it's going to take an additional one hundred successful listings on eBay to cover her fees, you have to ask if that's doable or not.

A couple of other things to keep in mind when hiring a Web designer:

- Your Web designer should be just that—a designer only, who makes your website look pretty; all decisions about website content should be made by you or your management team.
- If you allow your designer to have too much ongoing control over your website, she will become indispensable to you after a while and will have tremendous power over what does and doesn't happen on your website.

That makes it difficult for you to change designers (or take over the reins yourself) when the time comes.

- You should always own the Internet domain name (URL) for your website. Never work with a designer who insists that ownership be in her name "for security reasons," as she will then be in a position to hold your website hostage if you get into a dispute.

Q: ***"Should I hire student interns to help with the more mundane aspects of selling on eBay, such as listings and answering buyer e-mails?"***

A: Just about every community college in the United States has a graphic design program, and the kids who take these classes are hungry—starving, sometimes—to do Web-related work, because they realize that's where the money will be in a few years. Hiring interns can be a very cost-effective way to manage a business on eBay, as well as doing good for your community by giving young people their first real work experience and marketable skills.

Just keep a few things in mind before you hire your first intern:

- Interns are generally inexperienced, and the quality of their work will be erratic. Make sure you view samples of their Web design work before you hire, and make sure you will be able to teach them to do things your way.
- Student interns are teenagers, for the most part, with all of the issues that teenagers have everywhere in the United States. By hiring interns to work in your office you are acting in loco parentis ("in the place of the parent") and will be responsible for everything the interns do, both online and off, while they are working on your premises.
- Because they are teenagers, student interns haven't always learned to distinguish business from personal issues. Make sure your interns are emotionally stable and mature (at least for their age) before you allow them to deal directly with your buyers and other eBay community members.
- Student interns are employees when they are working even part-time for you. Make sure all interns sign a W-4 form and an I-9 form when they come on board, show you proof of U.S. citizenship or legal residency, and

otherwise comply with federal and state child labor laws (see Chapter 20 for details).

- Some states (such as California) have laws regulating the number of hours student interns can work, as well as working conditions, which you must comply with. Just because they are low-wage employees doesn't mean you can treat your interns as indentured servants.

7 My Winning Bidder Is a Jerk. What Do I Do Now?

Seller-Buyer Disputes, in General

Q: *"I've got this bad/crazy/evil buyer, and . . ."*

A: It's amazing how many of the postings on eBay's Answer Center and community bulletin boards begin just like that.

According to eBay, 99.9 percent of all transactions on the site go without a hitch—either the transaction closes smoothly (the buyer pays, the shipper ships, everybody leaves positive feedback for each other, God's in his Heaven, all's right with the world), or the transaction doesn't close at all (nobody bids on the item or the seller's reserve price—the minimum amount below which the seller won't sell the item—is not met).

At the same time, there are millions of items available on eBay at any given time. Do the math, and you will conclude that a fair number of transactions simply don't go as expected on eBay. Sooner or later, you will encounter a difficult situation with a buyer on eBay, and how you handle that situation may make all the difference between success and failure in your business.

Generally, there are six types of problem you might encounter on eBay after a listing closes:

1. The buyer doesn't pay for the merchandise.
2. The buyer claims you never sent the merchandise.
3. The buyer claims the merchandise arrived in damaged condition.
4. The buyer claims the merchandise is different from what you offered for sale in your eBay listing.

5. You agree to a refund, and the buyer returns merchandise that is different from the merchandise you shipped to him or her.
6. The buyer leaves negative feedback about you without contacting you or offering you an opportunity to set things right.

Let's discuss each of these in turn.

1. Unpaid Item (UPI) Disputes

This is the easiest of the five situations to deal with, and the one for which you will get the most support from eBay and PayPal. When an eBay listing closes, the buyer has seven days to pay for the item unless you agree to a longer period (if the buyer e-mails you and says he or she is going on vacation, for example). If the buyer fails to pay within the seven-day period, you report the transaction as a UPI to eBay, eBay gives you a credit for the *final value fee* for that transaction, the buyer gets a black mark (called an *unpaid item strike*) on his or her eBay account (too many of these and the buyer gets booted off eBay), and you can either relist the item on eBay or offer your underbidders in the first listing a *second chance offer* to acquire the item. For a step-by-step tutorial on this process, go to http://pages.ebay.com/help/tp/unpaid-item-process.html.

All of this presumes, of course, that you still have the item in your possession. One of the dumbest things an eBay seller can do, bar none, is to ship an item before receiving payment from the buyer. Fully 95 percent of all your UPI problems on eBay can be resolved simply by requiring payment (and if payment is made by check, requiring that the check clear your bank) before you ship.

2. Item Not Received (INR) Disputes

If a buyer pays for an item but then doesn't receive it, he or she can open an *item not received* dispute with eBay (see http://pages.ebay.com/help/tp/inr-snad-process.html). Basically, this is a mediation process by which you and the buyer each present your side of the case while eBay tries to get you to agree on a settlement. (Note: If PayPal was used in the transaction, eBay will refer your dispute to the PayPal Resolution Center, as only PayPal can make the appropriate debits and credits to your account if a settlement is reached.)

The surest way to avoid INR disputes is to ship items in such a way that you always receive *tracking numbers* from the carrier (U.S. Postal Service, UPS, or Federal Express). That way, you can track down the item and find out whether it was actually delivered—many times the item is sitting at the buyer's backdoor, but the buyer doesn't realize it because he or she never looks there for packages. A big mistake many eBay sellers make is to allow the carrier to leave packages without a signature. Doing so gives the buyer wiggle room to argue that although the carrier may have delivered the item, a neighbor (or the neighbor's dog) stole the item from the back porch and he or she never actually received it. If the item was lost in transit, this will show up when the item is tracked, and you will get either a refund from the carrier or the amount of insurance you took out when you shipped the item (something you should *always* do for unique or irreplaceable items, whether the buyer pays for it or not).

For many smaller or high-volume items, it isn't practical to require a tracking number and delivery with signature because the cost of those services is prohibitive. Few intelligent buyers on eBay will purchase a $5 item with a $15 shipping and handling charge. There isn't much you can do to avoid an INR dispute if the buyer wants to make trouble—all you can do to avoid negative feedback on eBay is to refund the buyer's money, bar the buyer from your future listings, and hope you can make up the loss on the next sale.

3. Item Significantly Not As Described (SNAD) Disputes

The process by which a buyer claims the item received is different from the one you offered for sale is basically the same as for an INR dispute (http://pages.ebay.com/help/tp/inr-snad-process.html). The problem in these cases is determining whether the buyer is right that the item you advertised isn't the item you actually shipped or whether the buyer is pulling a "switcheroo" by substituting another (lesser-quality) item for the one actually received from you.

Unless you have a video (unedited) of you actually packing the item in the shipping container, delivering it to your local post office or UPS Store, waiting in line, and shipping the item to the buyer, there is little, in practice, you can do about switcheroos. For high-priced items, some eBay sellers use invisible tags (such as can be made with an ultraviolet pen) to mark their merchandise before shipping it, but this is not practical for smaller, high-volume items. EBay gives you the option of shipping a replacement item in these types of disputes, which may enable you to resolve the dispute without incurring great cost.

4. "Item Lost, Damaged, or Destroyed in Transit" Disputes

These are often the most unfortunate disputes between eBay sellers and buyers, because both parties are innocent—the "bad guy" in these cases is the carrier, who is not a party to the dispute.

Under the law of just about every state, it is the seller's responsibility to deliver an item to the buyer in good condition. If this doesn't happen because the item is lost, damaged, or destroyed in transit, it is the seller's responsibility to make good. Period. If the seller has not properly insured the item with the common carrier, the seller has no recourse against the carrier and is basically out of pocket and out of luck.

For a seller to disown responsibility for lost, damaged, or destroyed items, two things must happen:

1. The seller must *require* the buyer to purchase insurance for the item in the amount of his or her winning bid or the fair market value of the item. Making it optional is not enough.
2. The seller must *notify* the buyer that if the item is lost, damaged, or destroyed in transit, the buyer's sole recourse will be an insurance claim against the carrier.

If either of these two steps is not followed, the seller remains liable for merchandise that is lost, damaged, or destroyed in transit.

Since it is often not feasible to require the buyer to purchase insurance on all items you sell on eBay, most eBay sellers adopt the following commonsense policies to keep damaged or destroyed item disputes to an absolute minimum:

- Package all items extremely carefully, and follow the carrier's packaging rules to the letter.
- Require the buyer to purchase insurance if the item is unique, high-priced, or irreplaceable.

- Offer insurance as an option on all eBay listings, regardless of the item's value, size, or cost (and tell bidders up front what the insurance will cost).
- If the buyer fails to buy insurance even though you offered it as an option, and the item is unique, extremely valuable, or irreplaceable, buy the insurance yourself and treat it as part of the selling cost of that item. (*Do not* include it as part of your shipping and handling fee, as that violates eBay policies—see Chapter 8.)

5. You Agree to a Refund, and the Buyer Returns the Wrong Item

In order to keep your reputation on eBay and maintain a high positive feedback rating, sometimes you have to agree to refunds with difficult buyers that you would rather not grant. Giving them their money back when they don't deserve it is difficult enough, but then when the buyer returns an item that is different from the one you originally shipped . . .

This is another example of a switcheroo, and one that is very difficult to win because it is your word against the buyer's. All you can do in this situation is return the defective item to the buyer along with a note saying you will not refund the money until you receive the correct item back in precisely the condition in which you shipped it. Then hope that your feedback rating is high enough that you can afford at least one negative one—what eBay sellers call "taking one for the team."

Because of the switcheroo problem, it is a good idea never to refund a buyer's money until you have received the item back and have evaluated it to determine that nothing suspicious has occurred while the item was in the buyer's hands.

6. The Buyer Leaves Negative Feedback

Negative feedback can have a disastrous effect on an eBay seller's reputation, especially for:

- Sellers with low feedback scores (because they are new to eBay)
- Sellers of extremely high-priced merchandise (such as motor vehicles and real estate) whose transaction volume may be extremely low or sporadic

eBay will not remove negative feedback except in cases where both parties, having cooled down and settled their disputes, mutually agree that the negative feedback should be withdrawn (see http://pages.ebay.com/help/feedback/questions/mutual-withdrawal.html).

If someone leaves you negative feedback on eBay and refuses to discuss the situation with you, there is only one recourse for eBay sellers: the online mediation service SquareTrade.com. By filing a case with SquareTrade and requesting *feedback withdrawal* as one of your remedies, SquareTrade will notify the other party and, if the other party does not respond to SquareTrade within fourteen days, SquareTrade will recommend to eBay that your negative feedback be withdrawn. If the other party does respond within the fourteen-day period, then SquareTrade will attempt to mediate the dispute in much the same manner as eBay's and PayPal's online mediation services. If the two sides cannot reach agreement, however, SquareTrade will not resolve the dispute.

SquareTrade charges a fee for its services (currently $29.95 per dispute, or $100 for disputes involving eBay Motors), which must be paid in advance before it will begin the review and mediation process.

Avoiding Bad Buyers

Q: ***"I'm just starting out selling on eBay, and I don't want to deal with any bad buyers. How can I keep from dealing with them?"***

A: By far the best way to deal with bad buyers is never to deal with them in the first place. Especially during the first few months of your business, when you are trying to build up that all-important 100 percent positive feedback rating, even one joker in the deck can be enough to kill your business before it gets off the ground.

Of course, you can never tell in advance who's going to be a bad buyer. Sometimes even buyers with high feedback scores can "go over to the dark side" if they think they can get away with it.

Having said that, there are a number of things you can do to keep the bad buyers at bay, at least until you have built up sufficient positive feedback that you can afford a negative hit every once in a while:

- Restrict bidders in your eBay listings to U.S. residents only. This can be done easily when setting up your eBay listings by indicating clearly that you will "ship within the United States only."
- Restrict bidders in your eBay listings to people with a high feedback score (over 25, at the minimum) and with a positive feedback rating of 99 percent or better.
- Avoid using high-risk categories within eBay (such as eBay Motors), where bad buyers tend to lurk in greater-than-average numbers.
- If you can, avoid dealing with buyers who are using "free" e-mail addresses such as hotmail.com and gmail.com. Statistics indicate that more than 50 percent of purchases made from these addresses are fraudulent—unless, of course, those e-mail addresses have built up a solid feedback rating on eBay.
- Bend over backward to give over-the-top customer service, so that nobody can claim that your inexperience, sloppiness, or negligence contributed to the problem.
- When a buyer complains about anything, give them anything they want to make them either go away or give you positive feedback.

I know this sounds wimpy, but it's really the best you can do until you can build a record on eBay that sends a signal to the powers that be that you're a professional, competent, and ethical eBayer and anyone who's got a problem with you is "guilty until presumed innocent."

Finding Information About a Buyer

Q: ***"I'm involved in a dispute with an eBay buyer and want to get their mailing address so I can pursue legal action outside of eBay. The buyer's contact information on eBay gives only his city and state. How can I get eBay to give me more detailed information about the buyer without violating any of their privacy policies?"***

A: The privacy of its members is a major concern for eBay, and they will not give out confidential personal information about eBay sellers or buyers until someone is (almost) literally holding a gun to their heads.

Because of this, you can request another member's contact information only if you are currently or recently involved in a bid or sale with that member. To request a member's contact information:

1. Click the Advanced Search link located at the top of most eBay pages.
2. On the left side of the page under Search, click the Find Contact Information link.
3. Enter the member's user ID and the item number of the item you're trading with that member.
4. Click the Search button.–The information you request will be e-mailed to your registered eBay e-mail address. The member whose information you are requesting will also receive your contact information.

When Buyers Have to Pay

Q: ***"I sold something on eBay, and the buyer hasn't paid yet. It's been several days, and he won't respond to my e-mails. At what point should I freak out and file an Unpaid Item dispute with eBay?"***

A: Buyers on eBay are required to pay immediately for their items, with three days after the listing closes being considered reasonable. Most eBay sellers give their buyers seven days to pay before filing UPI disputes.

In this situation, I recommend that you send the buyer an e-mail saying, "It's been *x* days since my listing closed. Please be advised that if I do not receive payment by the close of business on [date], I will have no choice but to file an unpaid item dispute with eBay." If you have one on your e-mail program, click the Receipt Confirmation box for this e-mail message so you can see when the buyer receives and opens it.

Seeking Help from eBay and PayPal: Online Dispute Resolution

Q: ***"Will eBay or PayPal take my side if I get into a dispute with a buyer?"***

A: Absolutely, positively not. Both eBay and PayPal take the position that they are "platforms"—playing fields, if you like—on which sellers and buyers interact directly. If you get into a difficult situation with a buyer, both eBay and PayPal expect that you and your buyer will resolve it directly, without their involvement. If you can't, well, that's why the legal system exists, isn't it?

Having said that, eBay and PayPal offer a number of resources to sellers and buyers who get into difficult situations, as follows:

- *eBay dispute resolution.* If a transaction did not involve PayPal (i.e., the buyer paid by check or money order), either party can submit their dispute to eBay for mediation (for full details, see http://pages.ebay.com/help/tp/problems-dispute-resolution.html); eBay will ask questions of both parties in an attempt to broker a negotiated settlement of the dispute, but it will not decide who is right and who is wrong.
- *PayPal's Resolution Center.* If the buyer paid via PayPal, either party can submit the dispute to mediation (for full details, go to the PayPal home page, click on Security Center, then click on Resolution Center). PayPal will ask questions of both parties in an attempt to broker a negotiated settlement of the dispute. However, it will not decide who is right and who is wrong unless either party accelerates their claim, in which case PayPal employees will review both parties' claims and render a decision, the vast majority of which will be in the buyer's favor.
- *SquareTrade.com.* If the seller or buyer in a dispute posts negative feedback on eBay and the other party feels it's uncalled for, he or she can file a claim with SquareTrade for a $29.95 fee ($100 for disputes on eBay Motors). If the party that posted the negative feedback fails to respond to the claim within fourteen days, SquareTrade will recommend that eBay remove the negative feedback (and eBay usually—but not always—goes along with SquareTrade's recommendation). However, if the other party does respond to the claim, SquareTrade will ask questions of both parties in an attempt to broker a negotiated settlement of the dispute, but it will not decide who is right and who is wrong.

So where is the "Judge Judy" who will hear both sides of the dispute and enter a binding ruling in favor of one party or the other? Answer: The small claims court in the state and county where the buyer resides is the only place that will render judgment in online seller-buyer disputes. Neither eBay, PayPal (unless prompted to do so), nor SquareTrade will render judgment. For details on how to bring an action in the small claims court where your difficult buyer resides and does business, see Chapter 6 of my book *The eBay Seller's Tax and Legal Answer Book.*

Q: ***"I'm in a dispute with a buyer right now; both of us want to do the right thing, but neither of us knows how to get this resolved and behind us. Do you have any suggestions?"***

A: Always remember that any dispute with a buyer on eBay is a *negotiation*—each side gives a little in order to get something in return—and that sooner or later a result must be reached. Instead of writing pages and pages of e-mails justifying your position and explaining why the other side should back down, make them a counteroffer and solicit a reply, along the following lines: "Since it's obvious you don't want this item, please return the item to me by UPS Ground and give me a tracking number. If the item is in the same condition it was in when I shipped it, I will refund 50 percent of your bid amount plus your return shipping. If that doesn't work for you, please tell me what will, as I'm happy to discuss any reasonable solution to this problem."

The buyer will almost certainly counter with a proposal of his or her own, but usually what happens is that the ground separating you gets smaller and smaller, such that at some point your difference is so small you can simply split it equally between you and move on.

For an example of how to negotiate a dispute with an eBay buyer, see pages 146–147 of my book *The eBay Seller's Tax and Legal Answer Book.*

Q: ***"I've been in a dispute with a buyer for several months now. I have used both eBay's and PayPal's online mediation services, and we still can't get to a resolution. Where can I go from here to get justice?"***

A: If you've tried negotiating with the buyer directly via e-mail or telephone (always the way to start when resolving disputes), and you can't get satisfaction from the online mediation services offered by eBay and PayPal, you have only three options:

1. Consider bringing a small claims court action against the buyer in the state where the buyer lives. (For advice on how to do this, see Chapter 6 of my book *The eBay Seller's Tax and Legal Answer Book.*) Showing the

buyer you're willing to spend the time and money to pursue him where he lives may just get his attention enough that he'll start working with you in good faith to resolve the dispute.

2. Relist the item on eBay, or offer the underbidders in the original listing a second chance offer, so you can recoup at least some of your losses.

3. Give up and take one for the team. Disputes with buyers take up a lot of time and emotional energy that are better spent putting new items up for sale on eBay. Sometimes it's best to write off a bad deal, chalk it up to experience, and (like Scarlett O'Hara in *Gone With the Wind*) realize that tomorrow's another day.

Reporting Bad Buyers to eBay

Q: ***"There's a buyer who has been playing games with several eBay sellers and violating eBay policies for some time now. I have reported him to eBay, but they haven't done anything. What can I do to get eBay's attention so we can stop this person once and for all?"***

A: It's always frustrating when buyers (and, to be frank, other eBay sellers) game the system and seek unfair advantage over folks who are following all of eBay's policies to the letter. Whenever you see bad stuff happening on eBay, eBay wants you to report it to them. There's a link called Report This Listing at the bottom of each eBay listing, and anyone can click on that link to report a violation of eBay's rules.

The problem is that eBay's resources, while considerable, are not unlimited. It costs a fortune to have hundreds of employees investigating and chasing down violations of eBay policy, and eBay's Trust and Safety team simply cannot investigate all of the alleged violations that are reported to them. Still, whenever you see bad stuff happening on eBay, it's always a good idea to report it, for the following reasons:

- To see what's happening on the site, eBay reviews seller (and buyer) complaints. If eBay's Trust and Safety department sees patterns or trends in the complaints being filed that indicate new or repeated abuses of the system, they will act eventually, either by programming their search bots to shut down members engaged in those abuses, by developing or tightening policies that prohibit or regulate that specific behavior, or both.

- If several members allege multiple violations of eBay policies by a specific user ID, those allegations are more likely to be investigated than a single complaint by a single seller.
- If the alleged violations are new or particularly egregious, especially if they threaten eBay's or PayPal's business models (for example, a new and creative way to avoid paying listing or final value fees), they are more likely to be aggressively pursued by eBay's Trust and Safety team.

Q: ***I always try to diligently report problems with bad eBay buyers whenever I see them, but I get frustrated sometimes that people on eBay get away with murder. It seems that in almost every dispute between sellers and buyers on eBay, PayPal and eBay take the word of the buyer. If the buyer claims an item is not as listed, or not received (if tracking is not available), PayPal reverses the transaction. I am concerned with eBay's policy on seller performance, since all of the negative feedback I have gotten is from customers who had no reason to leave negative feedback but just left it maliciously after they received refunds from me, or even if they never even asked for one. How can I be held accountable for these people? It seems that both eBay and PayPal take the position that the customer is always right, and, of course, I agree with that. But I have noticed an increase in dishonest buyers taking full advantage of this policy, just as they do at big stores like Lowe's and Nordstrom, where they can easily return items after they have been worn or used for a time, or even return items that they bought somewhere else or just decided they do not want anymore. This eBay policy does not allow me to set up any policies and do business in a fair and balanced way. I am not a large corporation that can absorb the costs of dishonest buyers who make false claims. What exactly are the eBay policies designed to protect sellers from malicious buyers?***

A: This isn't so much a question as what our French friends call a *cri de coeur*—literally, a "cry from the heart." It really hurts when you're doing everything you can to play by the rules in selling on eBay and you bump into the occasional buyer who's gaming the system and stealing stuff from honest sellers who are so concerned about maintaining a high positive feedback rating that they sometimes have to let the bad guys get away with murder.

I really, truly believe that eBay and PayPal have made the world a better place overall. Still, that doesn't mean that you will always have a perfect experience selling on eBay. Bad stuff happens sometimes, and there are bad people buying on eBay, just as there are bad people buying everywhere. Here are a few thoughts to give you some consolation.

Based on my (admittedly nonscientific) research of the questions posted on eBay's community Answer Center, slightly more than half are from buyers who are having trouble with difficult sellers, and the other half are from sellers who are having trouble with difficult buyers. Although that doesn't excuse bad behavior on anyone's part, I think it shows that sellers are not the only victims on eBay, and that eBay's system probably works as well as it can in the rough-and-tumble world of e-commerce. As we used to say on Wall Street, "If everybody walks away from the table a little unsatisfied, it means the deal probably was the best one that could have been negotiated."

Too many eBay sellers, in my humble opinion, are obsessed with trying to maintain a 100 percent positive feedback rating at all costs. While that's essential for newbie sellers, who need to earn their reputation on eBay, it becomes less and less important as your feedback score (your total number of transactions on eBay) grows. Only the most neurotic buyers on eBay will quibble with a feedback score of 99.5 percent if the seller has completed more than a thousand transactions on eBay, because everyone knows there are just some people you can't make happy no matter what you do.

Think you're alone? Go to any local department store on December 26 and watch what's going on at the returns desk. Do you honestly think every item being returned is defective? People shopping online want to have the same easy return privileges that they have in brick-and-mortar stores; they feel entitled to these, and they will feel cheated and angry if you deny them, even though your refunds and returns policy is crystal clear that they're not entitled to return merchandise just because they feel like it.

Just about every retailer recognizes that a small percentage—from 1 to 3 percent—of their transactions, on average, will turn sour. Accordingly, they establish a reserve for bad debts and build that into their chart of accounts (see Chapter 17). While you cannot deduct your reserve for bad debts on your income tax return, you can deduct actual bad debts as and when they occur. So the federal and state governments share in your loss to a certain extent.

Finally, I think it's important to realize that dealing with difficult buyers is just part of the retail lifestyle—when things get rough, remember that this is one of the many reasons why God invented liquor. ☺

8 I'm Having Trouble Packing and Shipping This Stuff

When Do You Ship?

Q: ***"I sold something on eBay last week while I was away on vacation. When I came back, there were several e-mails from the buyer screaming at me for not shipping the item, and demanding his money back! Do I have to do that, as I was away for only a few days?"***

A: In order for a transaction to qualify for PayPal's Seller Protection Policy, the item must be shipped within seven days of the listing close. Under federal law, a seller must ship an item within thirty days of accepting or receiving payment. Other than that, it is up to the seller entirely to determine when to ship an item to an eBay buyer.

The vast majority of eBay sellers put a sentence in their Terms and Conditions saying when they will ship an item. If you did that, then all you need do is point this out to the buyer. Many eBay sellers put a vacation notice up on their listings when they are going to be away for a lengthy period of time—this helps to manage the buyer's expectations and humanizes you as a seller.

Assuming you didn't indicate a shipping time on your eBay listing, then it becomes a question of how long you were on vacation. If it was longer than seven days after your eBay listing closed, I can understand why the buyer is getting a little antsy right now. If it was only a couple of days, then this buyer is being unreasonable, because it takes time for an eBay seller to pack and ship an item, and it can't always be done within twenty-four hours of the listing's closing date. In either case, ship the item immediately and send this buyer an e-mail explaining that you were away and apologizing for the slow response.

Although eBay does not require you to do this, it's always a good idea to send an e-mail message to buyers the minute you receive their check, money order, or PayPal payment, confirming that you received the payment and telling them approximately when the item will ship. This almost always puts buyers' minds at ease and lets them know they're dealing with a human being who will follow through on the commitment to sell the item. By not responding, you scared the dickens out of this guy—good thing he didn't report you to eBay as a nonperforming seller!

Q: *"How long after receiving payment must a seller ship the item to the buyer?"*

A: If payment occurred through PayPal and the seller wishes to make use of PayPal's Seller Protection Policy, then the seller must ship within seven days of receiving payment from the buyer. If payment was not made through PayPal, the seller must ship within thirty days of receiving payment, under a Federal Trade Commission rule.

While most good eBay sellers send buyers an e-mail letting them know when the item will ship, this is not required by law. A busy, harried seller might not send such a notice at all. As long as the seller ships on time, though, the failure to give notice does not give the buyer the right to post negative feedback or otherwise take action against the seller.

Problems with Buyer's Address

Q: *"Is it okay to ship to a buyer who does not have a confirmed address with PayPal?"*

A: It is never recommended to ship to a buyer who does not have a confirmed address with PayPal (see Chapter 11), because it gives buyers with dishonorable intentions the ability to claim (falsely) that they never received your shipment. Some buyers, of course, do not have PayPal accounts at all and won't have a confirmed address or an "ID Verified" address with eBay. In such cases you have to rely on the buyer's feedback score and rating to determine whether it's okay to ship to the address the buyer gives you.

If a buyer has a confirmed address with PayPal and asks that you ship the item to another address, be very careful—doing this renders the transaction ineligible for PayPal's Seller Protection Policy (see Chapter 11). Again, check the buyer's feedback score and rating and ask via e-mail why he or she wants the item shipped to a different address; if the buyer has a high feedback score and positive rating, and his or her explanation is plausible (for example, "It's a gift for my mom who lives out of state, and I don't want to have to lug it all the way up there"), it's probably okay.

Q: ***"I sold an item in an auction that was set up to ship only within the United States, but the winning bidder lives in Belgium! The shipping listed only domestic services and I made sure to mark that I shipped only within the states in the options feature when I first put it up for sale. However, I did just discover that I hadn't blocked bidders who were outside of my shipping area in my seller preferences. I changed my eBay seller preferences right away, but I'm still new to selling, so I'm not sure how I should handle this. What do I do?"***

A: Don't you just hate it when bidders don't read the fine print on your listings? Generally, you should monitor your listings to make sure bidders qualify under your Terms and Conditions. Whenever you state clearly that you will "ship only within the United States," that translates as "foreign buyers need not apply." Unfortunately, many foreign bidders don't read that far down the listing page, and you will get foreign bids. While the listing is pending, the best approach is to cancel their bid and send them a short e-mail message explaining why you did so.

Since your listing has closed, you have two options. You can either:

1. Find out how much it costs to ship the item to Belgium, and ship it anyway, especially if the buyer has a high feedback score and positive rating.
2. Report the user to eBay as an "unwelcome bidder"—eBay will credit you for your final value fee, and you will then be able to either relist the item or offer your U.S.-based underbidders a second chance offer to buy the item.

Shipping Charges and Shipping and Handling Fees

Q: ***"Can I post an eBay listing asking buyers to calculate their own shipping fees?"***

A: No—eBay requires you as the seller of an item to calculate and quote shipping and handling charges.

Q: ***"I sold something on eBay and discovered later that I had miscalculated the shipping amount. Can I e-mail the buyer after the auction closes and ask him to pay the corrected amount?"***

A: No. Your eBay listing is a legal contract between you and your buyer. While you are allowed to set your shipping terms, it is up to you to make sure your shipping calculations are accurate. If you make a mistake and shortchange yourself, as you did here, you cannot go back to the buyer and ask him to pay you more money. You will have to absorb the extra shipping cost in this case.

When quoting shipping charges in your eBay listings, there is no substitute for knowing exactly what the U.S. Postal Service, UPS, or Federal Express (or other carrier) will charge. If you can't do this in-house, package the item before you list it, bring it to your local UPS Store or post office, have it weighed, and have the postage applied right there. That way you will know to the penny what the shipping charges are, and you won't make any mistakes.

Q: ***"Do my shipping charges on eBay have to reflect 100 percent the actual amount I have paid for postage on each item I sell? Or can I estimate shipping charges to save time?"***

A: If you are selling multiple identical items, it's okay to estimate shipping charges to save time as long as you never ask the buyer to pay more than the amount you actually quoted in your listing for shipping (see the answer to the previous question).

If you are selling items that are not identical, then estimating your shipping charges becomes a bit riskier. Experienced buyers on eBay (especially those who are also sellers) have a pretty good idea how much postage costs for different sizes and weights. If they see you are off by a buck or two, they probably won't be too concerned, but if they see you are gouging them (for example, by charging $25 for shipping when the average shipping cost by U.S. Priority Mail is only $5), they will raise a fuss with both you and eBay. One of the surest ways to anger your buyers and get into trouble on eBay is to overestimate your shipping costs when setting up listings. The best approach is to make sure each shipping quote reflects your actual postage cost, to the best of your ability.

Q: ***"What do I do if the eBay Shipping Calculator shows one amount for USPS, but when I go to the post office they charge a higher amount?"***

A: eBay allows you to put a Shipping Calculator on each listing to help buyers determine what the shipping charges will be before they bid on the item. Like any software tool, the eBay Shipping Calculator is only as good as the information you put into it. Since, as the seller, you are the one who programs the Shipping Calculator with the size and weight of the item, your zip code and other pertinent information, any error is likely to be your fault (although there have been occasions when the calculator didn't keep up to the minute with changes in U.S. Postal Service rates). Generally, if you use the Shipping Calculator and the actual postage is greater than what the calculator determined, you cannot go back to the buyer and ask for more money.

There is no substitute for knowing exactly what the shipping charges are going to be for each item you sell on eBay before you list the item (see the answer to the previous question).

Q: ***"Can I charge my buyers a handling fee on top of my shipping charges?"***

A: Yes, you can, as long as it's reasonable. The Excessive Shipping Charges Policy on eBay is so important that it deserves to be quoted verbatim:

> Sellers may charge reasonable shipping and handling fees to cover the costs for mailing, packaging, and handling the items they are selling. While eBay does not prescribe exactly what a seller may or may not charge, eBay relies on member reports and its own discretion to determine whether or not a seller's shipping, handling, packaging, and/or insurance charges are excessive. Shipping and handling fees may not be listed as a percentage of the final sale price.
>
> Sellers who want to be sure they are in compliance with this policy [should] charge actual shipping costs plus actual packaging materials cost (or less).
>
> In addition to the final listing price, sellers are permitted to charge:
>
> **Actual Shipping Cost:** This is the actual cost (i.e., postage) for shipping the item.
>
> **Handling Fee:** Actual packaging materials costs may be charged. A handling fee in addition to actual shipping cost may be charged if it is not excessive.

Insurance: Sellers offering insurance may only charge the actual fee for insurance. No additional amount may be added, such as "self-insurance." Sellers who do not use a licensed 3rd party insurance company may not require buyers to purchase insurance. This is a violation of state law.

Tax: Only actual applicable federal, state, country, city, VAT, and equivalent taxes may be charged.

For cross border transactions, sellers may not collect tariffs and duties. However, buyers may be responsible for actual, applicable tariffs, and duties as requested by respective country laws.

Refer to http://pages.ebay.com/help/policies/listing-shipping.html.

So, for example, if you hire a student intern to pack boxes for ten hours a week, it may be appropriate to spread his or her weekly wages over the average number of successful listings and add that as part of your handling charge. It would not be appropriate, however, for you to value your time at $250 an hour and add your average packing and shipping time per listing as a handling charge (only we attorneys get to do that ☺).

Q: ***"Must I specify in my eBay listings how much is a shipping charge and how much is a handling charge?"***

A: No, you do not need to break these out. The total amount should appear in your listings as a shipping and handling fee. What you cannot do on eBay is post one amount in your listing as a shipping charge and then tack an additional handling charge on after the listing closes.

Shipping Large Items

Q: ***"Up to now I've dealt with mostly small items on eBay, but now I have an extremely large item that I want to sell. How do I deal with shipping for this extremely large item?"***

A: Unless you have access to someone (such as a UPS Store) who's experienced in packaging large, heavy, fragile, awkward, or unusually shaped items, you have two choices:

1. You can require the buyer to pick the item up locally (making sure you specify this in your eBay listing—use boldface or all-caps fonts for this, as many buyers will overlook it if they skim the listing quickly.

2. Use one of several Web-based services that provide trucking service for eBay sellers. Two of the best are http://www.freightnshipping.com and http://ebay.freightquote.com.

Pickup by Buyer

Q: ***"I listed a cell phone that someone bid on and then sent me a message saying that they live in the same city I do and would like to meet in person instead of having me ship it to them. I have mixed feelings about this; it would definitely save a few dollars in shipping costs, but I'm not completely comfortable with the idea of meeting someone and I really don't want them to come to my house. Also, I would have no way to prove that they received the item or that I delivered it."***

A: Since you have not specified "local pickup" as one of the shipping or delivery options in your eBay listing, you are not required to have the buyer pick it up. You may insist that the buyer pay the delivery charges specified in your eBay listing.

Having said that, though, check the buyer's feedback score and rating—if this is clearly a solid eBayer there's probably not much to worry about, although you should not meet the buyer at your home. Pick a neutral location, such as a local UPS Store, post office, fast-food restaurant, or diner. Also, do not accept PayPal for payment, as you will not have online proof of delivery and your transaction will become ineligible for PayPal's Seller Protection Policy (see Chapter 11).

Items Lost or Damaged in Transit

Q: ***"I mailed a buyer an item and when the package arrived at the buyer's home he said that it was "received without contents." I can assure you the package was mailed with the contents, and I show it as being delivered via***

USPS without insurance. Should I refund the buyer the selling price of the item or the full cost to include the shipping that I had to spend? Should I refund at all?"

A: Whenever an item shipped via the U.S. Postal Service is damaged or opened in transit, the Postal Service marks it in some way to limit its liability (for example, "received in damaged condition" or "opened in transit"). Ask the buyer to e-mail you a digital photo of the package with a close-up of the Postal Service's markings; if they can't do that, ask them to return the package to you for evaluation. If it appears that the item was damaged or lost in transit to the buyer, you are legally responsible for that and should refund the buyer's bid amount plus any shipping and handling charge. If the package bears no such markings (or if it appears that the markings were forged), then you are not obligated to make any refund, although you might want to offer the buyer something, to avoid negative feedback.

Q: ***"I shipped an item to a buyer that was totally trashed in transit. This person has bought from me before, so I know he's not playing games. I offer all my buyers the opportunity to buy insurance, but this one didn't. The item was unique, and I can't replace it. I want to do the right thing here, but I really don't think this is my fault. What should I do?"***

A: This is one of the most unfortunate seller-buyer scenarios on eBay, because both the seller and the buyer here are good guys who have done absolutely nothing wrong. The bad guy is the common carrier, who is not involved in the dispute.

Under the law of just about every state, it is the seller's responsibility to deliver an item to the buyer in good condition. If this doesn't happen because the item is lost, damaged, or destroyed in transit, it is the seller's responsibility to make good. Period. If the seller has not properly insured the item with the common carrier, the seller has no recourse against the carrier and is basically out of pocket and out of luck.

For a seller to disown responsibility for a lost, damaged, or destroyed item, two things must happen:

1. The seller must *require* the buyer to purchase insurance for the item in the amount of his winning bid or the fair market value of the item—making it optional is not enough.

2. The seller must *notify* the buyer that if the item is lost, damaged, or destroyed in transit, the buyer's sole recourse is an insurance claim against the carrier.

If either of these two steps is not followed, the seller remains liable for merchandise that is lost, damaged, or destroyed in transit.

Since it is often not feasible to require the buyer to purchase insurance on all items you sell on eBay, most eBay sellers adopt the following commonsense policies to keep damaged or destroyed item disputes to an absolute minimum:

- Package all items extremely carefully, and follow the carrier's packaging rules to the letter.
- Require the buyer to purchase insurance if the item is unique, high-priced, or irreplaceable.
- Offer insurance as an option on all eBay listings, regardless of the item's value, size, or cost (and tell bidders up front what the insurance will cost).
- If the buyer fails to buy insurance even though you offered it as an option, and the item is unique, extremely valuable, or irreplaceable, buy the insurance yourself and treat it as part of the selling cost of that item (*do not* include it as part of your shipping and handling fee, as that violates eBay policies; see Chapter 8).

For an actual transcript of an e-mail exchange between a seller and a buyer in exactly this situation, see pages 146–147 of my book *The eBay Seller's Tax and Legal Answer Book.*

Packaging and Packaging Materials

Q: ***"Can I ship an item in a box that has somebody else's logo or graphics on it?"***

A: Yes, you can do this, although it may look awfully cheesy to your buyers. If I'm buying expensive merchandise on eBay, I do expect that the packaging will be worthy of the item (I know that seems irrational, but buyers do think that way).

Here's a suggestion from several eBay experts: Take the box, disassemble it, turn it inside out, and then reassemble it before packing your item. That way, the outside of the box (formerly the inside) will be free of markings, while the inside of the box (formerly the outside) will be stuffed with packing material, so people won't see the markings.

Q: ***"I'm new to selling on eBay, and would like advice on keeping my costs down; specifically, where can I get good, low-priced packing materials such as bubble wrap , plastic packing peanuts, and boxes?"***

A: When you sell on eBay, you will become really good at scavenging items like these after a while. Visit local retailers (such as liquor stores) and ask them to give you any unused boxes or leftover packing material—offer to pay them a small weekly amount for doing this. Ask your neighbors to save any packing material on items they buy through the mail (although be careful—some of your neighbors won't want you to know where they buy stuff), and don't ever throw away packing material for things you buy through mail order or online.

You can order free U.S. Postal Service cobranded eBay/USPS boxes at http://ebaysupplies.usps.com. Use these boxes, and the Postal Service will charge a flat rate regardless of what the contents weigh. They will even deliver the boxes to your home! But be careful—if you use these, you must send everything by U.S. Priority Mail (the old first-class mail), and the Postal Service is extremely picky about these. If you overstuff one of these boxes so that the sides bulge even slightly, the Postal Service may assess additional postage and charge your buyer for postage due, which the buyer won't be happy about.

One of the best places to buy shipping materials is eBay itself. Go to the Sell tab on the eBay home page, click on Seller Resources, scroll down to the Selling Supplies section, and click on Packing and Shipping Supplies. You will see a list of eBay sellers who specialize in selling these materials to other eBay sellers.

Q: ***What are the different types of low-cost packing material, and how can I figure out which one is right for different types of merchandise?***

A: In my years of buying on eBay, I have seen the following materials used in sellers' packaging:

- Plastic packing peanuts
- Bubble wrap

- Cut-up Styrofoam
- Scrunched-up newspaper
- Shredded office paper
- Plastic grocery bags
- Styrofoam egg cartons
- Cut-up Styrofoam "pool noodles"
- Balloons
- Airbags
- Paper towel and toilet tissue cardboard cores
- Thin foam strips used in packing furniture

As for which type is right for which kind of merchandise, trial and error will teach you what works. For very fragile items, you might want to post a question on eBay's community Answer Center and see if any other sellers of similar merchandise have specific recommendations.

Learning More About Packing and Shipping

Q: ***"There's a lot to learn about packing boxes and all the different shipping rates when you're selling on eBay. Are there any good ways to learn about these things before you start selling lots of stuff?"***

A: When you're just starting out selling on eBay, this is one of the two big learning curves you will have to climb (the other is learning how to use a digital camera to photograph your items for best effect).

First, check the eBay Workshops page for packing and shipping workshops offered by other eBay members, the Postal Service, UPS, and others. Go to the Community tab on eBay's home page, scroll down to the Education section, then click on Workshops. If there are no packing or shipping workshops scheduled for the current month, check out the Archives section, as this almost certainly offers closed workshops that you can review. You can even contact the host of those closed workshops if you have questions.

Here's another possible approach—although it entails a bit of risk. In early to mid-November, visit your local UPS Store and volunteer your services as an unpaid intern for twenty to thirty hours a week during the holiday rush season. UPS Stores are incredibly busy between November 15 and December 31 each year, and most of them are extremely strapped for help during this crunch time. Many UPS Store owners welcome the offer of free labor during this difficult period.

Why is this a good way to learn about packing and shipping? Because for six weeks of your life this is all you will be doing—packing boxes, weighing boxes, calculating shipping rates for the different carriers (primarily UPS and the U.S. Postal Service, as UPS Stores are not allowed to ship via Federal Express and DHL), figuring out the most cost-effective way to ship something from Point A to Point B, and so forth. You won't get paid for this, but the education you receive will pay incredible dividends once you start selling seriously on eBay.

But be careful: Many UPS Store managers will be wary about letting you work in their stores if they see you as a potential competitor. Since UPS acquired the former Mail Boxes Etc. chain in 2002, they have restricted the number of shipping options available to UPS Store owners. As a result, many UPS Stores make most of their profits on packing, and they will be concerned about teaching you packing secrets that enable you to set up your own UPS accounts and compete directly with them.

9 Will eBay Kick Me off the Site If I . . . ?

Shill Bidding

Q: ***"I have a few items up for sale on eBay. I've received a couple of bids but nothing close to what the item is worth. Can I ask a friend to bid on these items to get some action going and possibly stimulate some interest in them?"***

A: ABSOLUTELY, POSITIVELY NOT!! (Yes, I know I'm screaming!)

This is called *shill bidding,* and it is absolutely illegal. If eBay catches you doing this, not only will they kick you off the eBay site forever, they will report you to your state attorney general's office for criminal prosecution.

Here's how shill bidding works. A seller asks a confederate (usually a friend or family member), called a *shill,* to enter bids in his auctions to drive up the price. If the shill wins the auction, no money changes hands; the seller and the shill exchange positive feedback on eBay and, after a decent interval of time, the seller relists the item on eBay. If other, legitimate bidders enter the auction, the shill backs off and lets the auction proceed to its natural conclusion on eBay.

A variation on shill bidding involves the use of eBay's popular Second Chance Offer feature. A seller posts an auction listing on eBay, and the confederate, or shill, places a "sniper" bid on the item at an outrageously high price. Legitimate bidders bid on the item, and at the very last second the sniper shill's bid is entered and wins the item. Because the shill bid is only a dollar or two over the second-highest bidder's maximum bid amount, that amount is now revealed to the seller. After a day or two, the seller announces that the high bidder wouldn't go through with the transaction and offers the second-highest bidder a second chance offer to purchase the item—at the maximum amount the second-highest bidder was willing to bid!

It's extremely difficult to prove shill bidding on eBay, because you have to prove the existence of a relationship, an agreement, or collusion between the seller and the shill bidder. If someone is bidding consistently on a seller's items and always comes in second when the listing closes, that person may or may not be a shill bidder. If the person is bidding at the request or urging of the seller, he or she is a shill bidder. If the person is simply a bidder who lacks the confidence to submit winning bids (an "always a bridesmaid, never a bride" bidder), he or she may be a loser but is not a shill bidder.

To read eBay's shill bidding policy, go to http://pages.ebay.com/help/policies/seller-shill-bidding.html.

Q: ***"I've been selling real estate on eBay for a while. Whenever I put up a listing I ask one or two of my friends to submit starter bids just to get the action going. Once real bidders start piling on, my friends back off and let the auction happen. Am I at risk for having my eBay listings taken down because of this?"***

A: I have a phrase for this: "shill bidding with good intentions." Unlike most shill bidding operations, the goal here is not for the seller to get an artificially high price for the item. The idea, rather, is to show bidding activity on an item so that on the search results it stands out from other items that have attracted no bids.

As buyers, we have all searched on eBay for popular items where there are many listings. If most of the items have attracted no bidders, but there are two or three bids on others, we tend to focus our attention on the latter, on the theory that these other bidders have already separated the wheat from the chaff for us.

But, to paraphrase Gertrude Stein, "a shill bidder is a shill bidder is a shill bidder." If sellers use shill bidders to create bogus bids to make the listing more attractive to legitimate bidders, they are manipulating the auction results just as much as a classic shill bidding operation does. The shill bidding policy on eBay is very clear: Any bidding that artificially increases the item's price "or apparent desirability" is shill bidding. Don't even think about doing it!

Q: ***"I have an item up for auction on eBay, and there's a lot of spirited competition for this item from several bidders. One of the bidders has been***

e-mailing me daily with questions about the item, and I've been answering his e-mails promptly. Is there any way I can get into trouble by doing this? Should I be sharing this information with some or all of the other bidders?"

A: Yes, to both questions. The shill bidding policy on eBay specifically includes "bidding by individuals with a level of access to the seller's item information not available to the general Community." By favoring this buyer with information that is not available to other bidders, he now has a "level of access to the seller's item information not available to the general Community." Think about it: If this buyer were a personal friend of yours, isn't this exactly how you would manipulate the auction to ensure that he wins the item? What you should do here is post his e-mail questions, and your answers, on the listing site so that all bidders can see your exchanges. You can do this by amending the auction listing.

Vigilantes on eBay and Bid Rigging

Q: ***"There's a seller on eBay who's clearly offering bogus merchandise and is making those of us who sell the same legitimate merchandise look bad. We've reported him to eBay several times, but nothing happens. What if several of us banded together and bid aggressively on his items until his prices were so high that no legitimate bidder would consider buying from him? Of course, we wouldn't pay for the items—we'll use new user IDs so the negative feedback won't affect our selling accounts. Sooner or later, he would have to stop selling on eBay. Can we get into trouble doing this?"***

A: Possibly. There's a name for people like you and your friends: *vigilantes.* In the Old West, vigilantes would take the law into their own hands and string up anyone they thought was guilty of a crime. The trouble is, they were wrong in a lot of cases and ended up lynching the wrong guy.

If you think someone on eBay is selling bogus merchandise, eBay wants you to report it to them and let them deal with the seller. By taking the law into your own hands, not only do you risk negative feedback from this seller, you might also be engaging in an illegal bidding ring and could be thrown off eBay for engaging in illegal auction practices.

Remember, what is bogus is often in the eyes of the beholder. The best advice here comes from the Bible: "Judge not, that ye be not judged."

Copying Other Sellers' Listings, Photos, and Item Descriptions

Q: ***"It's such a hassle to have to write new item descriptions and take photos for each item I sell on eBay. Is it okay to copy descriptions from other people's listings and cut and paste photos if I'm reasonably sure they're of the exact same make and model I'm selling?"***

A: No—eBay members are not allowed to use another eBay user's pictures or descriptions in their listings or About Me pages without the owner's permission. To see eBay's policy on this, go to http://pages.ebay.com/help/policies/vero-image-text-theft.html.

People who sell on eBay need to do everything possible to minimize the amount of time it takes to list items so they're not reinventing the wheel every time they put up a new listing (discussed in Chapter 6). Also, there are only so many ways you can describe certain merchandise, such as a particular make and model of laptop computer—put ten monkeys in a room with this item and they will all write the same description, pretty much word for word.

Common sense should rule here. You absolutely should not use someone else's description if the item you're selling is not 100 percent identical to the other item. I also strongly discourage your using anybody else's description word for word unless you are selling generic merchandise that can be described only one way. On the other hand, using several other sellers' descriptions of similar merchandise as templates or guidelines for drafting your own unique item description shouldn't get you into too much trouble on eBay. But if a particular seller is well known on eBay for using certain idiosyncrasies of grammar or syntax in his or her item descriptions, avoid copying them in your own because, although imitation is the sincerest form of flattery, plagiarism can get you kicked off eBay.

Selling Off of eBay and Communicating with Buyers

Q: ***"I recently closed an auction listing on eBay, but the buyer never paid for the item. Instead of relisting the item, can I e-mail the underbidders in the auction and offer the item directly to them?"***

A: Yes, but only if you use eBay's Second Chance Offer feature. For details, go to http://pages.ebay.com/help/sell/second_chance_offer.html. Otherwise, if you send e-mails directly to bidders in other auctions, you are violating eBay's spam policy, which can be found at http://pages.ebay.com/help/policies/rfe-spam-ov.html.

Q: ***"I have posted a reserve auction listing on eBay (a listing with a*** **reserve** ***price below which the seller is not obligated to sell); the reserve has not yet been broken, although the bidders are very close to doing so. Because he really wants this item, one of the bidders has e-mailed me and offered me twice whatever my reserve amount is if I will terminate the listing and sell to him privately. The offer is very attractive, as I don't think I will get twice my reserve price if the auction goes to closing. Can I take him up on his offer?"***

A: Absolutely not. This violates eBay's "offers off of eBay" policy, which can be found at http://pages.ebay.com/help/policies/rfe-spam-non-ebay-sale.html. Transactions off of eBay are strongly discoursaged for two reasons:

1. There is no assurance you will have the same degree of protection against fraud when you sell off of eBay.
2. When sellers pull their listings and sell off of eBay, eBay loses a fee.

If eBay discovers sellers engaging in practices that circumvent their obligation to pay fees to eBay, they will kick them off the site without hesitation. Say no to the offer.

Q: ***"I recently put an item up for sale on eBay in a reserve auction. While the listing was pending, I received an e-mail from an eBay member offering to purchase the item for a specified price off of eBay if the item did not sell because the reserve wasn't broken. Is this acceptable? Should I report this to eBay?"***

A: Technically, this is an offer off of eBay that violates eBay's policy. The difference between this and the previous question, however, is that the bidder here is not asking you to terminate your listing. If the listing closes and the item is purchased at a price above your stated reserve, then the bidder's offer becomes null and void. If the listing closes and the item does not sell because the reserve was not broken, you can choose to simply ignore the offer and relist the item. Still, it's an offer to purchase off of eBay that clearly violates eBay's fee circumvention policy.

I don't think you should report this to eBay, and I don't think you should accept this bidder's offer. Instead, wait for the listing to close. If the item does not sell, relist the item as a Buy It Now! listing at the price offered by the bidder and notify him via e-mail that the item is now available on eBay at his requested price. That way everybody wins—your item sells, the buyer gets the item he wants at the price he wants to pay, eBay gets their fees, and no policies have been violated.

Q: ***"I received an e-mail from a past eBay buyer offering to buy outside of eBay if I had more of the same items to sell in the future. Is this type of solicitation okay?"***

A: There is nothing wrong with this type of solicitation; it does not violate eBay's fee circumvention policy, which can be found at http://pages.ebay.com/help/policies/rfe-spam-non-ebay-sale.html. If you do have more of the same items, you have the choice of listing them on eBay (see the answer to the previous question) or negotiating with the buyer offline, as you choose. Be sure to check the buyer's feedback score and rating, though, as transactions off of eBay do not qualify for any seller protection offered by eBay or PayPal.

Q: ***"I have a fixed-price listing with less than twelve hours to go. A buyer has contacted me via e-mail offering a lower amount. Can I consider this offer, or should I ignore it?"***

A: Because your listing has less than twelve hours to go, you cannot make any changes to it at this point. The buyer has to accept your price.

What you can do is wait for the listing to end, relist it as a fixed-price listing, and add eBay's popular Make an Offer feature. Then send the buyer an e-mail letting him or her know you have done this. If the buyer doesn't want to pay the full price, he or she can make you an offer without violating any eBay policies. If the buyer's lower offer is acceptable, you can decide to accept it and pay eBay fees based on the lower price.

Transaction Interference

Q: ***"I'm selling a certain type of antique on eBay, and I noticed that another seller is selling similar merchandise but there are many mistakes in his item***

description that are clearly intended to mislead buyers. Should I send e-mails to his buyers notifying them of these errors? Sellers like this guy make all of us sellers on eBay look bad!"

A: You have the best of intentions here, but I'm afraid if you send e-mails to the seller's bidders you are violating eBay's Transaction Interference policy, which can be found at http://pages.ebay.com/help/policies/transaction-interference.html, even though your warnings may be 100 percent correct. And if they're not correct, you have committed libel and can be sued by the seller in a court of law outside of eBay.

Unfortunately, eBay does not allow you to post negative feedback for someone unless you actually are engaged in a transaction with that someone. Accordingly, there are two things you can do in this situation if you want to be a Good Samaritan:

- You can track this seller's listing and report each one to eBay—sooner or later they will take notice, especially if other sellers (and especially buyers) have filed reports similar to yours.
- If the item isn't priced very high, you can snipe the item from the seller, pay for it, and file an item significantly not as described (SNAD) dispute with the seller on eBay. This will permit you to post negative feedback for the seller, but be prepared that the seller is likely to do the same to you, especially when he or she finds out you are a vigilante who wasn't legitimately interested in the item when you placed your bid.

Excessive Shipping, Handling, and Insurance Fees

Q: ***"I offer my buyers U.S. Postal Service insurance on all shipments, but I recently found out where I can get shipping insurance at a lower rate than USPS offers. Since eBay does not have an option for me to charge insurance at the lower rate, can I still quote USPS insurance rates on my eBay listings and pocket the difference?"***

A: The Excessive Shipping Charges policy on eBay, which can be found at http://pages.ebay.com/help/policies/listing-shipping.html, does not allow you to charge anything but the actual cost of insurance. Even if eBay doesn't enforce this policy against you, I will feel very sorry for you if your buyers ever find out what you are doing here. Don't do it. Instead, give your buyers a small refund for the difference in insurance cost, and send them an e-mail explaining why they are getting it. You will receive positive feedback on eBay like you wouldn't believe.

Q: ***"Can I self-insure when I sell on eBay?"***

A: Absolutely not.The Excessive Shipping Charges policy on eBay, which can be found at http://pages.ebay.com/help/policies/listing-shipping.html, expressly prohibits charging your buyers for self-insurance. It's viewed as an excessive handling charge.

Q: ***"I have a couple of employees who help me pack and ship my eBay items. Can I add a few bucks to the handling charge I include in all my eBay listings to help cover their expenses?"***

A: You may add a shipping and handling charge to the purchase price in your eBay listings. While eBay's policies clearly prohibit you from charging excessive shipping fees, they are a little more flexible when it comes to handling charges. The only requirement is that your handling charge be "reasonable"—you do not have to specify what your handling charge covers.

Look at other eBay sellers with similar merchandise and see what they charge in terms of a handling fee. If your handling charge isn't grossly out of line with theirs, you shouldn't have a problem. If you must charge a handling fee that's out of line with other, comparable eBay sellers, include a paragraph in your Terms and Conditions section explaining why you charge what you charge. And if people stop buying or bidding from you, bring your handling charge back into line with what others are doing.

Q: ***"I sell a lot of stuff on eBay. Do my shipping charges have to reflect my actual cost of shipping, to the absolute penny, or can I average the charges over multiple items to save time?"***

A: You can average the charges over multiple items as long as your buyers don't feel they're being gouged. Nothing will get you into trouble on eBay faster than charging an excessive shipping fee. Experienced eBay buyers (especially those who are also sellers) generally know about shipping charges and will raise their eyebrows if they see you charging a shipping fee that is grossly out of line with their own experience on eBay. Generally, it's best to charge buyers what you actually pay for shipping. If you must average your shipping costs, put a paragraph in your Terms and Conditions explaining why you do that and assuring buyers that their actual shipping fee is never more than a few pennies more than your actual shipping costs.

Choice Listings

Q: ***"Can I take a photo of several items and list each of them separately on eBay with a photo of all items together?"***

A: Yes. This is a perfectly valid way to get buyers excited about your other listings on eBay, although a film loop is a lot more effective and classy looking.

Just be sure you clearly identify which item in the photo the buyer is bidding on—there have been instances in which buyers thought they were bidding on the second item from the left when they really were bidding on the second item from the right. If that happens, you probably will have to refund the buyer's money to avoid negative feedback, even if you thought your listing was crystal clear.

Q: ***"Can I post a Buy It Now! listing on eBay showing several items and offer my buyers the opportunity to pick the one they like?"***

A: No. This is a classic violation of eBay's Choice Listings policy, which can be found at http://pages.ebay.com/help/policies/listing-choice.html. These are prohibited because they enable you to list several items at once on eBay while paying only a single listing fee.

There are two exceptions to the prohibition:

1. Listings "may offer custom-made items or services that are created or customized to the buyer's specification. All offered options must be provided at no additional charge to the buyer."

2. Multiple-quantity listings (Multiple Item Listings, multiple-item fixed price, or Store listings) may offer a choice of color in otherwise identical items. However, the seller must be able to fulfill the entire quantity of every listing in any offered color even if every winning bidder makes ex-

actly the same color selection. It is not permissible to state: "The highest bidder gets first choice."

Choice listings may not be offered "subject to availability" or require the buyer to contact the seller to see which colors are available or what quantity is available. The exception for choice of color does not apply to single-quantity listings.

Sales Taxes

Q: ***"I just sold something on eBay. The bidder paid, but when I went to ship the item I saw that he is a resident of my state and I realized I should have charged sales tax. My auction listing didn't say anything about sales tax. Can I go back to the buyer and ask him to add sales tax to his winning bid at this point?"***

A: No. The law in just about every state I'm aware of prohibits you from tacking sales tax onto the buyer's purchase price if you did not say in advance that you were going to do so. That's why, in every one of your eBay listings, you need to include a statement along the following lines: "Note to Residents of State X [your state]: State and local sales taxes will be added to the winning bid or Buy It Now! price."

You are still required to pay sales tax to your state tax authority for this item. Unfortunately, you will have to take it out of the winning bid amount or Buy It Now! price.

Forced Sales

Q: ***"I just sold something on eBay and realized after the fact that I made a terrible mistake in the item description. I have apologized, explained the mistake to the buyer, and offered him a full refund of the purchase price plus shipping charges, but the buyer is furious and says I must go through with the transaction. Can eBay force me to sell this item? Can I be kicked off eBay if I refuse?"***

A: If there are good reasons for you not to sell an item, as there are here, eBay cannot force you to do so. Still, there is a risk that this crazy buyer will complain to eBay that you are a *nonperforming seller,* and you will be on the defensive.

I recommend that you ship the item to the buyer and refund the difference between what the buyer actually paid for the item and what you think the item is worth when correctly described. Then explain to the buyer via e-mail why you did what you did. Few buyers (even crazy ones) will complain about getting an item they want for a reduced price. If the buyer still is not happy and protests the transaction, you will look a lot better to eBay's dispute resolution team.

10 I Made a Mistake and Need to Cancel This Auction

Withdrawal of Listing by Seller

Q: *"I put something up for sale on eBay last week and then discovered it had a flaw. Can I pull the listing?"*

A: As long as there are twelve hours or more remaining in the listing, eBay allows you to terminate the listing by canceling each of the bids placed up to that time. Instructions for doing so are set out at http://pages.ebay.com/help/sell/end_early.html as follows:

> If you cannot complete your listing as planned, you can end your listing before the scheduled date. If there are bids on your item, you can cancel them.
>
> Reasons for ending listings early include:
>
> - The item is no longer available for sale.
> - There was an error in the starting price or reserve amount.
> - There was an error in the listing.
> - The item was lost or broken.
>
> **Note**: Your account will still be charged listing fees (such as the Insertion Fee) if you end your listing early. Consider revising your listing first if there are aspects of it you want to change or improve.

However, sellers are not permitted to cancel bids and end listings early in order to avoid selling an item that did not meet the desired sale price. This is considered to be *reserve fee circumvention,* and eBay is almost certain to investigate this if your reason for shutting down a listing early isn't a darned good one.

Q: ***"I posted something for sale on eBay last week and there are less than twelve hours remaining. I just realized I made a mistake in the item description. Can I terminate the listing now and make apologies to my buyers?"***

A: It's a lot more difficult to terminate a listing on eBay that has fewer than twelve hours to go. The eBay policy on this point says:

> When there are 12 hours or less remaining and the item has a winning bid, including a reserve met bid, sellers cannot make any changes to the listing, including:
>
> - Ending the item early. Sellers may cancel bids, but not end the item.
> - Adding to or changing the item description.
>
> **Note:** Canceling bids or making changes to a listing with bids when there are 12 hours or less remaining, can damage the buyer experience and can undermine trust in the marketplace.

You can still cancel bids, which will effectively terminate the listing, but you have to have a darned good reason for doing this.

Q: ***"I put something up for sale on eBay last week. Several bids were placed on the item, but then I received an e-mail from a buyer offering me twice the highest bid amount if I pull the auction and sell to him off of eBay. Can I do that?"***

A: No. This is someone offering to buy an item off of eBay, which is strictly prohibited—see http://pages.ebay.com/help/tp/isgw-fraud-non-ebay.html.

If your auction is a reserve auction and the item does not sell because the reserve has not been met, consider relisting the item as a Buy It Now! (fixed-price) listing at this buyer's proposed price, then e-mailing him to let him know that the item is legally available on eBay for the price he wants. That's really the only way to accept the buyer's offer without violating eBay policies.

Q: ***"I put something up for sale on eBay last week. Several bids were placed on the item, but they're not very exciting. I received an e-mail message from someone wanting to pay a reasonable price for the item. I'm not sure I want to sell to him off of eBay, so I'm thinking I should terminate the auction, relist the item as a Buy It Now!, and notify the buyer promptly so he can snap it up. Will that get me into trouble?"***

A: Probably not. In order to close the listing early, you have to cancel each bidder's bid, which means having to explain to them why you're doing that. As long as you don't make a regular practice of this, however, you shouldn't get into too much hot water on eBay. As long as you are relisting the item on eBay as a Buy It Now! listing, eBay is getting their fees, which is what they are primarily concerned about.

Q: ***"I purchased and immediately paid for a lot of three items last week for my son's second birthday. This morning, my PayPal funds were returned by the seller with a message saying his kids won't let him sell their toys. While I empathize with the seller, what are my options in terms of enforcing the valid contract I believe we entered into? If buyers are given a 'this is a valid/binding contract' warning upon bidding, shouldn't this work both ways? I have tried to find the same items in other auctions, but they are not all being offered."***

A: Generally, you cannot force someone on eBay to go through with their transaction—what we lawyers call "specific performance." This works both ways: A buyer can't force you to sell something you don't want to sell, and you can't force your buyers to cough up money for something they don't want. The proper remedy is to file the appropriate complaint with eBay—in the case of buyers, a nonperforming seller complaint, and in the case of sellers, an unpaid item dispute.

In this case, the buyer probably could file a nonperforming seller complaint against the seller—the seller clearly is bound to sell these items—but I would use good judgment here. Check out the seller's feedback score and rating. If it's extremely good (more than one hundred transactions, and a 100 percent positive rating), then I would cut the seller some slack here. Just make sure the seller gives you positive feedback for being such a "mensch." And keep your eye on his listings—if he puts the same stuff up for sale in the next week . . .

Q: ***"I sold something on eBay last week, but then discovered to my horror that I totally screwed up on the shipping fees. Can I ask the winning bidder to pay the actual shipping amount, or do I have to eat this? Can I simply undo the transaction and send the bidder her money back?"***

A: You have to eat the excess shipping fees—eBay expects you to get this right before you list an item, and they're pretty unforgiving when you screw up. If time permits, you can amend the listing and increase the shipping fees, but don't try to do this if there's less than twelve hours remaining in the auction. But your auction has already closed—chalk this one up to experience, and next time make sure you have the exact shipping charges for the item before you list.

Q: ***"I have just listed an item in an auction-format listing. The buyer wants me to add a Buy It Now! option so she can purchase this item. She has made me a nice offer—apparently, I don't know what I have. I would love to work with her, but someone else has already bid the minimum. What are my options?"***

A: At this point, none. Had this happened before you had a bidder, you could have ended the listing early and relisted it with a Buy It Now! option. Once an auction listing has at least one bidder, however, you are prohibited from adding a Buy It Now! option. All you can do at this point is ask this person or submit a bid, or perhaps snipe the item when the listing closes.

Q: ***"I have just listed my first items for sale and I think I made a mistake. I listed them as auction listings with a Buy It Now! option. I'm afraid now that my items are going to sell at a huge loss. Can I cancel these listings even though there are bids on them? If not, I guess this is just a learning curve thing I'll have to eat."***

A: Making a mistake on eBay can turn into an expensive lesson. You have bids, which is a good thing. But it also means you cannot cancel the auctions without creating a ton of ill will with your bidders.

It's too bad your first listings might cost you. Many sellers are under the impression that having a Buy It Now! saves them from low starting bids. But, as the eBay rules make clear, the Buy It Now! option is removed when there is a bid made. For details, see http://pages.ebay.com/help/sell/end_early.html.

You can end the listings, but you need to cancel the bids first. Read the instructions carefully because if you leave a bid active and then cancel the listing, the bid that is left becomes the winning bid.

Q: ***"I canceled an auction that had twenty-two people watching it. Will they be notified or will they just be left hanging?"***

A: No, watchers aren't notified. The auction will still be in their watch list (as ended). They can check the listing and see that you ended this listing early because of an error in the listing, and that it has been relisted.

Some sellers revise the description before ending the listing, to let people know why they are ending the listing early.

Retractions of Bids by Buyers

Q: ***"I put something up for sale on eBay last week. I've had several bidders, but the high bidder just e-mailed me and asked if he could retract his bid because he lost his job. Is this guy a crook? Should I agree to his request?"***

A: Generally, your bidders cannot retract bids just because they feel like it.Only a few narrow exceptions to this rule are permitted, where:

- The bidder made a *typographical error* and entered the wrong bid amount. For instance, the bidder bid $99.50 instead of $9.95. If this occurs, the bidder must reenter the correct bid amount immediately after he or she retracts the bid. If the bidder does not place another bid, the retraction is in violation of eBay's policy and could result in the bidder's suspension.
- The description of an item bid on has changed significantly.
- The bidder can't reach the seller. This means that the bidder tried calling the seller but his or her phone number doesn't work, or the bidder has tried e-mailing a message to the seller and it comes back undeliverable.

Timing is critical when it comes to bid retractions. Generally, if a bidder retracts his or her bid more than twelve hours before an auction listing closes, all of his or her prior bids are wiped out. After that point, only the most recent bid is retracted—any lower bids will remain in effect. This rule is designed to discourage *bid shielding*, whereby a bidder drives the auction price up to an unreasonable level in an effort to discourage bidding, and then retracts all bids at the last minute in order to "steal" the item at a bargain price.

In this case, however, I might make an exception. Pick up the telephone, call the bidder, and listen to what he has to say. If you are convinced that this bidder has truly lost his job and is in dire economic straits, don't be unreasonable—allow him to withdraw the bid. If the person bids on your next listing, however, and tries to pass off the same sob story . . .

For eBay's complete policy on bid retractions, go to http://pages.ebay.com/help/buy/bid-retract.html.

Q: ***"I just recently (last night) won a bid on an item. This item cost almost $2,000. The seller was selling an item for which he said he was an authorized dealer. I called the company that makes the item he sold to me and asked if he was an authorized dealer. His company name did not show up on their list. Also, I was told by this company that if I buy it through eBay, or pay through PayPal, the factory warranty is void; in essence, I will have paid $2,000 for this item and it will have absolutely no warranty with it at all. How do I deal with the seller without getting some kind of bad feedback? I don't want something new without a warranty."***

A: The time to do research is prior to or instead of bidding, as eBay advises, not after you have won.

By bidding, you have entered into a legally binding contract with the seller. You can either:

1. Beg the seller to accept a mutual agreement to cancel the transaction, which they are not obligated to do.

2. Pay for the item (this is the recommended course, since you were the one who made the bid).

3. Not pay for the item and risk receiving an unpaid item strike and negative feedback and possibly a small claims suit if the seller wishes to take it that far. The seller probably won't, but there is always that possibility.

Q: ***"I have a truck listed for auction. The high bidder has sent me an e-mail challenging me to prove that when we primered the truck, we didn't cover up rust, and if we have, then we're in violation of eBay policy, etc.—a whole paragraph of vitriol. A very unpleasant e-mail. I'm not sure how to respond to such a buyer."***

A: He should have questioned you before bidding, not after. If your listing goes into detail about the truck being rust free, then you better be able to prove it to the winner, whoever that might be.

You have two choices. First, cancel his bid and block him as a bidder from your future auctions. Second, respond with a guarantee that if he is not satisfied when he comes to pick it up, you will not hold him to the sale.

11 I'm Using PayPal (or Want to), and I Can't Figure Out . . .

Should You Use PayPal?

Q: *"Should I use PayPal to process payments for the merchandise I sell on eBay?"*

A: Absolutely, although PayPal is not mandatory. Accepting PayPal for the merchandise you sell on eBay gives you four huge benefits (among others):

1. You are able to receive payment immediately after a listing closes, without having to wait days for the buyer's check or money order to arrive in the mail and another several days for the check to clear your bank.
2. You are able to accept payments via credit card from your buyers without having to establish merchant accounts with each of the major credit card companies (a time-consuming and expensive proposition, especially for smaller seller).
3. If your listings qualify for PayPal's Seller Protection Policy (discussed in greater detail later), you have insurance for up to $5,000 each year for transactions that turn sour.
4. PayPal will handle foreign currency conversions so that you can accept payments from overseas buyers in U.S. dollars or any of fifteen other currencies.

PayPal charges you a fee for these services, of course, but the vast majority of eBay sellers think it's worth it.

PayPal Definitions and Types of PayPal Accounts

Q: ***"What's the difference between a confirmed and an unconfirmed address in the PayPal system?"***

A: According to PayPal Community Education Specialist and PayPal Radio host Jason Miner (www.wsradio.com/paypalradio), an address that shows as *confirmed* means that a buyer has a street address registered with PayPal that matches a billing address tied to a credit card on a PayPal account. In some cases, the confirmation may have come from PayPal examining the buyer's PayPal account history. Confirmed addresses are a part of the requirement to be covered by PayPal's Seller Protection Policy.

Q: ***"What's the difference between a verified and an unverified account in the PayPal system?"***

A: If a U.S. account has *verified* status, it means that the account holder has added a bank account and completed the verification process. When a bank account is added to PayPal, two small random amounts are sent by PayPal (at no cost to the account holder). The account holder logs in to his or her PayPal account and inputs the random deposit totals. This establishes that there's a good path between PayPal and the bank when sellers are ready to withdraw funds.

Q: ***"What is the difference between a Premier and a Business account on PayPal? What type of account do I need to have to sell on eBay?"***

A: To sell on eBay, you need to have a *Premier* or *Business* level PayPal account, according to PayPal Community Education Specialist and PayPal Radio host Jason Miner (www.wsradio.com/paypalradio). Many buyers start with *Personal* Paypal accounts, but those have limitations on how much money can be received. Additionally, Personal accounts cannot receive credit-card-funded payments for eBay purchases from buyers, although Miner points out that Personal accounts can receive a limited number of non-eBay credit card payments annually at a higher fee rate (see the PayPal Fees link at the bottom of any PayPal page to learn more). You can upgrade a Personal account to Premier or Business status from your Account Overview page after logging in.

A Premier account allows you to do business under your own name and receive any type of payment from your buyer (such as credit card, balance, or eCheck), says Miner. A Business account allows you to do business under a Business or company name. With a Business account, you'll be asked to provide some additional information about your main selling category, monthly payment volumes, and annual online sales revenue. You can also add a customer service e-mail address and customer service phone number to business accounts.

The biggest difference between Premier and Business accounts, according to Miner, is that Business accounts have an additional feature called *Multi-User Access*. This allows the primary account holder to create logins and passwords for employees to access the account and create selectable levels of access for those logins. "For example, the primary account holder may choose to have a webmaster with technical knowledge access the account to create logos, but limit that person's ability to withdraw funds or view the account's balance," says Miner.

Both Premier and Business accounts currently start out paying a fee of 2.9 percent plus thirty cents ($.30) per transaction for payments received within the United States, with a 1 percent additional fee for international transactions. Fee rates can be reduced with qualifying volumes. Learn more about this through the Fees link at the bottom of any PayPal page.

Your PayPal Account: How It Works

Q: ***"Somebody paid me via PayPal a month ago, but the amount hasn't yet shown up in my bank checking account. Can I report this to eBay as an unpaid item dispute?"***

A: When you open a PayPal account, it is entirely separate from your bank checking account. When a deposit is made to your PayPal account, it stays in the account—PayPal cannot and does not sweep funds from your PayPal account to your bank checking account unless you specifically authorize them to do that. Check your PayPal account balance, and you should see that the buyer's amount has been credited to your account. If you want to withdraw those funds to your bank checking account, simply tell PayPal to do that and they will, although it may take a day or two for the amount to show up on your checking account balance statement.

Q: *"What happens if PayPal debits my account and there are insufficient funds in the account? Can PayPal automatically charge my bank checking account?"*

A: If there are insufficient funds in your PayPal account, PayPal will send you a notice by e-mail demanding that you deposit funds into your account to pay any current debts. They may suspend your account if you don't respond promptly to this e-mail. But PayPal will never charge or automatically debit (ACH) your bank checking account.

Using PayPal Off of eBay

Q: *"If I have multiple business channels, can I use PayPal outside of eBay?"*

A: Absolutely. PayPal has a variety of features that allow for integration with websites. Simply log in to your PayPal account and click on the Merchant Services tab to learn more.

"PayPal offers functionality for building buttons on your website for buyers to make payments, shopping cart functionality for multiple purchases from the same buyer, and even processing payments through PayPal when your buyer doesn't have a PayPal account," says PayPal Community Education Specialist and PayPal Radio host Jason Miner (www.wsradio.com/paypalradio), adding that "the 'Merchant Services' tab on the PayPal home page allows you to tailor website solutions around the size and scope of your business and offers demonstrations of how many of its features work."

PayPal's Seller Protection Policy

Q: *"How do I know if a transaction on eBay qualifies for PayPal's Seller Protection Policy?"*

A: You can learn more about PayPal's Seller Protection Policy by visiting the Security Center link available at the top and bottom of any page at PayPal. Once in the Security Center, click on the Selling Safely link. There's a Seller Protection Policy overview that explains the protection and steps required to have a covered transaction. The policy covers most sellers for up to $5,000 (United States) and comparable amounts in foreign currencies on transactions that PayPal deems fraudulent.

"It should be noted that not all countries are covered by PayPal's Seller Protection Policy," cautions PayPal Community Education Specialist and PayPal Radio host Jason Miner (www.wsradio.com/paypalradio). "Currently, if you're selling in the United States, you can qualify for Seller Protection by meeting the appropriate criteria when receiving payments from United States, United Kingdom, and Canadian buyers. It is up to each individual business to determine an appropriate comprehensive risk management strategy, of which PayPal's Seller Protection Policy should only be one part."

PayPal's Seller Protection Policy is an actual insurance policy and can be found by clicking on the Protect Sellers link under the eBay Sellers tab on the PayPal home page, then scrolling down and clicking on the Seller Protection Policy link.

Section 11.3 of PayPal's user agreement, which describes the circumstances under which a transaction will be covered by the Seller Protection Policy, is so important that it deserves to be quoted verbatim:

> 11.3 Qualification Requirements. In order to qualify for coverage under the Seller Protection Policy, you must meet the following requirements:
>
> a. You must have a Verified Business or Verified Premier Account at the time of the transaction,
>
> b. The transaction must be between a United States, United Kingdom or Canadian buyer and a United States, United Kingdom or Canadian seller,
>
> c. The payment must be listed as "Seller Protection Policy Eligible" on the "Transaction Details" page,
>
> d. You must accept a single payment from one PayPal Account for the purchase,
>
> e. You must not charge a surcharge for accepting PayPal,
>
> f. You must ship the purchased item to the address listed on the "Transaction Details" page, and that address must be identified as a Confirmed Address,

g. You must ship the item to the buyer within 7 days of receiving payment,

h. You must have trackable online proof of delivery from an approved shipper to the address on the "Transaction Details" page. For transactions involving $250.00 U.S. Dollars or more, you must provide a proof of receipt that was signed or otherwise acknowledged by the buyer and can be viewed online (if you paid in a currency other than United States dollars, the following amounts apply for this section: 325.00 Canadian Dollars, 200.00 Euros, 150.00 British Pounds, 28,000.00 Yen, 350.00 Australian Dollars, 330.00 Swiss Francs, 1,600.00 Norwegian Kroner, 2,000.00 Swedish Kroner, 1,500.00 Danish Kroner, 800.00 Polish Zloty, 55,000.00 Hungarian Forint, 6,000.00 Czech Koruna, 400.00 Singapore Dollars, 2,000.00 Hong Kong Dollars, and 380.00 New Zealand Dollars), and

i. You must respond to PayPal's requests for information within the time period PayPal specifies.

Please note that in order to qualify for our Seller Protection Policy you must ship the item as required in this section. If you hand deliver an item, or provide delivery in any manner other than required in this section, your transaction will not qualify for the Seller Protection Policy.

Using PayPal When Selling Overseas

Q: *"How do I accept payments in different currencies when I sell internationally?"*

A: Log in to your PayPal account and go into the Profile area. It's available under the My Account tab, which is the default immediately after logging in. In the Financial Information section, there's a Currency Balances link. In addition to U.S. dollars, there are fifteen other currencies that you're able to toggle on or off, based on your preferences.

If you are carrying different currency balances, you will see a total U.S. dollar balance based on the amount you'd get if you opted to convert your funds completely to U.S. dollars at that time. You can convert other currencies to U.S. dollars within your PayPal account or prior to withdrawal. The conversion rate will be quoted to you, which includes a 2.5 percent spread to determine the retail foreign exchange rate. You will be given the option to convert at this rate or to decline and hold your existing balance in the other currency/currencies.

Q: ***"I understand PayPal accepts only certain currencies. What if I wish to do business in another currency?"***

A: At the time this book is going to press, you can use your current PayPal account to make or accept payments in:

- Canadian dollars
- Euros
- Pounds sterling
- U.S. dollars
- Yen
- Australian dollars
- New Zealand dollars
- Swiss francs
- Hong Kong dollars
- Singapore dollars
- Swedish kronor
- Danish kroner
- Polish zloty
- Norwegian kroner
- Hungarian forint
- Czech koruna

If you are doing business in any other currency, you cannot do business on PayPal.

Q: ***"I understand that you have to have a U.S. bank account to use PayPal. Is that true?"***

A: If you are doing business in a country where PayPal has a localized site, you can maintain your bank account with a bank in that country. At the time this is going to press, those countries are:

- Australia
- Austria
- Belgium
- Canada
- China
- France
- Germany
- Italy

- Netherlands
- Poland
- Spain
- Switzerland
- United Kingdom
- United States

In any other country, you will need to maintain a U.S. bank account.

Q: ***"I have a business with operations in several different countries. I want to use PayPal for all my eBay selling worldwide, but I understand PayPal has certain restrictions on what you can and cannot do on PayPal in each country. Where can I find out more about that?"***

A: Go to the PayPal.com home page, and click on "Learn more about PayPal worldwide." You will see a page called PayPal Offerings Worldwide. Choose your country from PayPal's list, click Enter, and you will see a page showing any restrictions on PayPal activity in that country.

Resolving Seller-Buyer Disputes on PayPal

Q: ***"I'm currently in a dispute with a buyer. I want to submit the dispute to PayPal's online mediation service, but I've been told not to bother because PayPal always takes the buyer's side. Is this true?"***

A: If PayPal was used to make payment for an item on eBay and the seller and buyer get into a dispute, you can elect to have the dispute mediated by PayPal's online dispute resolution system. To find this, go to PayPal.com, click on the Security Center link, then click on the Resolution Center link, and follow the prompts.

Keep in mind that this is a *mediation* system, not an *arbitration* system. PayPal is not going to listen to all the evidence, like Judge Judy, and then rule in one party's favor over the other. What PayPal does is ask you and your buyer a series of questions in an attempt to broker a settlement agreement between the two of you. Once you and your buyer have reached agreement on how to resolve the dispute, and either a full or partial refund is due to the buyer, PayPal will automatically debit your PayPal account and credit the buyer's.

One cannot say with absolute certainty that PayPal "always resolves disputes in favor of the buyer." However, in extremely close situations, where the facts do not clearly favor one side over the other, PayPal's mediation service (like eBay's own, to be fair) does tend to lean toward the buyer's side. There are two reasons for this:

- First, "the customer is always right." It is vital to eBay's and PayPal's success that buyers have trust and confidence in the system, and if a dispute is really too close to call, your conduct and behavior have probably contributed at least somewhat to the problem.
- Second, PayPal does not have the resources to let disputes drag on interminably while the parties go back and forth, back and forth, back and forth. At some point a resolution must be reached so that the parties (and PayPal) can get on with their lives.

Keep in mind that any resolution of a dispute through PayPal's mediation system is nonbinding and cannot be used as evidence in a court of law. If you truly believe that a buyer has gotten away with something, and the amount involved is too big to just write off, you can always sue the buyer in small claims court in the state where the buyer resides or conducts business. For advice on how to do that, see Chapter 6 of my book *The eBay Seller's Tax and Legal Answer Book.*

Q: ***"I have a buyer who wants me to ship goods and services to him first before he will pay for them. My eBay listing requires payment via PayPal, but he does not want to pay me through PayPal. Instead, he prefers to use Western Union, only when he receives the goods and inspects them. Should I go along with this?"***

A: No way. Any buyer who wants to inspect the goods prior to buying is violating the terms of your eBay listing (which he accepted by bidding on the item) and should be reported promptly to eBay. Western Union is a favorite tool of eBay fraudsters, as amounts and senders often cannot be traced. Insist on payment via PayPal if that's what your listing required; if the buyer doesn't pay within seven days, report it as an unpaid item and either relist the item or make a second chance offer to the underbidders.

Q: ***"I have several eBay listings up right now that require payment via PayPal, but I've just received notice that my PayPal account has been suspended. I***

think I can solve the problem with PayPal but not before several of these auctions close. What should I do?"

A: You have two choices here. You can terminate each listing (by cancelling the bids on each one) and send an e-mail to each bidder explaining why you are doing that. Or, if time permits, you can amend the listing to change your accepted forms of payment (for example, by adding checks and money orders and deleting PayPal) until such time as your PayPal dispute is resolved. Otherwise, a nasty eBay buyer can report you to eBay for a listing violation if his PayPal payment bounces.

Q: ***"I sold an item on eBay a couple of months ago. The buyer paid with PayPal and left positive feedback. Now, more than two months later, I have received a notice from PayPal saying this buyer has charged back the transaction on her credit card, and PayPal wants a refund. Do I have to give it after all this time?"***

A: Buyers using PayPal generally have sixty days in which to request a refund from a seller. Most of the major credit card companies, however, allow their members a longer period of time. If buyers have paid by credit card using PayPal, they can avail themselves of the longer period of time allowed by their credit card company to challenge what they perceive to be unauthorized or fraudulent transactions.

Because PayPal is not a bank, only an intermediary or payment conduit, PayPal often has no choice but to reverse the transaction and reimburse the credit card company upon demand. Once they reimburse the credit card company, PayPal will want to reimburse itself by debiting or suspending the amount from your PayPal account. Because you want to continue doing business with PayPal, you will have to reimburse PayPal and challenge the chargeback with the buyer's credit card company. This is hard to do, because when you receive payment via PayPal you do not know whether the buyer is paying by credit card or by automatic debit (ACH) from his checking account. You also do not know which credit card the buyer used—PayPal will not give you this information, in order to safeguard the buyer's privacy (after all, there's always the chance you are an identity thief trolling the Web for credit card numbers).

When PayPal is notified of a credit card chargeback, they notify you immediately via e-mail and suspend the amount of the chargeback in your account.

Whenever you receive such a notice, you are prompted to notify the PayPal Resolution Center immediately. The PayPal Resolution Center will provide you with transaction details (such as the reason the buyer gave for charging back the purchase, but not—again for reasons of privacy—the type of credit card the buyer used) and instructions on submitting additional information for the chargeback dispute. If you begin this process promptly, PayPal will leave the amount in suspension until the dispute is resolved.

PayPal has a team of chargeback specialists who, if you choose to fight back through PayPal's Resolution Center, help you build a case that they will then take to the buyer's credit card company. But don't hold your breath—even a successful dispute takes seventy-five to one hundred days, on average, to resolve, there is no assurance you will be successful, and the decision is entirely up to the buyer's credit card company no matter what the PayPal chargeback specialist (or you) tells them. Most credit card companies view the buyer, not you, as their customer and will resolve any close disputes in the buyer's favor. If your transaction qualifies for PayPal's Seller Protection Policy, you are entitled to a refund, even if the buyer's credit card company rules against you.

Also, let's face it, the law in this area tends to lean heavily in favor of consumers, and for good reason. Many credit card chargebacks *are* legitimate, either because:

- The buyer's credit card was stolen and the identity thief is buying stuff on eBay.

or

- The seller or merchant is a nincompoop who doesn't know what he's selling, doesn't know what he's doing, is trying to cheat buyers, or all three.

If you have ever had your credit card or your identity stolen, you thank heaven every day that your exposure was limited by federal law to $50 per card! You don't want to deal with angry phone calls from eBay sellers who were cheated out of merchandise by the fraudsters, no matter how much you may sympathize with their plight. You certainly do not want to make up their losses under any circumstances. You just want to get the fraudulent charges removed from your monthly statement, get a new card, and get on with your life.

In situations involving credit card or identity theft, there are two victims: the person whose credit card or identity is stolen and the merchants who unwittingly sell merchandise to the thieves, thinking they are honest buyers. In our legal system, disputes between two "good guys" (where an innocent person is going to suffer no matter which way the court rules) are usually resolved in the way that would best ensure the stability of our commercial system. In credit card chargeback cases, the law takes the view that merchants are better able to absorb these losses than consumers are, so close cases tend to be resolved in favor of the buyer. You shouldn't expect the credit card companies—or PayPal—to act any differently.

The only protections against credit card chargebacks when you sell on eBay are to:

- State clearly in your listing Terms and Conditions section exactly when you consider a transaction to be final and will no longer accept returns or process refunds.
- Do everything you can to keep fraudsters from bidding on your listings (for example, by excluding buyers from countries known to engage in massive Internet fraud, buyers using "free" e-mail accounts, and buyers with extremely low feedback scores).
- Make sure that all your transactions on eBay qualify for PayPal's Seller Protection Policy, and be sure to use PayPal's Resolution Center whenever credit card chargebacks occur.
- Not use PayPal as your sole source of payment; maintain other merchant and online payment accounts (or be willing to accept checks and money orders), so that if PayPal suspends your account due to chargeback activity you can continue to function and process your successful transactions without interruption.
- Like all online and offline merchants, accept the fact that not all of your transactions will go smoothly on eBay or PayPal no matter what you do, and maintain a reserve for bad debts accordingly. Remember that you can

deduct bad debts from your eBay income when preparing next year's tax return.

For two excellent articles on what online sellers can do when buyers charge back their credit card purchases (when the seller has established merchant accounts directly with the buyer's credit card company), see http://www.sitepoint.com/article/chargeback-challenge and http://www.merchant-account-services.org/article/chargeback-challenge/1.

12 When Do I Pay Income Taxes?

"Aw, Do I Really Hafta Pay Taxes When I Sell on eBay?"

Q: *"I sold a lot of stuff on eBay last year. Do I really have to pay taxes on the money I made?"*

A: Most eBay sellers do not intend to go into business for themselves when they first start out. They start selling stuff out of their attic, basement, or garage just to make a few extra bucks, and before they know it they've made $30,000 on eBay. By this time they know they have to do something about complying with the law, but they're not sure exactly what.

The short answer is "Yes, you do have to pay taxes if you made a profit selling on eBay." You do not pay taxes on your gross sales, only on your net profits, when you sell on eBay. If you sold stuff at a loss—the buyers paid you less money than you actually paid for the items—then you have incurred a loss for tax purposes and will not have to pay taxes on what the buyers paid you for your merchandise. You probably will not be able to deduct the loss, however (see discussion below).

If, however, you did make a profit selling on eBay—the buyers paid you more money than you actually paid for the items—then you must report the excess amount only (called *taxable income*) on your federal and state income tax returns and pay taxes on it.

It does not matter whether you treat your eBay selling as a business or as a hobby (see Chapter 1). If you made even one penny in profit selling on eBay this year, you are required by law to report it as income and pay income taxes on it. If you treat your eBay selling as a business, you file Schedule C on your federal tax return (and a similar form on your state tax return, if your state has an income tax). If you treat your eBay selling as a hobby, you report your income as follows:

- If the items you sold on eBay qualify as *capital assets* (almost everything you own for personal use or investment will qualify), then you would report your eBay profits as *capital gain* on your income tax return (federal Form 1040) and pay taxes at the (currently) favorable capital gain rates.

- Otherwise, you would report your eBay profits as *hobby income* on your income tax return (federal Form 1040) and pay taxes at the (currently) unfavorable ordinary income rates.

The definition of *capital asset* is a little tricky. Ask your accountant whether or not your eBay inventory qualifies, or read IRS Publication 544 (Sale of Capital Assets), which is available as a free download from the IRS website, www.irs.gov.

What if you lose money selling on eBay? That's when the difference between a hobby and a business becomes all-important.

If you treat your eBay selling as a business, you can deduct your loss on your federal and state income tax returns and apply it against income you earned from other sources (such as your day job). If you can't use the loss this year (because you didn't make any money), you can carry the loss forward and take it in future tax years. Business losses, while painful, are good things to have when tax time rolls around.

If you treat your eBay selling as a hobby, however, you can deduct your loss only if you have income from the same or a different hobby. So, for example, if you sell your rare coin collection at Sotheby's and make a $100,000 profit, and you lose $10,000 selling stuff from your attic on eBay in the same year, you can apply the $10,000 hobby loss against the $100,000 hobby gain and report only $90,000 in hobby income on your income tax return. (Because this gain came mostly from selling rare coins—which clearly are capital assets—you should qualify for reduced capital gain rates when paying taxes on the hobby income in this example.)

If you can't use your hobby loss this year because you have no hobby income to apply against it, you lose your hobby loss—you can't carry it forward into future years the way you can business losses. Hobby losses are not good things to have when tax time rolls around. They are basically useless, and many people don't even report them on their tax return if they don't have hobby income they can apply against it.

The bottom line is that you have to pay income taxes (and sometimes other taxes as well—see the following questions) whenever you make a profit doing anything, regardless of how you characterize it. If you've been making money selling on eBay and haven't been reporting your income on your tax return, now is the time to get yourself into compliance, before the IRS or your state tax authority finds out you have been running an illegal business behind their backs.

Should You Treat Your eBay Selling as a Business or a Hobby?

Q: *"Even if I made money selling on eBay last year, can I treat my eBay sales as a hobby rather than a business?"*

A: Yes. The IRS does not require you to file Schedule C if you don't want to. You would treat any profit you made selling on eBay this year as hobby income and report it as such on your federal and state income tax returns (federal Form 1040). If the merchandise you sold on eBay qualifies as capital assets (and most items will), you would pay taxes on your hobby income (basically, your gross sales, less what you paid for the item, less eBay and PayPal fees and other selling expenses) at (currently) favorable capital gain rates, although you will have to itemize your selling expenses on Schedule A to Form 1040.

Because of that, if you are making significant money selling on eBay I strongly recommend that you consider filing Schedule C and treating your selling as a real business—that way, you qualify for all sorts of business-related deductions (see Chapter 14) you cannot take if you have only a hobby.

Some people are afraid that by filing Schedule C they expose themselves more to an audit by the IRS or their state tax authority. While it is true that in general self-employed people tend to be audited more than "wage slaves" do (because they have more freedom and therefore more opportunity to make mischief on their tax returns), I don't think there's any greater risk of audit than if you file a Form 1040 showing a significant amount of hobby income. The IRS (and perhaps some other government agencies as well) may actually be more curious about a hobby that generates $100,000 or more in income every year.

Q: ***"How can I be sure the IRS will agree with my treating my eBay selling as a business rather than a hobby?"***

A: If you have made a profit in each of the last three calendar years, including the current one, the IRS will treat your eBay selling as a business if you choose to treat it that way on your income tax return. If you have been in business less than three years, or if, like most eBay sellers, you make money one year and lose money the following year, the IRS will still treat your eBay selling as a business if they see (when they audit you) that you are organized and disciplined, are keeping good records and regular hours, and are otherwise taking your eBay selling seriously.

If the IRS audits you and sees that you are lazy and disorganized, do not keep good records, and basically are just goofing off or having too much fun, all bets are off.

Q: ***"How do you record sales you make on eBay outside of your eBay business, such as personal items?"***

A: You don't report your gross sales to the IRS, only the income you made from your eBay selling activities. It's perfectly okay to sell personal items on eBay as well as having a real business on eBay, as long as you keep separate records of your activities in case you are ever audited. You would report any income from your personal selling as hobby income and file Schedule C to report any income or loss from your business selling. But don't go too crazy—if the items you're selling personally on eBay are similar to the inventory you are selling as a business (for example, you sell computers on eBay and want to sell your old office typewriter because you bought a new one), you probably won't get into too much trouble if you lump everything into your business and just file Schedule C each year.

Income Taxes Due for Prior Years

Q: ***"I started selling on eBay two years ago but just realized this year that I have to pay taxes. I will be filing Schedule C for my eBay business this year, but what about those sales from prior years? Will the IRS come back to me about those?"***

A: You have two choices here. You can file amendments to your prior years' tax returns, report the income from your eBay selling each year on the amendments, and pay the taxes you owed each year, along with interest and penalties imposed by the IRS for late payment. This is the way the IRS would prefer that you report your mistake. The downside, of course, is that you may be "waking a sleeping dog" at the local IRS office and opening the door to a thorough audit of *all* of your recent tax returns to see what other innocent mistakes you might have made.

The second choice, while not a perfect solution by any means, is what most people in your situation would do. Figure out the income (profit) you made from your eBay selling in past years, add it onto the income you report from your eBay selling this year, and report the total on Schedule C when you file next April 15, as if you made everything this year. It is unlikely that the IRS will inquire whether you were actually in business for prior years, although this might come up if you are ever audited. Even if they do discover your prior activity during an audit, by reporting the past income and paying taxes on it this year you will stop the accruing of interest and penalties on the overdue taxes—you will have to pay these only for the prior years for which you did not report income. More important, you will demonstrate to the IRS that your intentions are good and you are struggling to do things the right way; they will be less likely to come down hard on you than if they perceive that you have deliberately and willfully ignored your legal obligations.

Just be forewarned: If you choose to "forget" the income from prior years and make believe it didn't happen, and the IRS has reason to believe that you deliberately and willfully ignored it when you filed your prior years' tax returns (for example, because the amounts involved were too big to be overlooked), there is a small but real possibility they may view the situation as a fraudulent underreporting of income. There is no statute of limitations for underreporting income if the IRS believes you did so fraudulently (with intent), and the IRS can assess interest and penalties for fraud even if they don't discover it until many years from now. If there is even a shred of evidence that you willfully ignored your tax obligations, or if you are playing games with your taxes in other areas, err on the side of coming clean, filing amended returns for your prior years' activities, and accepting whatever consequences may come.

Q: ***"I am confused and sick in the stomach about the issue of selling on eBay and dealing with the IRS. I have things around my home that I have been***

saving and collecting for many years. My daughter is now twenty-two, and I have saved much of her childhood stuff also. Not to mention that I have always loved shopping at yard sales and thrift stores, which has caused my home to be very cluttered. I have made myself stop because I end up buying things I do not need. I also became addicted to eBay a few years back, and for about three years got caught up in buying way too many things—mostly dolls, teddy bears, and old toys—mementoes of my childhood. I have them all over the house. Some of them I have donated to thrift stores and some I have been selling on eBay. Much of the stuff I list on eBay does not even sell and when I pay eBay's fees I suffer a loss, but some things I have gained on. I do not count on this for my income and never considered it a business. The thought of having to go back over the past few years and amend our tax returns because I may have made a profit selling something on eBay or in my local pennysaver paper makes me feel ill from the stress. I take medication to deal with the problems of excessive worrying, depression, and anxiety, and this kind of situation could trigger them again, which scares me. Thanks so much for any help."

A: A lot of longtime eBay sellers are waking up and finding out they should have been paying taxes on their selling profits. Unfortunately, I can't give you the "get out of jail free" card you so badly want. Since you obviously didn't keep good records of what you sold and what you paid for it (most eBay sellers don't), you have no idea whether you made or lost money at the end of each year. The amount of any profit or loss was probably small, given that these were household items and not precious antiques . . . still, the law is the law is the law. If you have a hobby and you make as much as $1 in profit, the IRS wants you to report the profit as hobby income on Form 1040 and pay the taxes on it. If you fail to do so, and the IRS picks up on it during an audit, you're toast.

For peace of mind, if nothing else, you should go back and attempt to figure out whether you made a profit in any of the years you sold on eBay. If you can document that overall you lost money each year, then you're probably okay—the IRS does not require you to report hobby losses on your tax return (they actually prefer that you don't).

If the records show that you made a profit in one or more prior years, you have a difficult choice, and neither option will be stress-free. If you amend your tax returns for the prior years in which you made a profit, you will have to pay interest and penalties on the overdue taxes, and you may be "waking a sleeping

Rottweiler" in the form of an IRS audit to determine whether you've failed to report any *other* income. If you decide not to amend those returns, you will have many sleepless nights, hoping you won't get audited, until the statute of limitations on each return expires (currently three years from the filing date, unless the IRS suspects fraud, in which case there is no statute of limitations).

Is there anything you can do in this situation? Yes.

You can't change the past, but you sure can change the future. You should get into compliance this year, by keeping good records for any eBay listings and sales you make during the current tax year, which began on January 1. If you show a profit at the end of the year, you should pay the taxes due plus a little extra, say 5 percent.

Why the extra 5 percent? In a word, *penance* for your past sins and a little insurance in the event the IRS audits your past tax returns and discovers your goof. The IRS (and any other government agency, for that matter) is always going to go easier on someone who they see is working hard to get into compliance than they will on those who stick their heads in the sand and hope the bogeyman goes away. As an IRS agent once told me, "Even a dog knows the difference between being kicked and being stumbled over."

Income Taxes and Self-Employment Taxes (FICA and Medicare)

Q: ***"What is the minimum limit for filing income taxes when you sell on eBay?"***

A: Zero. I'm not kidding. There is no minimum amount of income you can earn on eBay without having to pay taxes. If you make even $1 in profit (income) selling on eBay, you have to pay taxes on it at your current tax rate.

There are three dollar amounts you need to be aware of when you sell on eBay:

1. If you make even $1 of profit selling on eBay in a given calendar year, you have to pay income taxes to the federal government (and your state government as well, if your state has an income tax).

2. If you make $400 or more of profit selling on eBay in a given calendar year, you have to pay self-employment taxes (FICA and Medicare) in addition to your income taxes.

3. If you have a tax liability of $1,000 or more from your eBay selling activities in a given year, you have to estimate your income and self-employment taxes and pay them in four quarterly installments (by April 15, June 15, September 15, and January 15) rather than in a lump sum by April 15 each year.

Q: ***"Do I really have to pay self-employment taxes such as Social Security when I sell on eBay?"***

A: Yes. If you make more than $400 in profit (income) in a given calendar year, you have to pay self-employment taxes (FICA and Medicare) to the IRS in addition to your federal income taxes. If your state has an income tax, you may have to pay similar amounts to your state tax authority as well. For more information, see IRS Publication 334, Tax Guide for Small Business, or IRS Publication 4591, Small Business Federal Tax Responsibilities.

Estimated Taxes

Q: ***"When do I have to pay estimated taxes?"***

A: When you have $1,000 of tax liability from self-employment activities (if you're making $5,000 or more in profit from eBay sales, you're getting close to this requirement and should talk to an accountant or tax adviser), you no longer can wait until April 15 each year to pay your taxes. You will have to estimate these and pay them in quarterly installments (the due dates are April 15, June 15, September 15, and January 15).

There are two ways to calculate your estimated taxes:

1. *The safe harbor method.* Take your tax liability last year (the amount you actually paid the IRS, not the amount of income that was subject to tax), add 10 percent, divide by 4, and pay that amount on each of the four payment dates.

2. *The SWAG method* (for "scientific wild-assed guess"). Sit down with a pencil and paper the day before each payment date, make your best calculation of how much you actually owe the IRS in taxes for that quarterly period, pay that amount, and pray to the Almighty that you're right at the end of the year.

Here are two (simplified) examples of estimated tax calculations:

- You paid the IRS $40,000 in taxes last year and want to use the safe harbor method this year. Take 10 percent of $40,000 ($4,000), add it to the $40,000 ($44,000), divide by 4, and pay the IRS $11,000 on each of the four payment dates.
- Your gross sales from eBay were $80,000 for the past three months, and you had $30,000 in eBay-related expenses during this same period. Using the SWAG method, report $50,000 in eBay business income and pay taxes on it using your current tax rate, hoping that your future sales on eBay will not throw you into a higher tax bracket for the year.

Calculating estimated taxes is extremely complex and difficult, and the preceding discussion merely grazes the surface of the IRS rules regarding estimated taxes. For more information, read IRS Publication 505, Tax Withholding and Estimated Tax, which is available as a free download from the IRS website at www.irs.gov. Then hire an accountant or tax adviser to help you with the calculations.

Income Taxes in Multiple States

Q: ***"If I move to another state, do I have to report the income I made from eBay sales in both states?"***

A: Yes. Report your income and pay federal income taxes as if you had never moved at all. You also have to pay state income taxes on all income earned while you were a resident of each state.

For example, let's say you moved from New York to California on June 30. You report your income from eBay selling for the period January 1 to June 30 and pay New York state income taxes for that period. You report your income from eBay selling for the period July 1 to December 31 and pay California state income taxes for that period. On April 15 of the following year, you will have to file three separate tax returns: a federal return for the entire year, a New York state return for the first six months, and a California state return for the last six months.

Keep in mind that some states do not have income taxes, some states do not have sales taxes (see Chapter 13), and at least one state (New Hampshire) has neither. Skiing, anyone?

Determining the Cost of Your eBay Inventory for Tax Purposes

Q: ***"If I sell something that was worth $10 about fifty years ago for $200, do I have to pay tax on the full $190 difference? Is there any adjustment for inflation?"***

A: Regrettably, our tax system in the United States is not indexed for inflation when it comes to calculating capital gain taxes. In this example, you would have to pay tax on a $190 profit.

Q: ***"If I'm selling stuff from people's estates, how do I go about determining the cost for purposes of figuring out my profit and taxable income?"***

A: The IRS gives you a break here. When someone dies and leaves you something (or the estate consigns something to you for sale on eBay), you do not have to figure out what the deceased person actually paid for the item. The cost of this item for your purposes is the *fair market value* of the item on the date of the person's death. You pay taxes only on the increase in value of the item since that time.

For example, Aunt Sadie bought a cookie jar in 1950 for $10. On the date of her death in 2006, the cookie jar had a fair market value of $100. Aunt Sadie left the cookie jar to you in her will, and you sell it in 2007 for $150. You would report only $50 as income from the sale of the cookie jar, not $140.

Since you are selling items on eBay reasonably soon after the person dies, the amount you realize for the item on eBay is probably pretty close to the fair market value of the item on the day the person died. If you are taking consignments, however, this won't protect you from paying income taxes on the sales commission or fee you agree to with your consignor—this is considered ordinary income for tax purposes, and you have to pay taxes on the full amount of it. Since in a consignment sale you technically don't have title to the items being sold, you can't avail yourself of the more favorable capital gain rates.

For example, Aunt Sadie dies and leaves all of her household belongings to Niece Jane, who hires you to sell everything in the house on eBay. You agree with Niece Jane that everything you sell in the consignment entitles you to a 30 percent fee. Niece Jane delivers the first item—a precious Ming vase—to you. You list it on eBay, and it sells for $1,000. You keep $300 (30 percent) of the sales proceeds and remit the $700 balance to Niece Jane. Niece Jane must pay income tax on the difference between $700 and the fair market value of the vase on the date of Aunt Sadie's death (the appraised value as set forth in Aunt Sadie's federal estate tax return) and can pay tax at the (currently) favorable capital gain rate because the Ming vase is a *capital asset*. You must pay income tax on $300 at the (currently) unfavorable ordinary income rate.

Q: ***"If I'm selling something I've had around for a long time and I can't remember what I paid for it, how do I determine its cost?"***

A: If the item in question is an antique or collectible and you remember roughly when you acquired the item, there are a number of research manuals and collector-oriented websites that give you access (sometimes for a small fee) to detailed records of auction prices for the same or similar items over long periods of time. For example, if you're selling an antique mechanical bank on eBay, you can check out the website of the Mechanical Bank Collectors of America (www.mbca.com)—click on Auctions and you will see a listing of auction sale prices going back thirty or more years for each make, model, and condition grade of mechanical bank made in the United States between 1870 and 1920.

If that's not feasible or would take up too much of your time, your safest bet is to treat the item as having a zero, or extremely minimal, cost. The IRS will never complain about your underestimating cost when calculating how much you owe in taxes.

Calculating Your Cost of Goods Sold (COGS)

Q: ***"When I determine how much money I made on eBay, do I simply subtract the eBay and PayPal fees from the winning bid amount?"***

A: No, I'm afraid it's a little more complicated than that. What you have to do is calculate the *cost of goods sold* (COGS) of the item you sold on eBay. For most items, your COGS will be the following:

- What you paid your vendor or supplier for that specific item, *plus*
- The sales taxes (if any) you paid to the vendor or supplier of the item, *plus*
- Any storage fees for that item, *plus*

- Your packaging and shipping costs for that item, to the extent (and only to the extent) these are not reimbursed by the buyer, *plus*
- Your insurance costs for that item, to the extent (and only to the extent) these are not reimbursed by the buyer, *plus*
- The sales taxes (if any) you are required to pay upon the sale of the item on eBay, to the extent (and only to the extent) these are not reimbursed by the buyer, *plus*
- Your eBay, PayPal, and other selling fees and commissions

Total these amounts for each item, and then subtract the total from the price the buyer paid on eBay, and—voila!—you have your net income for that item.

Note that you have to make this calculation on an item-by-item basis. If you are selling lots of stuff on eBay, it's best to invest in some software that will help you determine your profit on each eBay sale, such as Corey Kossack's ProfitBuilderSoftware (www.profitbuildersoftware.com).

Partnership Tax Issues

Q: ***"I have been selling on eBay for the past few months. My spouse helps me out a little bit by keeping the books and occasionally driving packages to the UPS Store, but I don't pay her anything for it. Obviously, everything we make goes into our joint bank account. Do we have to file our taxes as a partnership, or can I just file a Schedule C?"***

A: Generally, you file taxes as a partnership if two or more people are sharing in the profits and losses of a business. If you're a partnership, you file an *information return* on IRS Form 1065 each year, although many accountants think this isn't necessary if the only partners in the business are a husband and wife and each partner reports his or her pro rata share of the partnership income on Schedule C when they file their Form 1040 each year.

If you treat yourself as a partnership for tax purposes, then each of you is *jointly and severally* liable if the partnership gets sued. This means that if you make a mistake selling something on eBay, the buyer can sue both you and your wife, even though your wife had nothing to do with the business or the mistake you made. This is not a good thing.

Since this is primarily *your* business, you probably shouldn't treat it as a partnership for tax purposes because of the risks involved. I recommend that you talk to an attorney about the following:

- Have your spouse sign a document stating clearly that she has no interest in your business (this will be a lifesaver should you ever get divorced).
- Pay your spouse a reasonable fee for the services she performs for the business, and be sure to send her Form 1099 (see Chapter 20) if you pay her more than $600 total during the calendar year.
- Get a federal tax ID number for your business and open a separate checking account for it—no more commingling of funds in the family bank account.
- File Schedule C as a *sole proprietor* when you prepare your income tax return at the end of the year.

eBay Certified Education Specialists and eBay Certified Business Consultants

Q: ***"I am an eBay Certified Education Specialist and teach eBay classes at local colleges and adult education programs. What kind of tax form do I need to fill out for this? How do I pay taxes on revenue I generate through teaching, lectures, and private training sessions?"***

A: For those who don't know, an eBay Certified Education Specialist is someone who has been trained by eBay (for a fee) to conduct adult education and other classes that teach other folks how to sell on eBay. (If you're interested in becoming one, go to www.poweru.net/ebay for details.)

An eBay Education Specialist has to pay income taxes, just like anyone else, on the income from teaching classes, less expenses for training, instruction books, and other teaching-related costs. If you are a sole proprietor, you have to fill out Schedule C (income or loss from a trade or business) each year and pay your taxes on April 15. If your tax liability is more than $1,000 in any given year, you have to estimate your income taxes four times a year (by April 15, June 15, September 15, and January 15) and pay them in quarterly installments using IRS Form 1040-ES.

The good news is that in virtually all states, educational activities are exempt from state and local sales and use taxes. The bad news is that in many states, if you are using the word *education* or some variation in your company name, you have to get permission from your state education department to do so. Check with a local attorney to find out if this is necessary in your state; if it is, you have to pay a small fee and wait several weeks to get the education department's certificate authorizing you to represent yourself as being in an education-related business.

Consignment Sales and Drop Shipping

Q: ***"If I am taking goods for sale on consignment (for example, as an eBay Trading Assistant), do I have to pay taxes on the full value or on just the portion that I keep?"***

A: You pay income taxes only on the portion you keep under your agreement with each consignor. Because this is a sales commission and in a consignment sale you never take title to the item, you have to report this income at (currently) unfavorable ordinary income tax rates as compensation. Your consignor has to pay income taxes on the amounts you remit to him or her after deducting your commission. If you remit more than $600 total to a consignor during the calendar year, you must send the consignor Form 1099 within thirty days after the year ends (i.e., by January 31).

Q: ***"How do you handle income taxes when you are dealing with a drop shipper on eBay?"***

A: Basically, the same way you would handle income taxes for consignment sales. You pay income taxes only on the portion you are allowed to keep under your agreement with the drop shipper. Because this is a sales commission and in drop shipping you never take title to the item, you have to report this income at (currently) unfavorable ordinary income tax rates as compensation. Since the vast majority of drop shippers are corporations or other legal entities, you probably don't need to send them Form 1099 at the end of each year the way you are required to do for individuals who consign goods to you for sale on eBay.

Will eBay or PayPal Rat You Out to the IRS?

Q: *"Does eBay report member sales or earnings to the IRS?"*

A: Not yet. At present, eBay has said that if they receive a subpoena for information, they will honor it (so would PayPal), but to my knowledge no such subpoena has ever been issued. The IRS has an informative discussion of this issue on its website, www.irs.gov (go to the home page and type "online auction" in the site's search engine).

Whether or not it is reported to the IRS by another party, if you have gain or profit from selling on eBay, you are required to report it as income and pay income taxes on it. As this book is going to press, the IRS has drafted a new version of Form 1099-MISC and plans to require eBay to issue it to you if you have more than one hundred sales or more than $5,000 in auction bids during the calendar year. This may change, however, by the time this book is published. Talk to your accountant or tax adviser, or check the IRS website, for more up-to-the-minute information.

13 When Do I Charge Sales Taxes?

Registering for Sales Taxes When You Sell on eBay

Q: ***"If someone has been selling on eBay as a hobby and wants to get a sales tax number to sell as a business with a new name, should the person first take all their auctions off eBay, and if so, for how long? In my state, the rules for applying for a resale license say that you should not be conducting business for twenty days prior to applying for the resale license, and they warn that you could be fined up to $10,000 if you engage in business before you get the license, which takes approximately twenty days. I imagine a lot of people in this situation would just apply for the resale license and leave their eBay auctions going, but I'm wondering if there's a better answer about what to do."***

A: First, some basics. When you are selling stuff on eBay, you are required to register with your state tax authority to collect and pay sales taxes. When you register, you are issued a document that, depending on the state, is called a *sales tax permit*, a *business license*, a *resale license*, or a *certificate of authority*. The name on the document doesn't matter. What's important is the tax ID number, or *resale number*, that appears on the document. That number must appear on all sales tax and other tax returns you file with your state tax authority.

It doesn't matter whether you treat your eBay selling as a hobby or a business. When you sell stuff on eBay (or, indeed, anywhere on the Internet) to people who are residents of the same state you live in, you are required to collect and pay sales taxes (unless, of course, your state doesn't have a sales tax). Frankly, your sales on eBay right now might be in violation of that requirement—if you have sold anything on eBay to people living in your state, you are subject to the $10,000 penalty for doing business without a sales tax permit.

You are correct that most people in your situation would just apply for the sales tax permit, pay their sales taxes going forward, and not worry about their closed or pending eBay listings. Most people would not willingly pay the $10,000 penalty, even if they could afford it, for fear of "waking a sleeping dog" at the state tax authority and triggering a broader audit of their personal and business finances.

I recommend that you review your past eBay sales and, if there were any sales to residents of your state, calculate and pay the sales tax for those in-state listings to your state tax authority as soon as you have obtained your sales tax permit. It is unlikely that your state tax authority will inquire whether you were actually in business for prior years, although this may come up if you are ever audited. Even if they do discover your prior activity during an audit, by reporting your past sales and paying taxes on them this year you will stop the accruing of interest and penalties on the overdue taxes; you will pay these only for the prior year(s) for which you did not report them. However, if the $10,000 is a flat penalty (i.e., not dependent on the actual amount of taxes), you probably will still be liable for that. By demonstrating to your state tax authority that your intentions are basically good and you are struggling to do things the right way, it is much more likely that they will be lenient with you and work out a payment schedule or some other method by which you can pay the penalty without shutting down your business.

The problem here is that the punishment does not fit the crime. Many of these penalties were enacted into law a long time ago—before the Internet and e-commerce. If you owe your state tax authority only $100 in back taxes, then a $10,000 penalty is simply ridiculous. Seek some expert advice here—talk to a tax accountant or lawyer who deals with your state tax authority on a regular basis. It may well be that your state tax authority routinely forgives the penalty in situations like this and, if that's the case, then coming clean now would be to your advantage.

Sales Taxes: Seller and Buyer in the Same State

Q: *"When do I charge sales tax for selling stuff on eBay?"*

A: Under current law, you are required to collect and pay sales tax to your state (and sometimes also your local) government whenever you sell something on eBay to a resident of the same state in which you are operating. So, for example, if I live in Iowa and I sell something on eBay to an Iowa resident, I am required to collect and pay Iowa state sales tax. It doesn't matter that the other fourteen bidders in my eBay auction were from other states or that the winning bidder in the auction could have come from anywhere on earth. When it comes to sales tax, you always pay it whenever there's a same-state transaction—unless, of course, your state is one of several that doesn't have a sales tax at all.

There is currently no federal sales tax. You register for sales taxes with your state tax authority and file a sales tax return with it, usually once each quarter (every three months). If your city or town imposes a sales tax surcharge, you may have to register with your municipal tax authority as well.

Q: ***"Can I add the sales tax to the winning bidder's bid amount, or do I have to absorb the sales tax?"***

A: You can add the sales tax to the purchase price of an item, or the winning bid amount for an auction listing, but *only* if you warned the buyer in advance that you would do this. If you didn't, both eBay and your state law will have a problem if you try to tack on the sales tax after the listing closes.

Whenever you create an eBay listing, be sure to put the following sentence somewhere on the page (most sellers put it in their Terms and Conditions section): "Note to Residents of [your state]: State and local sales taxes will be added to your purchase price or winning bid amount." Use boldface type or an all-capital-letters font for this, so the sentence is clearly visible to your buyers.

If you don't warn your buyers in advance that you're planning to collect sales taxes from them, you cannot do so. You are still required, however, to pay sales tax on the transaction to your state tax authority if the buyer is a resident of your state. In that situation, you will have to absorb the sales tax out of your profits on the sale—although it is deductible and reduces your reportable income for income tax purposes.

Q: ***"I know I have to charge sales tax on the purchase price when I sell on eBay. Do I have to charge sales tax on the shipping and handling as well?"***

A: Some states require that you charge sales tax on the gross amount the buyer pays you, including shipping and handling charges. You should consult your accountant or tax adviser to learn about the rules in your state. Charging sales tax on shipping and handling when your state doesn't permit that violates eBay's Excessive Shipping Charges policy, which can be found at http://pages.ebay.com/help/policies/listing-shipping.html.

Sales Taxes: Seller and Buyer in Different States

Q: ***"Do I have to charge sales tax if the winning bidder lives in a different state than I do?"***

A: Under current law, the answer is no. You do not charge or pay sales taxes on interstate or international sales transactions unless you have a legal presence, called a *nexus,* in another state. *Nexus* is hard to define precisely, but some common examples are:

- You have a mailing address or post office box in another state that you use in your business.
- You are bidding on eBay as an employee of a company that has offices in other states.
- Your company has employees in other states who use their home offices as business locations (for example, they use their home addresses on your company's business cards).
- You are in partnership with someone in another state, and both of you are selling on eBay.
- You are drop shipping for a company that has offices in other states.
- You take consignments for sale on eBay from individuals who live in other states.
- You sell something on eBay and require a buyer in another state to come to your home or office to pick it up.
- You travel to another state and sell items at a flea market or garage sale there.

The law may be changing in the very near future, however, especially when it comes to Internet sales transactions. State and local governments have lost billions of dollars in sales tax revenue because of Internet commerce, the vast majority of which is interstate or international in nature and therefore not subject to state and local sales taxes. And they are hopping mad about that.

As a result of their anger, twenty-two states have adopted a law called the Streamlined Sales Tax Project, or SSTP. This statute requires you, as an Internet seller, to collect and pay sales taxes whenever you sell to a resident of a state that has adopted the SSTP. The tax is based on the rate in effect where the buyer is located, which means that you have to keep track of thousands of state and local governments in the twenty-two SSTP states that impose sales taxes on local transactions. If SSTP is adopted by all fifty states, you will have to keep track of roughly 7,600 sales tax jurisdictions in the United States alone.

Now, *don't panic*! Technically, the states that have adopted the SSTP are not in a position to enforce it, because of several U.S. Supreme Court decisions that prohibit states from imposing their sales and other business taxes on interstate commerce—state and local governments cannot legally enforce laws that the Supreme Court says violate the federal Constitution. Those Supreme Court decisions, however, can be overruled by an act of Congress—and every time there's a new Congress someone introduces a bill to do exactly that. So far, those bills have gone nowhere, but it's only a matter of time before Congress acts and the SSTP becomes enforceable in the twenty-two states that have adopted it. (And you just know the other twenty-eight will climb onto this bandwagon as soon as Congress acts, don't you?)

The states that have adopted the SSTP offer eBay sellers and other e-merchants a voluntary amnesty program, promising, in effect, that if you begin complying with the law now and start collecting and paying sales taxes when you sell to residents of SSTP states, the state tax authority won't audit you if and when Congress acts and the SSTP actually becomes enforceable. Extremely gracious, aren't they?

Avalara.com, based in Seattle, Washington, has developed a number of software products that will help you comply with SSTP if you wish to participate in the voluntary amnesty programs offered by the twenty-two SSTP states.

In the meantime, it's important for every serious eBay seller to join the fight to keep Congress and the states from passing legislation that would hurt the eBay community. The eBay Government Affairs department operates a website at www.ebaymainstreet.com, where you can sign up to receive news, information, and form letters whenever Congress or your state legislature is considering a bill that would hurt eBay sellers or the eBay community generally. These form letters are preaddressed to your federal and state government officials—all you need to do is print them out, sign them, and mail them to the officials whose names appear on the letters. The idea is to let these officials know just how many eBay sellers live in their districts and how unhappy those people will be if the officials vote for any legislation that would hurt their businesses.

When Do You Charge Another State's Sales Tax?

Q: ***"My sister and I are selling on eBay as a partnership. She lives in Texas, and I live in New York. Which state's sales tax do we charge?"***

A: You should charge sales tax whenever you sell to someone in New York or Texas, regardless of which one of you actually puts up the eBay listing. Partnerships have a *nexus,* or legal presence, wherever they have an office or physical location. In this case, your partnership has offices in both New York and Texas, and you should charge sales tax accordingly.

Have you ever ordered anything from a mail order catalogue, and the order form had a line that said, "If you are a resident of one of the following states, please add your state sales tax"? That's what's going on there—the mail order company has warehouses, sales outlets, or offices in those states.

Q: ***"If I am taking consignments of goods for sale on eBay, when do I charge sales tax to the winning bidders?"***

A: You charge sales tax if either you or your consignor (the person who delivers stuff to you to sell on eBay) live in the same state that the buyer does. So, for example, if you live in New York and are taking consignments from a person who lives in Connecticut, you have to charge the appropriate sales tax (either New York's or Connecticut's) whenever a buyer or a successful bidder lives in New York or Connecticut.

Q: ***"If I am selling stuff on eBay for a drop shipper, when do I charge sales tax, or is this the drop shipper's responsibility?"***

A: When you work for a drop shipper, you charge sales tax if the buyer or successful bidder lives in the same state as you or lives in a state where the drop shipper has an office, physical location, or nexus. Here are some examples:

- You live in Maine and are selling for a drop shipper in Ohio. If you sell to a Maine resident, you must charge Maine sales tax, and if you sell to an Ohio resident, you must charge Ohio sales tax.
- You live in New York and are selling for a drop shipper in Vermont that has offices or warehouses in California, Georgia, Montana, and Illinois. If you sell to a resident of any of the states listed in this example, you must charge that state's sales tax.

Whenever you deal with a drop shipper, you must make sure they give you a complete list of all states in which they currently charge sales taxes to their own buyers. Then, when you put up your eBay listings, you should include the following sentence in your Terms and Conditions section: "Note to Residents of the Following States: [list them alphabetically]. State and local sales taxes will be added to your purchase price or winning bid amount." Make sure the sentence appears in boldface type or an all-capital-letters font so that your buyers are sure to see it before they buy or bid on your drop shipper's item.

Q: ***"When I collect sales tax for a state other than my own, what do I do with it once I get it?"***

A: Go to your state tax authority's website (to find this, go to www.taxsites.com/state and click on your state when the map of the United States pops up), and look at their Forms and Publications section. Every state has a form for payment of out-of-state taxes. Print the form, fill it out, and then send it to *your* state tax authority (not the other state's!) along with a check for sales taxes you've collected from an out-of-state buyer, again made out to *your* state tax authority (not the other state's!).

When your state tax authority receives this letter and the check, they will remit it to the other state's tax authority.

Yeah, I'm laughing, too. . . . I really don't know if they'll do it or not, either. But by doing this you have done everything you possibly can to comply with *your* state's tax law, and that's all you're required to do, at least under current law.

Paying Sales Taxes on the Stuff You Buy

Q: ***"When I buy inventory for resale on eBay, the vendor sometimes insists that I pay sales taxes. Are they right to do that?"***

A: No. In the United States, sales taxes are imposed on retail sales only, not wholesale transactions. When you buy wholesale, you should not have to pay sales tax. However, some vendors charge you sales tax because they're really not convinced that you are buying the items for resale. To put their minds at ease, you need to give them a *resale certificate.* Do this, and they won't charge you sales tax.

You can find the form of resale certificate for your state on your state tax authority's website. To find that website, go to www.taxsites.com/state.html and click on your state when the map of the United States pops up. Go to the Forms and Publications section of your state tax authority's website and search for "resale certificate."

The resale certificate is basically an affidavit in which you swear to your vendor that you are buying his or her items with the intent of reselling them on eBay, not for your personal consumption. You will need a *resale number* to fill out the resale certificate—this is the same as your state tax ID number. If you have not registered with your state tax authority and obtained this number, you will not be able to use a resale certificate.

When you give resale certificates to vendors, they are excused from charging sales tax. If they ever get audited by your state tax authority for failing to pay sales taxes, they will wave your resale certificate in the auditor's face and then tell the auditor exactly where you live.

One more thing about resale certificates: It is a felony in most states to deliver a false or fraudulent resale certificate to a vendor. If you are buying a container of ten thousand bobble-head dolls for your own consumption, don't lie to the vendor and say it's a wholesale transaction. You can go to jail for that. Cough up the sales tax money and enjoy your new collection (if you can find enough room in your home to store it).

Q: ***"I often buy things at retail, and pay the sales tax, because I find I can resell them on eBay and make even more money. Amazing, but true. How do I account for the sales tax I pay to the vendors when I buy these items?"***

A: You add the sales tax to the cost of goods sold of each item, then deduct it from the purchase price when the item later sells on eBay.

Use Taxes

Q: ***"What exactly is a use tax? I see this listed on my state sales tax return, and I'm not sure whether I have to charge it, collect it, or pay it."***

A: A *use tax* is the opposite of a sales tax—I like to call it the sales tax's "evil twin."

A use tax is a tax on stuff you purchase for your own consumption, for which you do not pay sales tax (i.e., you don't pay use tax on your eBay inventory). Here are some examples:

- You go to your local Staples store and buy a box of paper clips for your eBay selling business, paying your state sales tax at the register. Because you paid your state sales tax on the paper clips, you do not have to pay a use tax on top of it.
- You live in New York and buy a laptop computer from a mail order house in Texas for resale in your eBay Store. Because the computer is inventory, it is not subject to use tax (because you bought it from an out-of-state vendor, there's no sales tax on it, either).
- You live in New York and buy a laptop computer from a mail order house in Texas, which you intend to use yourself in running your eBay Store. Because you did not pay sales tax on the computer and are intending to use it for your own consumption, you will have to pay use tax to the New York state tax authority when you file your next New York sales tax return.

Every state that has a sales tax also has a use tax; the tax rate is always the same as it is for the state sales tax. So if your state sales tax rate is 5 percent, the use tax rate will be 5 percent as well. At least they make *that* easy to understand!

One more point: While businesses are always required to pay use taxes in the states that have them, many states also require individual consumers to pay use taxes when they buy things for their own consumption from out-of-state vendors. Have *you* paid use tax on everything you've bought on eBay over the past ten years? Just a little something to keep you awake on those long, cold, winter nights . . . ☺.

14 What Can I Deduct on My Tax Return?

Auto Expenses and Mileage Deductions

Q: *"Can I deduct trips to the post office or to the UPS Store to pick up items I've ordered?"*

A: The IRS gives you two choices when it comes to deducting motor vehicle expenses. You can either deduct your mileage (the current rate is 46.5 cents per mile, but it changes every year, and sometimes even during the year) or deduct the actual cost of maintaining the car (e.g., gas, oil changes, garage repairs, car washes, and so forth).

Either way, the IRS does not allow you to deduct 100 percent of your mileage or expenses if you use your car or truck for both business and personal purposes. You must keep track of how much time you use your car for business as opposed to personal use.

I recommend that you buy a mileage log (available on eBay or from any store or website that sells office supplies), keep it in a convenient place (such as under the driver's side visor) along with a pen or pencil, and record your actual business mileage on a daily basis. This mileage log will come in handy when you prepare your annual taxes and if you are ever audited.

What counts as mileage? Basically, any miles you travel while actually conducting business for eBay selling. Here are some examples:

- Driving between your home office and the local post office or UPS Store to check your private mailbox and pick up ordered items that you are planning to sell on eBay

- Driving to and from your home office to your post office or UPS Store to drop off items you have sold on eBay for shipment to the buyer
- Driving to a seller's home or office to pick up items you plan to sell on eBay
- Driving to and from garage sales, flea markets, and the like, to purchase goods for sale on eBay
- Making personal deliveries of items you have sold on eBay to local buyers
- Driving to and from a local meeting of an organization of local businesspeople or eBay sellers, such as a networking group

Here's an example scenario: You leave your home office in your SUV with your three children and several packages of goods you have sold on eBay that have to be shipped. You drive three miles to your children's school and drop them off. Then you drive another two miles to the post office and mail the packages before returning the five miles to your home office. You can deduct the two miles you drove to the post office and the five miles you drove back to your home office, but you cannot deduct the three miles from your home office to your kids' school.

Compensation to Owner

Q: ***"In my eBay selling business, I sometimes take money out of the business checking account to pay my personal bills. How do I deduct these withdrawals for tax purposes?"***

A: You don't. As the sole owner of an unincorporated business, you cannot pay yourself a deductible salary. Instead, you must report 100 percent of all profits from the business as your personal income each year, regardless of whether you withdraw the money from the business checking account. There is no need to report periodic withdrawals from your business checking account (called *draws* in tax language) on Schedule C.

If you have employees in your business who are not also owners, then you can pay them a fixed salary each week or quarter and deduct it from your business income. Amounts you pay to employees who are also owners, however, are not deductible (see Chapter 20).

Computer Equipment and Software

Q: ***"Can I deduct the cost of a laptop computer I use in my home-based eBay selling business?"***

A: Yes, but only if you use the computer exclusively for selling on eBay. If your kids use it even some of the time for playing video games, or if your spouse uses it to crunch spreadsheets for his day job, you have to determine the percentage of time the computer is being used for selling on eBay and deduct only that percentage of the computer's cost.

Q: ***"Can I deduct software fees?"***

A: Software that you purchase can be depreciated over three years or less, if the software has a shorter useful life. For example, tax preparation software such as TurboTax is good for only one year, so it probably could be deducted outright in the year you buy it. On the other hand, an annual subscription fee to the KeepMore.net online accounting solution for eBay sellers probably can be deducted only in the year in which it's taken.

Cost of Goods Sold

Q: ***"Can I deduct the cost of my inventory directly against the winning bid amount?"***

A: No, I'm afraid it's a little more complicated than that. What you have to do is calculate the *cost of goods sold* (COGS) of the item you sold on eBay. For most items, your COGS will be the following:

- What you paid your vendor or supplier for that specific item, *plus*
- The sales taxes (if any) you paid to the vendor or supplier of the item, *plus*

- Any storage fees for that item, *plus*
- Your packaging and shipping costs for that item, to the extent (and only to the extent) these are not reimbursed by the buyer, *plus*
- Your insurance costs for that item, to the extent (and only to the extent) these are not reimbursed by the buyer, *plus*
- The sales taxes (if any) you are required to pay upon the sale of the item on eBay, to the extent (and only to the extent) these are not reimbursed by the buyer, *plus*
- Your eBay, PayPal, and other selling fees and commissions

Total these amounts for each item, and then subtract the total from the price the buyer paid on eBay, and—voila!—you have your net income for that item.

Note that you have to make this calculation on an item-by-item basis. If you are selling lots of stuff on eBay, it's best to invest in some software that will help you determine your profit on each eBay sale, such as Corey Kossack's ProfitBuilderSoftware (www.profitbuildersoftware.com).

Q: ***"I have started selling toys on eBay. How do I handle the toys I have been collecting and storing for many years and want to put up for sale now? How do I handle starting inventory for tax purposes? Many of the things I bought several years ago are highly collectible now."***

A: I think you are asking how you report the cost of goods sold of these items when you don't have accurate records of how much you paid for them.

You may have to rely on your memory about how much you paid for the item. In that case, record the cost but keep some type of written memo to the file, such as "Purchased at Danbury antiques fair, March 1966, for $10." You can also look at old auction catalogues and ads in antique toy collectors' magazines to see what specific toys were selling for at roughly the time you bought them. The IRS usually will accept that type of information.

Another (less reliable) approach is to show your toys to a local antiques dealer who's been around a while and get a rough written estimate of how much these items were selling for back then. Many dealers collect old catalogues and magazines and will do this research for you—for a fee, of course. Just don't sell your toys if the dealer offers to buy them—you'll often do better on eBay.

eBay and PayPal Fees

Q: ***"How do I deduct the various eBay and PayPal fees on my tax return?"***

A: You add these to your cost of goods sold (see the answer to the previous question) and deduct them when each item sells on eBay.

Design Services for Website or eBay Store

Q: ***"Can I deduct the cost of having my auction pages custom designed?"***

A: The World Wide Web is where you make all eBay sales, of course. Therefore, you can claim deductions for:

- Web-related design costs
- Internet access fees
- Website hosting

Insurance

Q: ***"Can I deduct insurance I provide for myself and other family members?"***

A: You can take deductions relating to:

- All insurance for employees, other than yourself or your spouse
- Health insurance for yourself, your spouse, and your dependents (unless you are eligible for insurance through your day job)
- Premiums for business insurance (e.g., liability, business interruption, property/casualty)
- Long-term care insurance for yourself, your spouse, your dependents (with some limits)
- Payments to a state unemployment compensation or disability fund

Net Operating Losses

Q: ***"Please address the issue of net operating loss (NOL) for business. Can bad years be safely woven in with better ones? Is this a red flag? Should losses be carried forward?"***

A: Generally, if you have an NOL for a tax year ending in 2005, you must carry back the entire amount of the NOL to the two tax years before the NOL year (the carryback period), and then carry forward any portion of the NOL you cannot use for up to twenty years after the NOL year (the carryforward period). You can, however, choose not to carry back the NOL and only carry it forward. See IRS Publication 536 for more specific information.

Although taking net operating losses is certainly not an audit trigger, make sure you're doing it right. If you find out next year that you should have taken an NOL in 2005, you will have to amend your 2005 tax return to claim the deduction retroactively, and that just might wake some "sleeping dogs" at the local IRS office.

Postage

Q: ***"Should the cost of postage be deducted, or should it be incorporated into the item cost for cost of goods sold?"***

A: Postage cannot be deducted right away but must be added to your cost of goods sold and deducted from the final sales price (the winning bid in your eBay auction) when the item is sold.

Sales Taxes

Q: ***"If I pay sales taxes to buy goods at retail and then resell them on eBay for an even higher price, can I deduct the sales taxes I pay as a business expense?"***

A: Taxes you have to pay to sell and buy on eBay (especially sales and use taxes) may be deductible if your buyer has not reimbursed you for them on top of the purchase price or winning bid amounts. Taxes that are deductible include:

- Inventory or "floor" taxes (if imposed by your state) on the year-end value of your eBay inventory
- One-half of self-employment taxes you pay (note, however, that you take that deduction on your Form 1040, not on your schedule C)
- Personal property taxes on equipment and supplies (if imposed by your state)
- Sales taxes you pay when you buy goods for resale on eBay
- Sales taxes you pay when you sell goods on eBay (unless you are reimbursed for these sales taxes by the buyer, in which case it is a wash—you don't deduct them, nor do you report the sales tax amount as income)
- Telephone service taxes (for a dedicated business telephone line)
- Use taxes (paid to your state when you buy items from out-of-state vendors for use in your business—not for resale—and when you don't pay sales taxes)

Shipping and Handling Fees

Q: *"If I charge my buyers shipping and handling fees, how do I account for that on Schedule C?"*

A: Most eBay sellers charge their buyers a shipping and handling fee precisely to cover the costs of postage, packaging materials, and other selling expenses. If you charge your eBay buyers a shipping and handling fee, then you cannot deduct the cost of these items, nor is the shipping and handling fee treated as income to you. It's a total wash, as if you took the buyer's shipping and handling fee out of one hand and paid it to the supplier with the other hand at the same moment.

For example, you buy $100 worth of inventory for sale on eBay, plus $10 for a cardboard box that the item fits in. You then sell the inventory on eBay for $100, plus a $10 shipping and handling fee to cover the cost of the box. You would include the $10 cardboard box in the cost of goods sold and report $100 ($210 minus the $100 item cost minus the $10 box) as income on your Schedule C, paying taxes on that amount. The $10 shipping and handling fee would offset the $10 you added to your cost of goods sold for the box.

Q: *"If I charge more for shipping than it actually cost me, how do I report this on my tax return?"*

A: This is not a recommended practice for any eBay seller. Not only might it violate eBay policies and get you kicked off eBay, but it might also violate consumer protection laws in your home state. If winning bidders find out you are inflating their winning bid by overcharging for postage or shipping materials, you are almost certain to generate negative feedback on eBay's Feedback Forum—not a good thing, especially for new sellers.

If you do engage in this practice, you will have to pay taxes on the excess shipping fees, which are income to you. The proper approach when filling out your tax return—and what the IRS would prefer you to do—is to total all the shipping fees you receive from winning bidders on eBay and report the total as Other Income on Schedule C. Then, total up your actual postage and shipping costs and report the total as deductible Materials and Supplies on Schedule C. If you do it right, the net income subject to tax is the total amount of your excess shipping and handling fees, which is where you should end up.

Be forewarned: If you are ever sued by an eBay buyer (or eBay itself) for fee gouging, the first thing a lawyer will ask to see are copies of your Schedule C.

Shipping and Packaging Materials

Q: *"Should the cost of shipping materials (such as plastic peanuts and duct tape) be deducted, or should it be incorporated into the item cost for cost of goods sold?"*

A: Shipping materials, such as boxes, peanuts, and bubble pack, used for wrapping merchandise, cannot be deducted right away but must be added to your cost of goods sold and deducted from the final sales price (the winning bid in your eBay auction) when the item is sold.

Start-up Expenses

Q: *"What expenses qualify as business start-up costs?"*

A: Start-up costs are business expenses you have before you start your business selling on eBay. General preliminary costs, such as researching whether you want to sell on eBay, are not deductible, but conventional expenses of setting up your eBay selling business are deductible. For example:

- Legal and accounting costs of getting a tax ID number and/or forming a limited liability company (LLC)
- Office stationery and business cards
- Preopening advertising (such as in the Yellow Pages)
- Rent, telephone, and other expenses you incur before you make your first sale on eBay

Under current IRS rules, the first $5,000 of start-up expenses is fully deductible in the year you incur them. Beyond that, start-up expenses must be amortized over a period not to exceed five years (sixty months).

If you haven't made your first sale on eBay, wait until you do. Everything you spend money on after that point is deductible as a business expense, and you won't have to worry about IRS start-up cost rules.

Time Spent on eBay Selling Activities

Q: *"Can I deduct my time, such as the time spent traveling to the post office or preparing my tax return?"*

A: Unfortunately, although time is often the single biggest expenditure you make in a business selling on eBay, it is not deductible.

Travel, Meal, and Entertainment Expenses and Education Expenses

Q: *"Can I deduct trips to conventions, such as eBay Live!?"*

A: If you are a frequent seller and are treating your eBay selling as a business for tax purposes, then the answer is clearly yes. But there are a few rules:

- You must be an established seller. If you are just starting out on eBay, the IRS may not let you take these deductions because attending eBay Live! will be seen as training you to enter a new business, not helping you improve your skills at an existing business.
- You can deduct only 50 percent of meals and entertainment expenses, although you can deduct 100 percent of qualifying travel expenses to and from the convention.
- Unless your spouse is a partner in your business (e.g., you file IRS Form 1065, have a formal partnership agreement, and split profits and losses with him or her based on an agreed-upon percentage), you can deduct only your own travel, meals, and entertainment expenses—not your spouse's.

Q: ***"I want to improve my understanding of import and export laws and rules. The university in my town has a great class. There is also a very good class in Tampa, Florida, about forty miles from my favorite vacation islands (Sanibel and Captiva). Can I take the Florida class and still deduct the cost of the air tickets, the class, the hotel, and meals?"***

A: If you are already an eBay seller and have at least some international sales, you should be able to deduct all travel expenses, including hotel, meals, and entertainment—within reason.

If you are a newbie and are just thinking about selling on eBay someday, be careful: The IRS does not allow you to deduct educational expenses for getting into a new business, and the rules are highly technical here. You might want to hold off until you actually have sales before you sign up for this seminar.

More Information About Deductions

Q: ***"Where can I get more information about deductions for eBay sellers?"***

A: Chapter 9 of my book *The eBay Seller's Tax and Legal Answer Book* has an overview of tax deductions a typical eBay seller can take.

Appendix E to this book contains a fairly detailed checklist of items that a typical eBay seller can deduct, while Appendix F to this book contains a fairly detailed checklist of items that a typical eBay seller cannot deduct. In using these checklists, please keep in mind that:

- They are not comprehensive.
- Some of the deductible and nondeductible items listed are subject to conditions, limitations, and restrictions that are not included in the checklist. To find out more about these, talk to your accountant or tax adviser.

Finally, for a comprehensive list of small business deductible expenses in an easy-to-read format, see the books *422 Tax Deductions for Small Business*, by Bernard Kamoroff (Bell Springs, 2007), and ***J.K. Lasser's Small Business Taxes 2008: Your Complete Guide to a Better Bottom Line (J.K. Lasser's New Rules for Small Business Taxes; John Wiley & Sons, 2008)***, by Barbara Weltman.

15 Should I Set Up an eBay Store?

Should You Have an eBay Store?

Q: ***"What is an eBay Store?"***

A: An eBay Store is your own personal website within eBay where you can showcase the items you sell, link all of your auction listings in one place, and feature fixed-price merchandise (what eBay calls Buy It Now! items) that is available only within your eBay Store and, for the most part, not elsewhere on eBay.

An eBay Store, according to Janelle Elms, eBay expert and author of *The eBay Stores Success Video* (www.storessuccessvideo.com), makes sense in many situations, especially if you aren't ready to head into the world of owning your own website, or if you have your own website but want to use an eBay Store as an extension of your business.

Q: ***"Why should every business (online and brick-and-mortar) consider an eBay Store in their business/marketing plan?"***

A: "No one can tell me where their customers are coming from anymore," says Elms. "It used to be that they would come in off of Main Street USA into your Store, but now they are looking for you on YouTube, MySpace, Google, eBay, Yahoo!, Facebook, etc., and you don't know where your customers are shopping, so you need to have a presence where the maximum number of people are congregating and looking to buy things." With over 233 million registered users, eBay is not the only, but is definitely the largest, such space.

Elms believes an eBay Store is one of three points of what she calls the "triangle" of e-commerce success: "your own Website, eBay auction listings, and an eBay Store."

In total agreement is eBay Store designer and consultant Rebecca Shapiro, of Oasis Connect (www.oasisconnect.com): "Every e-business should have an eBay Store as part of their online business strategy. The reason why is because eBay purchases billions of dollars of keywords each year in their search engine advertising. When your store is correctly optimized, and you use the great and free marketing tools eBay provides for eBay Store owners, you can take amazing advantage of eBay's spending power." For less than $16 per month, Shapiro points out, your eBay Store can show up on the first page of relevant searches on Google within less than two weeks, while most stand-alone websites, when optimized for search engine visibility, can take anywhere from six to twelve months before being picked up and ranked by the major search engines.

Q: ***"Why should I open an eBay Store?"***

A: When it first began, eBay was an auction site for which people cleaned out their attics and haunted garage sales for products to sell there. Now eBay is a massive marketplace with over 223 million registered users and 600,000 eBay Stores.

Says eBay Store designer and consultant Rebecca Shapiro (www.oasisconnect .com), "The nice thing about eBay stores is that they are a basically a website in a box with a complete shopping cart and check out system. Try to build one of those on your own and you're looking at some big dollars!"

According to Shapiro, eBay offers a wide range of eBay Store templates to help you build a professional-looking website and listing template. You can also hire professional designers and consulting companies that specialize in building and optimizing eBay Stores.

A professionally designed eBay Store is attractive to both the buyer and the vendors whose products you sell. A custom-designed listing template also helps minimize the auction-style look of traditional eBay listings.

Shapiro maintains, "eBay Stores that are professionally designed have fewer problems when developing new vendor relationships because they appear to be a legitimate business."

Q: ***"How will having an eBay Store help me sell more on eBay?"***

A: If you are more than just a casual eBay seller and you have not yet opened an eBay Store, you are missing the real power of the eBay platform. With a basic eBay Store (currently $15.95 per month), you can use the following eBay top-seller strategies to dramatically impact your bottom line, according to eBay

PowerSeller and Certified Education Specialist Jack Waddick of Chicago, Illinois (www.oakviewtraining.com).

Example 1. "You can auction a big brand-name searchable hot item (such as a Motorola Razr V3 Cell Phone), and then offer all the add-on/accessory items in your eBay store . . . the car charger, long-life batteries, belt clips, colored faceplates, Bluetooth headsets, fancy leather carrying case, and so forth," says Waddick, who recommends including the words "See our eBay Store for ALL Your Phone Accessories" in each of these auction listings. "Always, always, always put a link to your eBay Store in every one of your auction listings," emphasizes Waddick.

Example 2. "Start your auction item at a low initial bid price, then offer the *same item* in your eBay store at full-profit 'buy it now' pricing. When I first started using this strategy in my PowerSeller business, it felt like I would be competing with myself, but after trying it (and selling 6 of the items in a 7-day period—the first in the auction, then five in my eBay Store), I realized the power of this strategy," says Waddick. When using this strategy, says Waddick, be sure to include the words "Don't Want to Bid and Wait? . . . See my eBay Store for a Great 'Buy it Now' Price."

Example 3. "Offer the most popular size and color in your auction listings and then list all the other sizes and colors in your eBay store. I once used this strategy with a shopping cart full of men's Ashworth golf shirts I bought at a Chicago retailer at the end of golf season for $5 each. I auctioned the popular size large white shirt, and then listed all the other sizes and colors in my eBay store for $39 each," says Waddick, who adds that when using this strategy be sure to include the words "Need S/M/L/XL? Blue, Yellow, Green, Red? See my eBay Store for a full selection" in your auction listings.

The preceding example is also an excellent way to market your depth of inventory without violating eBay's policy that prohibits you from offering a choice in a single listing.

Types (Levels) of eBay Stores

Q: ***"What are the three levels of eBay Stores and which one should I choose?"***

A: There are three levels of eBay Store, as follows:

Basic: Currently $15.95 per month

Premium: Currently $49.95 per month

Anchor: Currently $299.95 per month

Janelle Elms (www.janelleelms.com), an eBay expert, recommends that you start off with the Basic eBay Store, for a simple reason: "You're going to spend at least a couple of weeks, and maybe longer, getting your store design right, your search engine keywords right, and stocking your eBay Store with the first several items of inventory, and I don't think you should be paying $300 a month while you are in your 'learning phase.' "

Elms says that choosing the right level of eBay store is a cost-benefit decision: Look at the additional marketing tools eBay gives you with each progressive level of eBay Store and then decide if the additional cost is worth it. "In my experience, 80% of sellers on eBay should be using the 'Premium' level of eBay Store as they are set up now," advises Elms.

Your eBay Store Inventory

Q: ***"Is an eBay Store just for fixed-price items, or can I put my eBay auction listings there as well?"***

A: It is perfectly okay, and is actually advisable, to have both auction listings and fixed-price items in your eBay Store, according to Elms. An eBay Store consists of two types of listings: a list all of your eBay listings (fixed-price and auction-style) and fixed-price items that are available only in your eBay Store (called *store inventory* in eBay lingo).

Store inventory listings are items that you make available in your eBay Store at a fixed price for up to thirty days, or indefinitely (under eBay's Good 'Til Cancelled (GTC) option, eBay will relist an item every thirty days automatically for you as long as you have quantity left in your listing). When people search for items on eBay, they will see all of your auction listings in the search results, but if there are less than thirty results for a particular item, eBay will also automatically search the eBay Stores database and list store inventory items.

Even if there are more than thirty search results for a particular item, people shopping on eBay will often search the eBay Stores database separately looking for items that aren't available in the auction listings or that they wish to purchase immediately without the risk of being outbid in a traditional eBay auction.

Q: ***"Should I offer the same things in my auction listings and eBay Store or is there an advantage in keeping my store inventory separate from my auction stuff?"***

A: Your goal with an eBay Store is to achieve synergy between your eBay Store and auction listings so that they feed each other. People see your auction listings, want to know what else you've got, and click on the link to your eBay Store. Once they realize you've got great merchandise, they will bookmark your store, visit repeatedly, and check out your auction listings for special deals that may not be available in your store.

Generally, it's not very productive or exciting to list one type of merchandise in your auction listings and another in your eBay Store. There is no law, however, against having multiple stores featuring different types of merchandise—it's actually recommended, as that way you can build separate "brands" for your merchandise. People aren't going to buy laptop computers from "Suzies-Fantasies," nor are they going to buy Barbie dolls from "laptopguy123." Having multiple eBay Stores helps you achieve brand recognition over multiple eBay categories without confusing your marketplace.

Optimizing eBay Stores for Search Engines

Q: ***"What are the top three areas of an eBay Store that a new owner should pay attention to?"***

A: According to Janelle Elms, eBay stores are powerful marketing tools, but only if they are optimized for search engines. If you have ever searched for something on Google, Yahoo!, or another search engine and an eBay Store popped up on the first page of the search results, you know that the owner of that store has taken advantage of this. Elms emphasizes that you are the one who has to do the actual optimizing—selecting the keywords that will attract the search engine spiders and get your store on page one of the search results (for related questions on this topic, see Chapter 16).

Elms says there are three places within an eBay Store that should be optimized for search engines the minute you set the store up:

- The eBay Store name—"you can call yourself 'Cliff's Collectibles,' but calling yourself 'Cliff's Ancient Roman Coins and Antiquities' gives the search engines keywords that more precisely describe your store inventory," says Elms.
- The description of your eBay Store.
- The categories of product you carry in your eBay Store.

Q: ***"I have heard eBay experts say that 99 percent of eBay Stores are set up wrong. What do they mean by that?"***

A: There are three big mistakes people make with their eBay Stores, according to Elms:

1. Not taking the time to optimize each page of their stores properly, both for eBay buyers searching on the eBay site and for search engine spiders
2. Not taking advantage of the very powerful marketing tools eBay makes available to store owners, such as custom pages, RSS feeds (which enable readers to "subscribe" to your blogs or other regularly updated Web content), and e-mail newsletters
3. Not understanding basic business principles—for example, listing many items in their store for a price that won't generate a profit

Designing Your eBay Store

Q: ***"Should I have a designer create my eBay Store, or should I use one of eBay's custom templates for an eBay Store?"***

A: "Rome wasn't built in a day, and neither will your eBay Store," says Elms, who suggests that if you do design your own eBay Store you do it in stages, designing only the pieces you have the time and money for. So, for example, use eBay's standard template when you launch the store, then when you have the time and money, change the header. When you have more time and money, start using one of eBay's templates (which don't cost anything), and when you have the time to make changes to the template, customize your eBay Store. "eBay does have some nice templates, and many eBay Stores will not need to [be] customized beyond them," says Elms, "but the design can definitely make your success. I have seen many 'paper' sellers come and go, but that is because they use the standard eBay template and look like every one else. However, www.periodpaper.com can easily attribute a huge majority of their success to their beautiful, award-winning design. It's all about the 'experience' you provide for people. Buyers buy two things—security and confidence; if you can't sell them that, they will go somewhere else. If you look like a garage sale store . . ."

Q: ***"Where can I find a Web designer who knows how to put together an eBay Store?"***

A: Many otherwise qualified Web designers have never designed an eBay Store before. For a list of designers that have been certified by eBay to help community members set up and maintain eBay Stores, check out the following page on the eBay site: http://pages.ebay.com/storefronts/designdirectory.html.

Linking Your eBay Store to Other E-Commerce Sites

Q: ***"Can I link my eBay Store to my website and other e-commerce venues?"***

A: With one exception, eBay will not allow you to link your eBay Store to your website or any other e-commerce venue outside of eBay. Doing so would violate eBay's strict fee avoidance policy (http://pages.ebay.com/help/policies/listing-circumventing.html). The exception is your About the Seller page in your eBay Store, in which you are allowed one mention of your website URL, along with the street address of your brick-and-mortar retail store, if you have one.

Not only does eBay allow you but it encourages you to link your website and other e-commerce venues to your eBay Store and auction listings to build traffic on eBay and even provides free tools to help you and your webmaster do so. For details, go to the Help section on eBay, click on A–Z Index, click on the letter "L," and scroll down to the Linking Your Website to eBay link. After signing in with your eBay user ID and password, you (or your webmaster) will be taken step-by-step through the linking process.

Finding Information About eBay Stores

Q: ***"eBay is constantly changing and updating its offerings for eBay Stores. How can I get the latest information so I can keep my eBay Store up to date?"***

A: To find out what's new in the eBay Store universe:

- Bookmark the following eBay page and check it frequently: http://pages.ebay.com/comingtostores.
- Join the Stores News Group: http://forums.ebay.com/db2/thread.jspa?threadID=1000288496&tstart=0&mod=1148423702150.
- Read the Stores discussion boards: http://forums.ebay.com/db2/forum.jspa?forumID=21.

16 How Can I Use My Website and My eBay Store to Market My Product?

Online Marketing, in General

Q: *"What do people look for when they search for stuff on eBay?"*

A: When people search online, there are four things they are looking for (some people look for all of these, others just one or two).

First, they are looking for *information.* The Internet is all about content and making it accessible to interested people free of charge. Your website should not just be a laundry list of stuff you've got around the house you want to sell. It should be a source of information about certain types of antiques and collectibles that people are interested in knowing more about.

And not just any kind of information. Everything that appears on your website should be cool, compelling content. People these days have short attention spans and expect to have a measure of fun, excitement, or drama when they do stuff online. Your content must be interesting, captivating, and entertaining—the sort of stuff people will e-mail their friends about, creating positive buzz for your website.

Second, they are looking for *stuff they can't find in their local stores.* I have a Smith Corona typewriter that I bought in the early 1990s. Because I'm a fairly fast typist, I just find it a lot easier to use an old-fashioned typewriter to address envelopes and create mailing labels than printing them from Microsoft Outlook. Needless to say, I'm not able to find replacement parts, print wheels, ribbon cartridges, and correction spools for a 1990s-era typewriter in my local Staples or Office Depot outlet. So where do I get these typewriter supplies when I need them? From eBay! There are several eBay Stores that actually specialize in typewriter parts, and I'm one of their best buyers.

If you're selling antiques and collectibles on eBay (or anywhere else online), do some research and find out if there are any antique or collectible categories that are underrepresented on the Web. Online retailers generally do best when they focus on a niche and become known for their knowledge and expertise within that niche. So, for example, you might want to focus your website on "tobacciana" (tobacco-related paraphernalia, usually from the 1800s) or "hippie/counterculture artifacts" from the 1960s.

Third, people are looking online for *stuff they* can *buy at their local stores but at deep, deep discounts.* To put it bluntly, a lot of people online are shopping for wholesale prices; they won't pay retail on eBay or anywhere else online if they can find the products locally at the same price.

If you've got a baby, you need diapers. Lots of diapers. You can always find them locally, and if you need to buy in bulk, there's a Wal-Mart, Costco, or BJ's Wholesale Club within a short drive of your home (although no drive is short enough with a screaming infant in the backseat). If people are shopping for diapers online, they are looking for prices that beat even Wal-Mart's "regular low, low prices." If you can offer bulk lots of diapers for half the big-box retail prices or less, you probably can find customers for them online. Otherwise, don't sell diapers online.

Fourth, and finally, people are shopping online for *people with like-minded interests.* Social network sites such as MySpace and Second Life are built on the principle that people are still interested in living in villages or communities, but no longer strictly geographical ones. Like it or not, the communities of the future are likely to be virtual ones—you might find you have more in common with someone in Timbuktu than you do with the person who lives on the other side of the privet hedge in your backyard.

Always have a space on your site where buyers and other visitors can interact with you and each other. This can take the form of a weblog, or *blog,* a community chat room, a discussion board, or a series of webinars on topics of interest to the people who buy from you. If you sell cast iron antiques from the 1800s, for example, you might want to post a request for tips from collectors on how to remove rust from these items without damaging them. Trust me, you will get responses, and the search engine spiders love stuff like that.

One more thing: Always be sure that everything on your website is what your customers want to see, not what you think they should see. I read a lot of blogs in my line of work, and far too many of them remind me of that old song from the 1970s movie *Midnight Cowboy:* "Everybody's talkin' at me, I don't hear a word they're sayin', only the echoes of my mind . . ."

Q: ***"How can I increase my Internet exposure and buzzworthiness?"***

A: There are over one billion users on the Internet these days. That's a lot of people and information cruising around cyberspace. Naturally, people want to organize that information so it is more manageable. Web 2.0 is helping buyers sort all this information into social networks related to interest, genre, theme, and so on.

The ubiquitous eBay is a popular Web 2.0 site, according to eBay Store designer and consultant Rebecca Shapiro (www.oasisconnect.com) because it helps people shop according to niche market, and the eBay stores that are the most successful are those that capitalize on the power of social networking. "These eBay Stores use the free marketing tools that eBay provides such as Guides, e-mail marketing and custom pages to position themselves as experts in their niche market," says Shapiro. "This, in turn, builds buyer confidence and loyalty. Those happy customers then tell their friends and family who shop and tell their friends and family. Social networking is all about buzzworthiness and word of mouth."

Owners of eBay Stores also take advantage of other social networking sites to increase their exposure and drive traffic back to their eBay Stores. Many eBay Store owners experience significant traffic and sales coming from their MySpace blogs, Squidoo lenses, and YouTube videos (which can now be used in eBay listings).

Q: ***"What is a niche market?"***

A: Selling in a *niche market* means that you're selling to a select group of people who share a common interest—for example, people who love baseball, Hummel figurines, or anything designed by Coach. Why should you bother to define or refine your niche market? Because it can be very lucrative, says eBay Store designer and consultant Rebecca Shapiro (www.oasisconnect.com). "When you're the very best in a healthy niche market you're the big fish in a small pond," says Shapiro. "You will either be alone or in very limited company in a niche market; other small businesses may not be aware of your niche and large businesses won't want to bother with it."

The trick, according to Shapiro, is to find or develop a niche that has customers, is growing fast enough, and is not already owned by a group of established vendors (like the supersaturated electronics, clothing, and jewelry categories). Then start expanding and refining your target market carefully so that you don't grow beyond the boundaries of your niche. Explains Shapiro, "If you're selling everything related to cats, you should think twice before you expand and start selling everything related to birds, turtles, gerbils and dogs. There's Petco for that!"

Successful eBay Stores are those that capture their niche market and use their expertise and experience to build healthy businesses in the eBay marketplace.

Your E-Commerce Website

Q: ***"I'm planning to set up an eBay Store. Do I also need a website of my own? I know eBay has a rule that prohibits people from directing buyers to sites off of eBay, and I don't want to get into trouble there. But I've got some really great stuff that I'm not sure will sell on eBay."***

A: When you are selling online, you absolutely should have a website of your own, even if you have an eBay Store. There are two reasons for this.

First, if you develop a following on eBay, excited buyers will naturally want to know what else you've got for sale, and they will be looking for your website. These days, everybody expects you to have a website, and you will look like an amateur if you don't have one.

Second, and more important, there is one place and only one place on all the Internet where you can sell stuff and keep 100 percent of the profits—and that's your website. Whenever you create a retail presence on another website—be it eBay, Yahoo!, Amazon, or anywhere else—that other website is going to want a piece of the action and charge you a fee for the privilege of basing your operations there.

All online retailers need to have at least one place where they don't have to share their profits with anyone else. Every online retailer needs his or her own website.

Having said that, of course, there are rules you need to follow when you have your own website and an eBay Store operating at the same time:

- You absolutely *can* link your website to your eBay Store and eBay auction listings—not only won't this get you into trouble, but eBay actually *wants* you to do this and makes tools available for you to create these links, free of charge.

- You absolutely *can* link your eBay auction listings to your eBay Store, and vice versa (in fact, you are crazy not to do that).

But

- Except for your About Me page (for an eBay Store, this is called the About the Seller page), you absolutely *cannot* link your eBay auction listings or eBay Store to your website or any other location off of eBay—this violates one of eBay's strictest policies.
- If you are using eBay to send newsletters to your frequent buyers, you *cannot* mention your website URL in your newsletters.

Q: ***"Can I use my website URL as my eBay user ID?"***

A: No—eBay prohibits you from using a website URL as a user ID, and will kick you off the site if they see a ".com," ".net," or ".org" in your user ID name.

However, eBay does not prohibit you from using your company name as your eBay user ID. So, for example, if you are doing business offline as Cliff's Antiques and your website URL is www.cliffsantiques.com, having "cliffsantiques" as your eBay user ID is only a natural thing to do. As long as it's not too obvious what you're doing (e.g., picking a business name that's so unusual that its only purpose is to create a unique website URL and user ID), you shouldn't have any trouble. Buyers on eBay are fairly smart—if they see "cliffsantiques" as your user ID, they probably will guess that your website URL is cliffsantiques.com.

Q: ***"Can I use my website URL as part of a trademarked logo and use the logo as my eBay Store name?"***

A: A lot of businesses with names that cannot legally be trademarked (such as "Cliff's Antiques") do this as a way of getting a federal trademark registration. They create a unique logo with the name "Cliff's Antiques" included as part of the logo design and then submit the logo for trademark registration. Very often, that works and the logo is registered as a trademark by the U.S. Patent and Trademark Office (www.uspto.gov).

I wouldn't try that on eBay, however, since eBay's search engine spiders are pretty adept at picking up ".com" names in eBay Stores and auction listings, and that might be pushing the envelope a bit too much. Keep in mind that if eBay kicks you off the site because of a name violation, you won't ever be able to use that name on eBay again, even if they let you open another eBay account down the road, using a different name. You don't want to build a following on eBay only to lose your "brand" overnight because you were recklessly stupid in setting up your eBay Store.

ProStores

Q: *"What are ProStores, and do I need one?"*

A: When you are selling on eBay, you need an eBay Store, but you also may eventually need your own website. ProStores, owned by eBay, will help you create a website that is branded by eBay and synchronized with your eBay Store, your eBay auction listings, and other elements of your eBay world.

The main advantage of setting up a ProStores website, according to eBay expert Janelle Elms (www.janelleelms.com), is that their tools work well with eBay, and they will manage and run your shopping cart and other technical aspects of your e-commerce-enabled ProStores website.

The main disadvantage, according to Elms, is that a ProStores website is not integrated to work with other e-commerce channels like Amazon.com. Also, when you set up your website (as with any other branded website) with ProStores, ProStores gets a percentage of everything you sell there.

Marketing Your eBay Store

Q: *"What are some of the more powerful marketing tools you can use to market your eBay Store?"*

A: According to Janelle Elms, eBay author and founder of the Online Success Institute (www.OnlineSuccessInstitute.com), there are several that are very effective:

- Getting other relevant websites to link to your eBay Store
- Making sure your eBay Store is optimized for search engines

- Using the custom pages in your eBay Store to create information about the items you sell on eBay that will attract search engine spiders

But by far the most powerful marketing tool for an eBay Store, according to Elms, is an e-mail newsletter. "This is an amazing tool that eBay gives to eBay Store owners for free," says Elms, adding that you would pay "hundreds of dollars" in the world outside of eBay to have someone create and distribute an e-mail newsletter for your business.

If you have an eBay Store, eBay allows you to send a newsletter free up to 5,000 e-mails a month (for a Basic store), up to 7,500 e-mails a month (for a Premium store), or up to 10,000 e-mails a month (for an Anchor store). The maximum frequency for an eBay Store newsletter is once per week, but eBay allows you to have up to five different newsletters at the same time, according to Elms, so it's a very powerful tool for sellers carrying multiple lines of merchandise.

"An e-mail newsletter allows you to get in front of your buyers and make sure they remember your name," says Elms. "I hate it when I can't remember a good seller's name because I haven't bought from them in a while; if I'm getting a newsletter every seven days from them I'll be sure to remember them when I need to buy something they've got."

According to Catherine Seda, Internet marketing expert and author of *How to Win Sales & Influence Spiders* (www.CatherineSeda.com), "You may already have newsletter subscribers—even if you don't have a newsletter! When people visit your eBay Store, they can subscribe to the 'Seller Newsletter' after clicking the 'Add to My Favorite Stores' link at the top of the page," Seda explains. "If you have an eBay Store, log into your account. You may be surprised to see how many people are waiting to hear from you."

Q: ***"I offer a variety of merchandise on both my website and my eBay Store. I have a number of things I would like to put up on my website but don't know how much legal trouble I will get into. Three things in particular I would like to post on my website: testimonials from satisfied customers—basically letters and e-mails they have written me; an e-mail from an organization thanking me for speaking at their monthly meeting; and an e-mail from a prominent celebrity offering to tell my customers and patients how really great I am in exchange for a link to his website."***

A: Using testimonials from customers and others can be a very effective way to promote your business. After all, everybody expects you will say great things about yourself in your advertising. But an unsolicited rave review from a satisfied customer or industry leader? Solid gold.

Still, there are rules. Let's examine these three items one at a time.

Letters from customers. Customers who are delighted at getting superior service often write thank-you letters, but that doesn't mean they are authorizing you to use those letters in your promotional efforts. Unless the letters state specifically that it's okay to use them in your marketing literature, write or e-mail them and ask for specific written permission to reproduce all or parts of the letters on your website. If they don't respond to your request for permission, view that as denying you the right to post the letters online.

Letters from organizations. You can be a lot less concerned about posting the letter from a local organization that praised your abilities as a public speaker. Such letters help build your credibility as an expert in your field and do not involve the disclosure of private information about individuals. Besides, posting this letter will give the organization some free publicity, which they are unlikely to complain about.

Still, you should ask the organization for permission to reproduce the letter, but if they don't respond, it's probably all right to post it anyway. If the organization objects to your use of the letter, they will send you a cease and desist letter before considering any formal legal action against you. That will give you the opportunity to pull the letter from your website and avoid a lawsuit.

Celebrity endorsements. Legally speaking, these are very tricky. You should first ask: Is this a celebrity whose endorsement will make a difference? If the celebrity is a prominent authority on the type of merchandise you sell, his or her endorsement might well boost your business. If the celebrity is a television or movie actor, well, how much more than average folks do actors know about this merchandise? If you are selling salad dressing on your website and you get an endorsement from Paul Newman (movie star and founder of Newman's Own), that's fabulous. If you are selling antique mechanical banks on eBay and you get an endorsement from Paul Newman, well . . .

Here are several rules about celebrity endorsements:

- Celebrities cannot say that they use your products and services, unless they actually do and you can document it (for example, by copies of cancelled checks showing the celebrity has actually purchased your stuff).

- If celebrities are receiving anything in return for their endorsement (in this case, a link to the celebrity's website), you must clearly state that the endorsement was given for promotional consideration.
- Look out for false or misleading information in the celebrity's endorsement—for example, a celebrity with a PhD in English literature who calls himself "Doctor" to mislead people into thinking he is competent to speak on health care issues.

Having said all that, I think every eBay business should seek endorsement and promotional support from people whose judgments and views are likely to be respected by customers—perhaps a nationally syndicated small business columnist and eBay author.

Q: ***"What are some things I can do offline to get people into my eBay Store?"***

A: Interestingly, some of the most effective ways to build traffic for your eBay Store and auction listings have nothing to do with the Internet. Cindy Shebley, eBay marketing expert and author of *Easy Auction Photography* (www.ezauctionphotos.com), offers the following suggestions:

- Make sure your eBay Store URL appears on all your business cards and stationery.
- Print flyers and postcards, give them out to everybody you know, and put them in your packages whenever you ship eBay merchandise to buyers.
- Make sure your eBay Store URL appears on the signature at the bottom of every e-mail message you send out, as a clickable link to your eBay Store.
- Make sure your eBay Store URL appears prominently on any swag—promotional giveaways you hand out at trade shows, eBay Live!, and other conferences and networking meetings.

Linking Strategies

Q: ***"How can I get other websites to link to my eBay Store?"***

A: According to Catherine Seda, Internet marketing expert and author of *How to Win Sales & Influence Spiders* (www.CatherineSeda.com), you can buy a link in a business directory, such as Yahoo!, for a couple of hundred dollars. If you belong to a business or trade association, your membership may include a free link from their website to yours. Seda suggests that you follow up with these associations to make sure you're getting that free link.

But by far the best links, according to Seda, are from websites and blogs that are relevant to the merchandise you're selling on eBay. For example, if you're selling antique mechanical banks from the 1800s, a link from the Mechanical Bank Collectors of America (MBCA) website is even more valuable than a link from a general antique website. Why? Well, there are two reasons. First, the MBCA's audience would be a better match for your business; they're more likely to buy from you. Second, link relevancy is key to getting higher free rankings in the search engines. In ethical search engine optimization (SEO), ten links from relevant sites are better than one hundred links from nonrelevant ones. So don't bother getting a link from your cousin Johnny's fishing site—it won't help you.

Seda advises that you join in the conversations on blogs that are relevant to your business on eBay. "When you post a comment on a blog," she reveals, "you'll get a link to your website URL, and search engines love that. Blogging is quick, easy and FREE."

Search Engine Optimization and Search Engine Advertising

Q: ***"Are search engine optimization (SEO) and search engine advertising (SEA) the same thing?"***

A: Although the two terms are often used interchangeably, they generally refer to two different things.

When you search for something on Google, Yahoo!, or any other popular search engine, the search listings that show up on your computer screen are called *natural search results. Search engine optimization* is the process of setting up your website, eBay Store, or other Web location in such a way as to increase the odds of appearing on the first or second page of the natural search results. Generally, *search engine optimization* involves selecting certain keywords that most accurately describe the merchandise you're selling and the contents of your

Web location and making sure those keywords appear prominently and repeatedly in those portions of your Web location that are visited regularly by search engine spiders such as Google's Googlebot.

When you search for something on Google, Yahoo!, or another search engine, in addition to the natural search results you will also see advertisements on the results page for businesses offering products or services for sale that relate to the object of your search. These are called *pay-per-click ads* or *search engine ads. Search engine advertising* is the process of creating advertisements for your business and asking the search engine to place that ad on the results page whenever someone searches for a certain keyword or combination of keywords. In return, if someone searches for something, sees your ad, and clicks on it (which directs them to your website or eBay Store), you agree to pay the search engine a certain amount of money in exchange for that click, whether or not the person searching actually buys something from your Web location. The more you agree to pay the search engine for each click to your website or eBay Store, the more likely it is that your ad will appear prominently in the search engine results for the keywords you have selected.

So, for example, let's say I create an ad on Yahoo! that I want to appear on the search engine results whenever someone searches for "small business attorney." If I agree to pay Yahoo! ten cents for every click on that ad, Yahoo! guarantees that my ad will appear on page 36 of the search results for "small business attorney." How many times, however, have you looked at page 36 of the results when you search for something online? My ad isn't likely to generate a lot of traffic for my website, is it? In order for Yahoo! to assure me that my ad will appear on page 1 of the search engine results for "small business attorney," I would currently have to pay something like $50 for each click on that ad.

Interestingly, Google's search engine system works a little differently. When you buy an ad using Google's search engine advertising program (called Google AdWords), your ad appears in the search engine results based not only on how much you agree to pay for each click, but on how closely your website, eBay Store, or other Web location relates to the keywords a person is searching for. Given the choice between a tightly targeted website that offers $5 a click and a totally irrelevant website that offers $25 a click, Google will often favor the former over the latter and put the former website's ad on page 1 of the search engine results, on the theory that it's better to get revenue from a few clicks at $5 each than to get no revenue from zero clicks at $25 each.

Search engine optimization and search engine advertising are as much art as they are science. To learn more about them, see some of the books and other resources mentioned in Appendix A of this book.

Q: ***"Will eBay help me optimize my eBay Store for search engines, such as suggested appropriate keywords?"***

A: In order to optimize their website for search engine spiders, eBay will do a lot behind the scenes, but they will not help you find appropriate keywords for your eBay Store. "If you've ever searched for something on Google and an eBay Store pops up on page 1 of the search engine results, you can thank eBay for that," says eBay expert Janelle Elms (www.janelleelms.com). "All we have to do as eBay sellers is come up with the keywords, which shouldn't be that hard as after all we know our merchandise better than eBay ever will."

According to Catherine Seda, Internet marketing expert and author of *How to Win Sales & Influence Spiders* (www.CatherineSeda.com), a top tool for finding appropriate keywords for your eBay Store is the Google AdWords Keyword Tool (http://adwords.google.com), which is absolutely free. "Type in a relevant keyword, and Google will suggest additional keywords for you," says Seda. "Spend some time with this tool. You'll find a lot of keywords that will work for your eBay Store." Seda also notes that Google shows you the search volume for each keyword. Consider a mix of high- and low-volume keywords. That's because even though high-volume keywords get more traffic, there's more competition over them these days. So optimize your eBay Store for both kinds of keywords.

What is Seda's number one tip for finding profitable keywords? Go after tail terms. A *tail term* is a low-volume, highly targeted keyword for your business. Generally, it's a phrase containing three or more words. Back to the mechanical bank example: Don't just focus on "banks," because you'll be competing with a lot of eBay and non-eBay businesses trying to get search engine rankings for that keyword. "Mechanical banks" would be better. But a great tail term would be "antique mechanical banks" or "cast iron mechanical banks." Yup, according to the Google AdWords Keyword Tool, people are searching for these tail terms. Shoppers searching for tail terms are more qualified prospects. Seda says these shoppers are much more likely to become your customers.

Q: ***"What are some tips for optimizing an eBay Store for search engines?"***

A: Here are six from Catherine Seda, Internet marketing expert and author of *How to Win Sales & Influence Spiders* (www.CatherineSeda.com).

First, choose a good store name because it'll turn into your store URL. Make sure to include keywords here—if you have a choice between "Cliff's Attic" and "Cliff's Antique Mechanical Banks," go with the latter because the search engine spiders can look at your URL.

Second, choose some appropriate keywords for the stuff you sell and make sure to include them in the meta-tag fields in your eBay Store account.

Third, create an eBay Store description and include relevant keywords in it—eBay gives you up to two hundred words for this.

Fourth, create keyword-based category names when setting up your eBay Store. Don't use something generic like "Category 1" or "Category 2." Using keywords in your category names helps your shoppers quickly and easily find what they're looking for, too.

Fifth, create an About the Seller page (similar to the About Me page for an eBay seller or buyer who doesn't have an eBay Store), and sprinkle relevant keywords throughout this page. But Seda warns, "Don't do keyword spamming. You don't want to repeat your keywords over and over again. Search engines hate that and eBay doesn't allow it."

Sixth, create *custom pages* in your eBay Store that answer questions about the items you are selling. For example, if you are selling antique mechanical banks in your eBay Store, create a page about the history of mechanical banks manufactured in the United States during the late 1800s. This information-rich page will be filled with delicious keywords spiders like.

Should you optimize your actual item listings when you have an eBay Store (eBay optimizes everything for the search engines, whether you spend time optimizing different areas of your eBay Store or not)? "I pick only the products I know I'm going to have listed for the long term," says eBay University instructor Steve Lindhorst. "Once a search engine sees these, I want to be sure the product is there when people come to my store; I don't spend a whole lot of time optimizing listings for items with very low inventory levels."

eBay marketing expert Janelle Elms (www.janelleelms.com) points out, however, that optimizing each listing has its benefits: "Even if you're not optimizing each listing for the search engine 'spiders,' you want to make sure that buyers searching for your listings on eBay find them." She adds that even if the item sells quickly, a closed listing that is properly optimized will still contain information that will direct someone to your eBay Store if they find it on Google and click on it.

Q: ***"What areas of eBay have an effect on search engine optimization (SEO)?"***

A: Basically, any page on eBay that is rich in content and is designed to stay in one place for a while will affect SEO. So your eBay auction listings probably don't have much effect on SEO because they are posted for such a short period of time.

Your blogs, your Reviews and Guides, your About Me (or About the Seller) page, your MyWorld page (if you have one), and the long-term listings in your eBay Store are the pages most likely to attract search engine spiders.

Q: ***"What areas of an eBay Store have an effect on search engine optimization (SEO)?"***

A: "A ton of them," according to Elms, including:

- The store title.
- The store description.
- The product categories listed down the left-hand side of your eBay Store page.
- Your custom pages for the store.
- Your About the Seller page.
- Your shopping feeds.—When you have an eBay Store, eBay aggregates all listings and sends them out to online retail portals such as shopping .com and froogle.com. "You do have to turn this feature on when you set up your eBay Store, but after that it just happens automatically, and you don't have to think about it," says Elms.

Q: ***"Can people get into legal trouble if they choose the wrong keywords when optimizing their eBay Stores or auction listings?"***

A: Oh, yeah; eBay has a fairly detailed policy that prohibits keyword spamming—the use of keywords that don't have anything to do with the stuff you're selling on eBay that are intended to distract buyers looking for other things. So, for example, if you list a handbag for sale on eBay with the description "1970s no-brand handbag, kinda looks like a Gucci," you are keyword spamming because people looking for genuine Gucci merchandise will see your listing when they search the keyword "Gucci."

Keyword spamming is one of the surest ways to get kicked off eBay, because other eBay sellers selling merchandise using the correct keywords get so furious you're doing it that they'll turn you in to eBay. The Keyword Spam policy for eBay appears at http://pages.ebay.com/help/policies/keyword-spam.html—be sure to read this before you set up an eBay Store.

eBay Marketing Tools

Q: ***"What are the Reviews and Guides on eBay, and how can I use them to sell more?"***

A: One of the best ways to build traffic on eBay is to become an expert on the stuff you're selling. Reviews and Guides are *Consumer Reports*–type reviews of products available for sale on eBay, written by community members.

When you have an eBay Store, you should consider posting Reviews on products you know about—for example, a review of the most recent iPod saying what you liked and didn't like about it. When you create a Review or contribute to a Guide, eBay allows you to link it to anything on eBay, including the auction listings or eBay Store where the merchandise can be found.

Q: ***"What is a MyWorld page, and how can I use it to make more money?"***

A: The popularity of social networking websites such as MySpace and FaceBook has led eBay to create its own networking section of the eBay site called MyWorld.

You automatically get an eBay MyWorld page when you become an eBay member. A MyWorld page gives members of the eBay community ways to create customizable, personal pages that feature content they create themselves.

When you customize your eBay MyWorld page, you can add features and include what makes you unique, such as:

- Links to the items you sell
- Photographs of yourself

- Highlights from your eBay blog, if you have one
- A guest book so that visitors to your page can leave comments and notes for you

Then, you can e-mail everyone you know and tell them to visit your page. Your eBay MyWorld page's URL uses the following format: myworld.ebay.com/youruserID.

Q: ***"Should I have an About Me page?"***

A: Absolutely. All eBay sellers are entitled to create an About Me page describing themselves, their off-eBay world, and the merchandise they sell. If you have an eBay Store, your About Me page is called your About the Seller page.

Generally, eBay discourages sellers from directing buyers to their websites or other locations outside of eBay—in fact, they will kick you off the site if they catch you doing that. There is one exception: You are entitled to mention your website URL in your About Me page and put one link to your About Me page in each of your eBay listings. Savvy eBay buyers know this and will check out a seller's About Me page if they see stuff they like on eBay and want to know what else the seller has got lying around the house.

If done correctly, a seller's About Me page can also attract search engine spiders who will index it to keywords describing the merchandise the seller is selling. "Too many people on eBay use their 'About Me' pages to talk about their kids and dogs," says eBay expert Janelle Elms (www.janelleelms.com), "when they should be describing their merchandise and the information they know about."

Blogs, Blog Marketing, RSS Feeds, and Squidoo Lenses

Q: ***"Does it make sense to have a blog on eBay? Or, indeed, anywhere else?"***

A: A blog (short for *weblog*) is a website that takes the form of an online journal or diary—you post entries to the blog every day (or week, or month, or whenever you feel like it), and people can respond with postings of their own, ask questions, or give you a hard time if they disagree with what you're saying in your blog.

Elms believes blogs can be a powerful marketing tool for eBay sellers if they are used strategically. "Blogs are a great way to communicate with your buyers on a regular, ongoing basis because you can get them to open up and tell YOU what they want to buy."

Among the questions Elms says you should frequently ask readers of your eBay blog are:

- "I just got a bunch of stuff [list items]. What should I put up on eBay first?"
- "I'm going on a buying spree next week with some of my sources. What should I be looking for that you might be interested in?"
- "I'm ready to order more of item X; are you looking for anything that's not on eBay?"

"People are fascinated by reality TV shows," explains Elms. "Blogs are not static pages some copywriter wrote—they are by real people, with real emotions, and real situations, and real products. It's a view into someone else's private world and, let's face it, we're all voyeurs to some extent."

Properly done, a blog can also help your eBay business attract search engine spiders. Here's a tip from Elms: Write an article for your e-mail newsletter, then change it a little bit and put it up on your eBay blog, then change it a little bit more and put it on one of your eBay Store custom pages, then change it a little more and put it up on your website. Why all the changes? Why not simply post the same article in all four places? "Because search engine 'spiders' hate viewing the same exact content over and over again," explains Elms. "They don't see it as unique content. By changing your article around a little bit each time you repurpose it, you are tricking the 'spider' into thinking it's four different articles and they will index them as such, boosting your search engine rankings."

Q: ***"What exactly is a Squidoo lens, and should I have one?"***

A: A *lens* on Squidoo.com is a hybrid between a blog and a static website, according to Cindy Shebley, an eBay marketing expert and Certified Education Specialist (www.clovercitysells.com). "Squidoo.com operates a lot like a Website affiliate program," says Shebley. "You put up a blurb about something you know and love, and by using what Squidoo calls a 'Plexo' you can link that blurb—called a 'lens'—to your eBay Store, your 'affiliate' page on Amazon.com, and other online retail venues." Shebley says that Squidoo lenses are showing up in the top rankings of Google search results.

Direct-Marketing Your Listings to Other eBay Community Members

Q: ***"If I am selling something on eBay and I see the same item being offered by someone else, can I contact the bidders in that other auction and tell them about my listing?"***

A: Absolutely, positively *not.* By approaching another seller's bidders directly, you are interfering with that other seller's auction, and if he finds out you've done that, he will raise a fuss with eBay. Believe it or not, you can actually be sued on those grounds—it's called *interference with contract* (or sometimes *tortuous interference with contract* or *inducing breach of contract*). Don't do it—if you've listed your item correctly on eBay, the buyers who know and collect this stuff will find you, including that other seller's bidders if your item is clearly superior to his.

Q: ***"If I am selling something on eBay and I see that an auction for the same item closed recently, can I contact the underbidders in that other auction and tell them about my listing?"***

A: The good news is that probably would not be considered interference with contract or transaction interference (see previous listing). This might, however, violate eBay's antispamming policy (see http://pages.ebay.com/help/policies/rfe-spam-ov.html), as you are sending unsolicited e-mail messages to other eBay members. If you've listed your item correctly on eBay, the buyers who know and collect this stuff will find you, including another seller's bidders if they regularly check eBay for new merchandise, as most buyers do.

Q: ***"When I ship stuff to winning bidders on eBay, is it okay to include some brochures and price lists for my brick-and-mortar antiques store?"***

A: Absolutely yes—doing this almost certainly wouldn't violate eBay's fee circumvention policy (see http://pages.ebay.com/help/policies/listing-circumventing.html). Keep in mind, though, that most of your buyers will view this as junk mail, and some will think less of you and your eBay business for promoting yourself that way.

Videos and YouTube

Q: ***"Should I consider adding videos to my eBay listings? What are some tips for creating eye-catching videos?"***

A: You absolutely should consider adding video to your eBay listings, says Cindy Shebley, eBay photography expert and producer of the DVD *Add Video to eBay Auctions* (www.ghostleg.com). "Online retailers report an average 72% increase in their sales when they add audio or video to their Websites," says Shebley, adding that "while video listings are still pretty new to eBay, there's every reason to believe you'll be just as successful as off-eBay sellers are using video."

Shebley says you don't need fancy equipment, such as a state-of-the-art video recorder, to shoot a video for eBay. "If you have a Webcam for your Internet telephone calls (such as Skype(r), which is owned by eBay), you can use that; even a cellphone or 'still' digital camera has the capacity to take short videos, which is all you need," says Shebley.

Shebley has the following tips for shooting eBay video:

- Use a tripod to stabilize your video camera, because "you don't want your viewers to get seasick."
- Shoot your eBay items indoors and control the lighting. "Use a couple of daylight balance fluorescent bulbs—the little spiral kind—and you should be okay."

Can you post your video on YouTube.com with a link to your eBay auction listing? Absolutely, says Shebley. In fact, Shebley recommends posting your video on Google, America Online (AOL), and MySpace as well—eBay is optimized for all of these. Shebley doesn't currently recommend posting your video on MSN.com, but only because the technology is in transition. "Make sure to include the URL of your eBay Store or auction listing in any video you post on YouTube or anywhere else," says Shebley.

Public Relations (PR) Strategies

Q: ***"How can I get more visibility on the Web for my business?"***

A: According to Catherine Seda, Internet marketing expert and author of *How to Win Sales & Influence Spiders* (www.CatherineSeda.com), try press releases.

"Thanks to the Internet," says Seda, "press releases are more powerful today than ever before. Not only can the media see them, so can consumers. The press release you send out once through a newswire service can be re-published on hundreds of websites or blogs all across the web." A one-time distribution fee can range from $80 to $200 or more. Seda recommends PRWeb and Newsforce because these are low-cost services that also include search engine optimization features. "Regardless of the service you choose," advises Seda, "look for one with SEO benefits, like the ability to hyperlink keywords from within your press release to your website."

Finding More Time for Marketing

Q: ***"All this marketing stuff sounds great, but I don't have time to write a blog or a custom page or a Squidoo lens, because I spend all my time listing. Is there any way I can market my eBay Store and auction listings without investing a lot of time?"***

A: This is perhaps one of the biggest mistakes small business owners (not just eBayers) make. Marketing is the one essential activity when you run your own business—stop doing it, and sooner or later your sales wither and die. If you're in business for yourself, 20 to 25 percent of the total time you spend on your business should be spent on marketing activities.

There are a number of ways you can free up more time for marketing, says Cindy Shebley, eBay marketing expert and Certified Education Specialist (www.clovercitysells.com), including the following:

- Automate as much of your eBay listings as possible, using eBay software tools such as Turbo Lister 2, Auctiva, Blackthorne, or Selling Manager Pro.
- Hire a student intern for $10 to $20 an hour to help you with your listings.

- Go to elance.com or craigslist.org and advertise for a freelance writer who can write your blog, your Squidoo lens, and other online marketing material for you. Just be sure they sign a copyright assignment, so that when you pay them, you own all of the content that appears on these pages.
- Repurpose your content as much as possible. Write an article for your blog, then change a few words and post it on your Squidoo lens, then change a few words and put it on one of your eBay Store content pages, so that you don't have to reinvent the wheel each time you sit down at the word processor.

17 How Do I Keep Track of Everything in My Business?

Using an Accountant Versus Accounting Software

Q: ***"I'm just starting an eBay business. Am I better off hiring a bookkeeper or accountant or using a software product such as QuickBooks?"***

A: When you're in business, sooner or later everything boils down to numbers. As a dear friend of mine who taught college-level statistics used to tell me, "In business, if you can't quantify it, it's only a rumor."

One of the biggest mistakes eBay sellers make is not putting systems in place from the beginning to track their eBay listings, fees, gross merchandise sales, and profits. If you are beginning to sell regularly (i.e., more than a few times a year at odd intervals), the time is now to put a bookkeeping and accounting system in place.

You have two choices: You can buy a software package and learn to do it yourself, or you can hire an accountant to help you with your books and records.

Whichever way you decide, here are some tips to make sure you are on top of your numbers at all times:

- Take an evening course on basic accounting and bookkeeping at your local community college. Accounting is the language of business, and a basic understanding of accounting terminology and procedures will help you immensely whether you buy a software package or hire an accountant. A basic course should be all you need—you're not sitting for your state CPA exam, after all; you just want to learn the difference between accounts receivable and accounts payable.

- If you are using an accounting software package, such as QuickBooks Pro, learn to do as much of the data entry yourself as you can. There are two reasons for doing this. First, you will save a ton of money in accounting fees—roughly 80 to 90 percent of a typical bookkeeper's bill is for data entry and inputting services, and you can save that by learning to do much of the grunt work yourself. Second, by inputting your own data, you will see patterns, trends, and weird things that you wouldn't see if you used an outside accountant, and that the outside accountant wouldn't mention to you. Doing your own data entry enables you to spot problems and opportunities before they become overwhelming.
- If you are using an accounting software package, make sure it integrates with the eBay and PayPal systems, so that you don't have to manually upgrade your chart of accounts each time a listing on eBay closes.
- If you are using a live bookkeeper or accountant, keep in touch with them on a regular basis. Don't just send them your shoebox full of invoices in February with a note asking them to please prepare your tax returns by April 15. Ask them instead to prepare financial statements for you on at least a quarterly basis (every three months)—you should do this monthly once you hit PowerSeller status—then schedule a meeting with them to go over your financial statements and get feedback on how your business is running. Many accountants will not volunteer information, either because they're afraid of liability or because they're simply too busy, until you ask them for it.
- There are a lot of accountants and CPAs out there who only prepare tax returns. That's not the type of accountant you need for your eBay selling business. You need an accountant with business savvy and street smarts, who can not only prepare your tax returns each year but also:
  - Do basic financial analysis to find out whether you're making money or not.
  - Troubleshoot problems and alert you to them before they get out of hand.
  - Communicate regularly with you in the English language.

If your accountant can't do any of these, forget about the beautiful framed diploma on the wall and the fact that he or she got a perfect score on the state CPA exam. Get yourself another accountant you can work with.

- If you're thinking about a live bookkeeper or accountant, find one who understands how eBay and PayPal work. Accountants who are also PowerSellers would be the ideal choice, provided they don't compete with you on eBay. If you visit their office and you see that there's no computer or laptop on the desk, they're still using Number 2 pencils, and they think *eBay* is Pig Latin for *bee,* run screaming from the room. With a little effort, you should be able to find an accountant in your city or town who understands what you're trying to accomplish on eBay.

Live Bookkeepers and Accountants

Q: ***"How do I find an accountant or bookkeeper in my area who understands eBay?"***

A: The best way to find one is on eBay itself. Go to eBay's Community section, click on the Groups link, and find the eBay seller's group for your region of the country (while you're at it, join the group, as you will get a wealth of local information from other sellers that you won't get anywhere else on eBay). Post a question on the group's discussion board asking for a referral to local accountants—give them your city, state, and zip code, as you want to find someone as close to your home as possible. Trust me, you will get responses—if the same name crops up more than once, give the person a call. If nothing else, you will get an earful about some local accountants you *shouldn't* call under any circumstances.

Q: ***"Is there a difference between an accountant and a bookkeeper, and which is better for an eBay business?"***

A: As a practical matter, there isn't much of a difference between a bookkeeper and an accountant. Most accountants do some bookkeeping for their clients, and vice versa.

The technical distinction is this:

- A *bookkeeper* takes your raw data (your invoices, sales receipts, and all the other pieces of paper in your shoebox), organizes them, and assembles them in ledgers or charts of account that accountants and other financial professionals can understand.
- An *accountant* takes the information the bookkeeper has prepared and prepares financial statements and tax returns that tell the story of how your business is performing.

Generally, you need both a bookkeeper and an accountant for your business on eBay. Your goal ultimately is to learn to do as much of the bookkeeping as possible yourself—either by hand or using a software program such as QuickBooks—so that you force yourself on a daily or weekly basis to review the numbers and stay on top of things. The more chores you delegate to outsiders, the more you risk losing control of your business because you don't know what's going on and don't have the time to ask the outsiders for information.

Q: ***"What is the difference between an accountant and a Certified Public Accountant (CPA)? Which one is best for an eBay selling business?"***

A: The licensing of accountants varies widely from state to state—in most states you don't need a license to be an accountant or prepare people's tax returns—which means that the quality of accountants varies widely as well.

A CPA is an accountant who has passed a state examination and is certified to perform specific functions, mostly for publicly traded companies. Generally (although not always), a CPA knows more about tax law and compliance than regular accountants do.

You don't really need a CPA for an eBay selling business, but a CPA can fit the bill if he or she:

- Understands your business
- Is familiar with the accounting software you are using and can work with it
- Has street smarts as well as knowing how to fill out tax forms

Q: ***What is an enrolled agent, and when do you need one?***

A: An *enrolled agent* is a former IRS employee who is empowered to help people with their taxes even though he or she hasn't taken the CPA examination and is not licensed by the state to practice accounting. The idea is that after twenty years with the IRS, somebody probably knows as much about taxes as the typical accountant and shouldn't have to observe all of the licensing formalities.

An enrolled agent is extremely useful to have at your side should your business ever be audited by the IRS. If (heaven forbid) that ever happens, who would you rather have on your side—someone with book knowledge of the tax laws or someone who has had lunch with your IRS auditor every day for the past twenty years and knows the hot buttons that particular individual looks for when auditing a small business? Enough said.

Every state has an organization of enrolled agents. To find the organization's website, type "enrolled agent [your state]" into your favorite search engine. Then check out the organization's directory of members to find an enrolled agent in your area.

Bookkeeping and Accounting Software Solutions

Q: ***"What is the best accounting software product for eBay businesses?"***

A: There is no right answer; many small or start-up eBay sellers don't use software at all; they just keep records manually.

Sooner or later, though, you will want to automate your accounting system. The sooner you become familiar with one of the popular software packages, the easier it will be to make the transition, before you develop bad habits.

When it comes to small business accounting packages, there is QuickBooks and . . . there is QuickBooks. The vast majority of eBay sellers begin by using either QuickBooks Basic or QuickBooks Pro. I generally recommend starting with QuickBooks Pro, as you will outgrow QuickBooks Basic's features fairly quickly, especially if you are maintaining a large and diverse inventory of products for sale on eBay.

To customize QuickBooks for an eBay selling business, you may want to download eBay Accounting Assistant, a free QuickBooks template"owned by eBay that helps you import eBay and PayPal data directly into your QuickBooks files (http://pages.ebay.com/accountingassistant). Note that you need to have QuickBooks already loaded onto your desktop or laptop computer in order to use eBay Accounting Assistant.

Two things to keep in mind, though, when using eBay Accounting Assistant:

1. If you are using QuickBooks to run more than one business, you may have to run a separate installation of QuickBooks for your eBay selling business before you can use eBay Accounting Assistant.
2. I have heard reports from numerous eBay sellers that eBay has been extremely slow to update and fix software bugs in eBay Accounting Assistant, and that eBay's technical support for this product is uneven at best. You should read the member postings in the Technical Issues section of the eBay community Answer Center to get more information about this product and eBay's commitment to it.

Another great accounting software product for eBay sellers is KeepMore.net, a Web-based accounting solution offered by Sagefire, Inc., of Boulder, Colorado (www.keepmore.net). KeepMore.net helps you keep track of your income and expenses without getting bogged down in accounting and bookkeeping minutiae that have nothing to do with selling on eBay. By adding the Yes! feature to your KeepMore account, you preserve an entire year's worth of eBay transaction data—plus loads of reporting on your bought and sold items—in one concise place, so you can:

- Identify your top buyers and sellers
- See your sell-through rate
- Know your average selling price

KeepMore.net with Yes! allows you to import data directly from eBay and PayPal and automatically imports all of your eBay transactions every hour, allocating them as income or expense for you. For a demonstration of the product in action, go to KeepMore.net's home page and click on Live Demo.

Q: ***Where can I get a chart of accounts and other QuickBooks templates that are specific to eBay businesses?***

A: A chart of accounts is basically a list of income and expense items organized by categories. Whenever you sell something on eBay, your bookkeeper (or your bookkeeping software) enters amounts in the appropriate categories—for example, by debiting "inventory of SKU 1234" by one item, crediting "cash" for the purchase price, and crediting "sales tax" if the buyer paid sales tax on the item.

No two charts of accounts for an eBay seller will ever look exactly the same, but taking a generic chart of accounts for a retail business and then customizing it for an eBay selling business will take lots of time and patience. Cathy Aiello, an eBay PowerSeller and CPA from Portland, Oregon (www.allegroaccounting.com), specializes in developing and selling customized charts of accounts and QuickBooks data files for different types of eBay sellers, beginning at $19.98. For about $150, Allegro Accounting will also help you set up QuickBooks and eBay Accounting Assistant for your eBay selling business and provide a one- to two-hour tutorial on how to use it (for details, see www.web-bookkeeper.com).

Q: ***"Is there a software product that will help me determine which of the items I'm selling on eBay are profitable and which aren't?"***

A: There are actually several, but the ones most commonly used are:

- QuickBooks Pro with eBay Accounting Assistant
- KeepMore.net with Yes!, offered by SageFire, Inc., of Boulder, Colorado (www.keepmore.net)
- Easy eBay Accounting System, offered by Allegro Accounting of Portland, Oregon (www.allegroaccounting.com)
- ProfitBuilderSoftware, offered by eBay PowerSeller and author Corey Kossack of Phoenix, Arizona (www.profitbuildersoftware.com)

Keeping Separate Business and Personal Selling Accounts

Q: ***"I have a business selling on eBay, but I also occasionally sell personal items. Do I have to break those out in my records?"***

A: It's probably a good idea to do so. The IRS vastly prefers that your business finances be completely separated from your personal finances. While it's not actually illegal to mix them, when your finances are mixed together (*commingled* is the technical term), it's much easier for the IRS to claim that your personal income is actually business income and/or that your expenses are personal, not business (especially when the expense could be either one, which is most of them).

You should also consider using a second eBay user ID for the personal items, which will make it much easier to correctly track your sales.

Cash Basis Versus Accrual Basis Accounting for Inventory

Q: ***"What is the difference between cash and accrual basis accounting, and why should I care?"***

A: The IRS allows small businesses to use two different accounting methods: the cash method and the accrual method.

Under the *cash method* of accounting, you report sales when, and only when, you actually receive the cash from your winning bidder. So if someone buys something from you on eBay and pays with a check or money order, you do not report the sale until the check or money order has arrived. If you hold onto the check for a few days before depositing it in your account (as many folks do, especially in late December, when they're trying to push income into the next tax year), it doesn't matter—you record the sale when the buyer's check hits your mailbox.

Under the *accrual method* of accounting, you report sales when you have the legal right to payment, even if you haven't received the cash yet. So if someone buys something from you on eBay and pays with a check or money order, you can report the sale as having occurred the moment the auction ended, even though it will be a few days before you receive the buyer's check or money order.

Under either the cash or the accrual method of accounting, holding onto a check or money order for several days before depositing it does not affect in any way the recording of the sale. You record the sale either when the check or money order arrives in your mailbox (cash method) or when the eBay auction closes and the winning bidder has been identified (accrual method). If you have a PayPal account and use the cash method of accounting, you record a sale when the buyer's payment hits your PayPal account.

Q: ***"Am I required by the IRS to use accrual basis accounting because I have inventory that I sell on eBay?"***

A: If you have more than $1 million in sales each year, the IRS requires you to use the accrual method of accounting, whereby you record sales when your customers have a legal obligation to pay (not when you actually receive the cash). The IRS is more flexible when it comes to smaller businesses, but get into the habit of using the accrual method, because it more accurately reflects the operating results of a business that maintains inventory, which virtually all eBay sellers do.

Finding and Retaining Your eBay Selling Records

Q: ***"I used to download all my eBay history at the end of the year and then do my taxes. To my horror, I find that eBay now allows you to download only the last four months! What can I do to get my history for the past year, including eBay fees?"***

A: This is the most important reason for using an auction management software program (see related questions in Chapter 6). Your My eBay page keeps accurate records of your auction and fixed-price listings on eBay, including information about eBay fees, but the information disappears after a period of time (currently, four months). However, there is one last resort: Go to your Seller's Account page, dig around a little bit, and you will find that eBay saves copies of your seller invoices (the documents you send to buyers after a listing closes) for eighteen months. Print these out, get a calculator, and you should be able to deduct all the information you need from those records.

Sellers who use only their My eBay page as a record-keeping device should get into the habit of printing out their My eBay transaction information every thirty days or so and keeping the information in a file somewhere so that they will have accurate information about their eBay sales when it comes time to prepare their taxes for the year.

Your PayPal transaction records are kept online for at least a year, so they are less of a concern.

Q: ***"I have been keeping copies of purchase receipts from thrift shops, Goodwill, and garage sales for the stuff I sell on eBay. Sometimes I have only one receipt for lots of different items. Do I have to break out the cost of each item?"***

A: You cannot determine your cost of goods sold on an aggregate basis—each item you sell on eBay must be assigned a cost. Having said that, if you purchased lots of substantially identical items, the IRS will allow you to average the cost among specific items. So, for example, if you purchased one hundred second-hand blouses from a thrift shop for $300, you should be able to use $3 as the cost of each blouse when you sell it on eBay.

Q: ***"Generally, how long should I be keeping records for all my eBay transactions? Or, to put it another way, when can I safely destroy this stuff?"***

A: I'm a big believer in keeping copies of your federal and state income and sales tax returns forever—they don't take up a lot of space (all my returns since 1970 are in a box of copy paper in my attic, and there's still plenty of room), and you never know when you might need to produce a copy on short notice.

Keeping all the backup material—copies of checks, invoices, and other supporting documents—is another matter. Generally, most statutes of limitations expire after three years, so you should keep this material at least that long. If the IRS thinks you have understated or "hidden" income from them, however, they can go back six years. If you have the room in your attic, basement, or garage, keep these records for at least six years.

If the IRS thinks you have committed fraud, there is no statute of limitations—they can go all the way back to the day you filed your first tax return. If things have gotten that bad, keeping copies of backup material probably won't help you very much. What you need now is a good criminal defense attorney.

18 I Just Got a Buyer from Timbuktu. What Do I Do Now?

Should You Sell Internationally?

Q: *"Should I offer my eBay listings worldwide?"*

A: Over 50 percent of eBay's total business is conducted outside the United States, and half of eBay's estimated 233 million registered users live in foreign countries. If you are selling only within the United States, you may be missing out on some incredible opportunities to build your business—there are sometimes huge markets overseas for items that you can't even give away here!

If you do decide to offer your eBay listings to a worldwide audience (rather than just the United States or certain regions of the world), there are several points to consider, according to eBay Certified Education Specialist and PowerSeller Jack Waddick of Chicago, Illinois (www.oakviewtraining.com), as follows:

- When setting up your eBay listings, selecting the "will ship worldwide" option means your listings will appear on all twenty-seven eBay websites around the world (at no additional charge). Your listing will appear in English unless you also provide a translated language.
- Every item you ship outside the United States must have customs papers attached.–You can print domestic and international shipping labels and customs papers through the PayPal Shipping Labels feature.
- PayPal is accepted in 190 countries and regions around the world covering sixteen currencies, and PayPal can easily convert the currency for you.

- PayPal's Seller Protection Policy covers shipments to the United States, United Kingdom, and Canada only.
- Sellers are required to maintain a United States bank account if they intend to use or accept PayPal, unless they are located in one of the few countries in which PayPal maintains a legal presence.

Q: ***"The auction on one of the items I was selling just ended, and the winning bidder is from the United Kingdom. I stated clearly in the auction that I would not ship internationally. Am I obligated to sell to this bidder or can I go right into a second chance offer to the next highest U.S. bidder?"***

A: You are not obligated to sell to this bidder, since he clearly did not read your selling Terms and Conditions. You should list this person as an "unwelcome bidder" and either relist the item or offer the underbidders a second chance offer to buy the item.

Customs Duties and Paperwork—When You Export

Q: ***"Who is responsible for paying customs duties when I ship internationally to a buyer?"***

A: Legally, it's the buyer's responsibility to make sure an imported item clears customs in his or her country. If you, as the seller, do not fill out the customs forms properly, however, the goods will be held up at the port of entry in the buyer's home country (which may be several hours' drive from where the buyer actually lives), and the buyer will have to deal with it at his or her own expense of time and money. The buyer won't like you for that and might leave negative feedback on eBay, even though you did everything else correctly.

Q: ***"I just sold an item on eBay to a Canadian buyer. The winning bid amount was over $500. I plan to ship the item via the U.S. Postal Service, but the buyer has asked me to check the 'gift' box on the form and state only a $50 value. When I asked him why, he replied that the Canadian customs duties would 'kill him' financially. He also suggested that I declare the item as a 'used light fixture' having a value of only $20. I am very nervous about doing this—is it legal?"***

A: Absolutely not. What this buyer is asking you to do is commit *customs fraud*—a felony in the United States. Checking the "gift" box or declaring a minimal value for an item robs Canada of customs revenue. If you are caught, they will refer you to U.S. authorities for prosecution.

The rules are that you must declare an item's actual value when filling out customs forms—for an eBay seller this will almost always be the winning bid amount or Buy It Now! purchase price. The one legal exception is if the item sells on eBay for much more than its current fair market value—for example, a situation in which two or more bidders engage in a bidding war that drives the price up to astronomical levels (you should be so lucky!). In that case, you are allowed to declare the lower fair market value of the item to save the buyer some customs duties; just be sure you have documentation supporting your calculation of fair market value.

You can be sure that if the authorities in either the United States or Canada catch you understating an item's value—and, believe me, they will, as they are wise to the ways of wily eBay sellers by now—your buyer will disavow any knowledge of your intentions and claim that, of course, he would not encourage an overseas seller to engage in any sort of illegal or fraudulent transaction. Your buyer should have read your listing and, before he bid on your item, determined how much in customs duties and value-added tax he was willing to pay.

To learn the finer points of filling out customs and international shipping forms, check out the book *Export/Import Procedures and Documentation,* by Thomas Johnson. It costs around $75 but is well worth the price. Intended as a training manual for corporate employees involved in import-export activities, the book is chock-full of examples of how to fill out international shipping forms for each of the major United States–based carriers, as well as some foreign ones.

Q: ***"What are some dos and don'ts for eBay sellers when it comes to customs documents?"***

A: You don't need to be specific on the declaration, when it comes to the contents. If you sell an antique mechanical bank, for example, it is sufficient to declare the contents as "coin bank" to deter or mislead thieves.

The declared value is, however, very important.

You do not have to declare the value your item sold for on eBay if the winning bid is greater than the actual retail value. So, for example, if you bought something at retail for $20 and it sold on eBay for $90, you could declare $20 on the customs form. If the item sold below what you paid for it, it is okay to declare the winning bid amount on the customs form.

You should not, however, declare a value of zero for any item; that's a red flag for customs officials overseas, and they are then free to set a customs value themselves. In many cases, the buyer will end up having to pay more duty/taxes than necessary. You should also exclude shipping and handling costs from the declared value.

If you include an invoice in the package to the buyer, the best invoice to supply is a copy of the auction listing or an invoice generated through the eBay system. Ensure that the value you indicate on the enclosed invoice matches the information on the customs form. The customs authorities at destinations do not really require an invoice, since they will go by the customs form. Customs will, however, request an invoice from the buyer if the value stated on the customs declaration seems unbelievable (for example, a laptop computer with a value of $10).

Customs Documents and Paperwork—When You Import

Q: ***"I just ordered $5,000 worth of merchandise from a supplier in China and received a notice last week that the goods are being held up in U.S. customs. What do I do?"***

A: You need help. Generally, when you import goods into the United States in a single shipment having a total value of more than $2,000, you have to obtain a *formal clearance* from U.S. customs before the goods can legally enter the country. Find a customs broker (there are some good ones listed in eBay's Seller Resources section), or enlist the help of a U.S.-based product-sourcing company such as Worldwide Brands Inc. in Orlando, Florida (www.worldwidebrands.com).

Export Licenses

Q: ***"When do you need an export license to sell overseas?"***

A: A U.S. export license is generally not necessary unless you are selling computers, software, marine systems, or other technology with potential military applications. You need an export license to sell *anything* to buyers in Cambodia, Cuba, Libya, Iran, or North Korea (although at the time this is being written, Libya is under reconsideration—check the U.S. Treasury's "sanctions" page at http://www.ustreas.gov/offices/enforcement/ofac/programs/index.shtml for more updated information).

If you are selling to an overseas business-to-business (B2B) customer, with the understanding that your buyer is buying for resale to third parties, you may need the buyer's written confirmation that it will not resell to a country with which the United States does not trade.

Import Licenses

Q: ***"When do you need an import license to bring stuff into the United States?"***

A: Generally, if you need a state license to sell something in the United States (such as wine, beer, or tobacco), you need a federal license to import it from overseas. If imported goods are subject to quotas, you need a license from the country of origin for *each shipment;* once the quota from that country has been filled, you're out of luck until next year. A partial list of goods that are subject to U.S. import quotas appears in Joseph Sinclair's book *eBay Global the Smart Way: Buying and Selling Internationally on the World's #1 Auction Site.*

Shipping Overseas

Q: ***"A recently shipped package to Brussels, Belgium, was returned to me in the United States due to a failure of the local post office to successfully deliver it. According to the buyer, no one was home when the delivery attempt was made, and no notice was left. The buyer wants me to resend the item, but the U.S. Postal Service is requiring that I pay a second shipping fee. Can I insist that the buyer pay this second fee?"***

A: Absolutely. As a seller on eBay based in the United States, you cannot be held responsible for the failure of a foreign post office to deliver an item or leave a notice of delivery. To preserve your good relations with this buyer, ask him if he has a preferred method of shipment he would like you to use. Find out what that service would charge, and then ask him to prepay the shipping before you ship again. That way the buyer will become part of the solution and will have a tougher time claiming a refund if the package isn't delivered a second time.

Selling in Different Currencies

Q: ***"When selling goods internationally on eBay, is there any advantage to listing the item price in U.S. dollars as opposed to an overseas currency?"***

A: Currencies float in value over time. If you sell something on eBay to a foreign national in U.S. dollars, and the dollar declines in value between the time you list the item and the time you receive payment, you lose. But if the dollar increases in value between the time you list the item and the time you receive payment, you win.

Similarly, if you sell something on eBay to a foreign national in the buyer's local currency, and the U.S. dollar declines in value between the time you list the item and the time you receive payment, you win. But if the dollar increases in value between the time you list the item and the time you receive payment, you lose.

It isn't recommended to engage in currency speculation when selling on eBay. If you are listing the item on eBay's U.S. website, the item should be priced in U.S. dollars. Period. Also, if you list lots of items on one of eBay's overseas websites exclusively in the local currency, there's an argument that you are legally doing business in that country and should be subject to all the laws, taxes, and regulations that country imposes on its own domestic businesses.

Dealing with Foreign Laws and Taxes—When You Export

Q: ***"When I sell stuff on eBay's overseas auction sites, am I subject to local laws and taxes in that country?"***

A: Generally, no. If you are selling only on eBay's U.S. website and someone from a foreign country buys or bids on your item, you are legally doing business only in the United States, not in the country where the buyer resides.

There is a growing body of Internet law, however, that says you may be doing business in a foreign country, and will be subject to that country's laws and taxes, if you maintain a "legal presence" there or appear to be "targeting" your sales to residents of that country. Here are some examples:

- You list items for sale exclusively on one of eBay's overseas websites (such as eBay France) and exclusively in the host country's language (French).
- You list items regularly on one of eBay's overseas websites and sell a significant volume of items to residents of a particular country.
- Your items are shipped to foreign buyers from a local address under your name or your company's name.

The law in this area is developing rapidly, and there is currently no certainty about exactly when a foreign country will consider you to be "doing business" there. If you find yourself selling lots of stuff to residents of a particular country, and especially if you are listing certain items on only one of eBay's overseas websites, the best advice at this time is to make friends with an eBay seller in that country and find out the likelihood of being pursued legally as a result of your eBay selling activities there. Go to eBay's Community section, click on Groups, find the User Group for that country, and post a question asking for help.

Q: ***"What exactly is a VAT, and do I have to pay it when I sell on eBay to overseas buyers?"***

A: VAT stands for "value-added tax," and almost all countries on earth (except, interestingly enough, the United States) have one. In Canada, the VAT is referred to as a *general sales tax* (GST).

A VAT is a national (or federal) sales tax, with one big difference. While sales taxes in the United States are imposed only on retail sales (see Chapter 13), VATs are applied at each stage of the manufacturing process—so, for example, whenever a United Kingdom manufacturer sells to a United Kingdom wholesaler for resale on eBay, a VAT would be charged to the wholesaler. That wouldn't happen in the United States.

When you sell on eBay to an overseas buyer, you are not responsible for paying or withholding VAT—the buyer is responsible for doing that. Because many overseas buyers are unaware of this, however, it's usually a good idea to put a sentence in your listing Terms and Conditions as follows: "Note to Overseas Buyers: Your purchase on eBay may be subject to customs duties, value-added tax, and other laws and taxes in your home country. Please consult with your legal or tax adviser before bidding on anything being sold by a U.S. seller on eBay."

Paying Use Tax on Imported Items

Q: ***"Two years ago, I bought something from an antiques dealer in the United Kingdom, which I then resold on eBay. Last week I got a notice from my state tax authority telling me I have to pay use tax on this item. What's up with that?"***

A: If your state has a *use tax* (virtually all states with sales taxes do), you are required to pay it whenever you buy an item for your own personal consumption for which you did not pay sales tax (use taxes are discussed in greater detail in Chapter 13). Most things you buy from out-of-state or foreign merchants are subject to use tax if they are for your own consumption.

In this case, the item you imported from the United Kingdom was inventory that you intended to sell on eBay—it was not an item you personally used. If you still have records of your eBay listing, photocopy them and send them to your state tax authority along with a letter explaining how the transaction went down. If your sale on eBay occurred reasonably soon after you imported the item into the United States, that should make them go away, at least until you import something else.

Foreign Nationals Doing Business on eBay in the United States

Q: ***"I am a citizen of Peru. For the past couple of years, my husband and I have been living in the United States on a student visa. We have paid U.S. taxes throughout this time. During our time in America I started selling things on eBay. My husband and I will be returning to Peru in a few months, and I want to keep this business going. I want to take PayPal payments, but the PayPal rules say you must have a bank account in the United States. PayPal currently does not operate in Peru. Is there any way I can operate legally in***

the United States without actually being a resident or citizen? I am more than willing to pay United States taxes."

A: Under current rules, you don't have to be a citizen or permanent resident of the United States to operate a business here legally. You need to talk to an attorney for specific advice, but here is one way it might work (no guarantees, now).

First, find a state (such as New Hampshire) in which there are no state or local income, sales, or other business taxes—if your business has any sort of presence in a state, you are considered to have a *nexus* there and must pay that state's sales, use, and other business taxes.

Then, hire an attorney in that state and set up a limited liability company (LLC) with yourself as the sole owner (you cannot form a Subchapter S corporation because you are not a U.S. citizen or green card holder). For a small annual fee, the attorney (or a registered agent service such as National Corporate Research Ltd., www.nationalcorp.com) acts as your *registered agent* in that state and makes sure all LLC paperwork is forwarded to your attorney so that he or she can deal with it.

Next, find a UPS Store or Mail Boxes Etc. in the state where the LLC is located (www.theupsstore.com or www.mbe.com) and obtain a private mailbox there. This is like a post office box except that you actually get a street address (such as "123 Main Street, # 456, Anytown, Anystate, USA"). Use the mailbox address as your LLC's business address, and instruct the UPS Store employees to forward all mail in the mailbox overseas to you (or to your U.S. attorney) at least once a month.

Then, obtain an *Individual Tax Identification Number* (ITIN) from the IRS (for details. go to www.irs.gov, click on Forms and Publications, and download IRS Publication 1915 along with IRS Form W-7). An ITIN is like a Social Security number for people who are not U.S. citizens or green card holders. It does not give you the rights that citizens have—for example, you cannot vote in U.S. elections or receive Social Security benefits. But with an ITIN you should be able to open a bank account (an LLC with one owner and no employees is not currently required to obtain a federal tax ID number), which in turn will enable you to set up a PayPal account for your business.

Finally, hire a good accountant in the state where your LLC is located, and pay him or her well to file U.S. federal tax returns and pay taxes for the LLC each year. But be very careful—the IRS has been tightening the ITIN requirements to prevent abuse. Also, keep in mind that after the terrorist attacks of September 11, 2001, the federal government watches these arrangements closely to make sure there is no illegal money laundering going on. If the U.S. government even suspects your business is a front for a terrorist operation, they will come down on you with full force. Don't say I didn't warn you!

Q: ***"I am looking into opening a business on eBay. I am from France, currently doing an internship as part of my education requirements at a university in the United States. I am on an F-1 (student) visa, I have an Individual Tax Identification Number (ITIN), a bank account for four years, and a state driver's license. I looked into applying for an E-1 visa (entrepreneur visa) but I realize that you need $1 million to open one, and I won't be making that kind of money for quite some time. Are there any other kinds of business I can operate legally in the United States while I am here?"***

A: I am not an expert on F-1 visas, but I do know they strictly limit what you can and cannot do while you are in the United States. You are supposed to be studying here and getting a degree that will help you get rich when you return to France. You are not here to get rich at the expense of your U.S. competitors. You really need to talk to an immigration attorney to find out what you can and cannot do in the United States with an F-1 visa (to find one near you, go to www.findanimmigrationattorney.com, www.lawyers.com/immigration, or www.findlaw.com). But take a look at the answer to the previous question—it may give you some ideas.

Also, there is absolutely nothing to prevent you, as a French citizen, from setting up a French company with your relatives in France and selling stuff on eBay France and other French e-commerce websites. And if your French company is also selling on eBay in the United States . . .

Repatriation Laws and Selling Antiquities and Cultural Heritage Items on eBay

Q: ***"I sell ancient Roman coins on eBay. I've been reading about foreign governments suing U.S. museums and auction houses over the sale of items that were illegally looted from archaeological sites and graves in their countries.***

Is that a risk for eBay sellers? How can I find out if an item I'm selling might be seized by a foreign government?"

A: Yes, it is a risk, and it is likely to be a growing issue for eBay sellers in the future, especially those selling antiquities (items more than five hundred years old) or high-value artwork and antiques from other historical periods. At the time this is being written:

- The government of Cyprus has retained U.S. law firms to search for Byzantine icons and other religious items that may have been illegally looted from churches on the island during the Greco-Turkish civil war of the 1960s and 1970s.
- A number of Jewish organizations regularly troll auction catalogues and listings looking for artwork and religious items that may have been looted by the Nazis or Russian troops during the Holocaust.
- The British government strictly forbids export of items—including Roman coins—dug up by metal detector hobbyists without an evaluation by the local coroner's office (!) and the issuance of a certificate declaring the item to be "without historical or cultural value" and permitting the item to be exported.
- The government of China currently forbids the export of any antique or artwork more than one hundred years old without an export permit.
- On the domestic front, the National Museum of the American Indian in Washington, D.C., maintains a repatriation service that will put you in touch with the appropriate tribal authorities if you suspect a Native American artifact you own was illegally looted from a Native American gravesite.

There is currently no foolproof way to determine whether an item you're selling on eBay will be seized by a foreign government, other than to do your best to determine the provenance of an item when you acquire it and deal only with low-priced or common items (such as Native American arrowheads or low-grade Roman coins) that are unlikely to attract scrutiny as having "significant historical or cultural value" by the country of origin.

When in doubt, have the item reviewed by an established, reputable dealer in antiquities and get an opinion (preferably in writing) as to the likelihood of it being a "cultural patrimony" item you will have to repatriate to the country of origin. Any dealer who is a member of the London-based Antiquities Dealers Association (www.theada.co.uk), the National Antique & Art Dealers Association of America (www.naadaa.org), or the Antique Dealers Association of California (www.antiquedealersca.com) should fit the bill. Avoid dealing with "antiquities experts" who advertise in the back pages of popular magazines such as *Archaeological Digest* or *Biblical Archaeology Review,* because many of these folks are not dealing in genuine antiques but, rather, in what are euphemistically called "genuine replicas."

19 Can I Work Out of My Home?

Complying with Local Zoning Laws

Q: ***"I live in a gated community, and the association's rules specifically prohibit doing any sort of business out of your home, including selling on eBay! Is that legal? Can they do that?"***

A: Yes. Technically (and I hope you're sitting down), just about every home-based business is an illegal business.

You read that correctly: Just about every home-based business (including yours and mine) in the United States today is technically an illegal business. Why? Because every town or municipality in the United States has a *zoning ordinance.* This is a law (actually, it's a map) that divides your town into sections (called *districts*), and it dictates what sort of activity is legally allowed in each of those districts. Except for a growing number of enlightened municipalities that have created *mixed-use business and residential districts* in their zoning laws to specifically allow home-based businesses, just about every zoning ordinance prohibits you from running a business in a residential district. Therefore, virtually all home-based businesses are technically illegal.

So why is it that there are fourteen people working out of their homes on your street and nobody's doing anything about it? Why aren't prisons filled to the rafters with home-based business criminals?

Because, although every community in the United States (just about) has a zoning ordinance, hardly any community has "zoning cops" going door-to-door asking if people are operating illegal businesses. Don't get me wrong—every community that has a zoning ordinance also has a *planning and zoning board* that interprets the ordinance, issues *variances* from the ordinance, and so forth. But, generally, your local zoning board has no enforcement mechanism—except one: your neighbors. Local zoning boards rely on the community (that's you and everyone who lives near you) to tell them when violations of the zoning ordinance occur.

Generally, as long as you keep a low profile for your home-based business so that your neighborhood doesn't start looking like a commercial district, you should be allowed to work indefinitely from your home. After all, many of your neighbors are operating businesses out of their homes, and they wouldn't want you finding out about that, either.

The rules are slightly different, however, for gated communities such as yours. Condominium and cooperative boards are free to regulate their members' lives in ways that are sometimes almost tyrannical. It is not illegal or unconstitutional for these boards to ban home-based businesses altogether, and if they do, there's nothing you can do about it. You will either have to rent commercial space outside your home or else use a local UPS Store or other private-mailbox location (see the answer to the next question) to run your eBay selling business, and use your home office only for administrative functions (such as putting up your listings and keeping your accounting books and records) and other office activities that won't arouse your neighbors' suspicions.

Q: ***"What are some of the things I can do to keep a low profile for my home-based business, so my neighbors don't report me to the local zoning authorities?"***

A: When doing business out of your home, it is essential to conduct it in such a way that your neighbors do not turn you in to the local zoning authorities. If your business is conducted in a way that changes the character of your neighborhood, you are likely to get your neighbors riled up. Here are some tips:

- Don't see clients, customers, or vendors in your home. If your neighbors see a line of cars outside your home every day and people lounging on your front lawn waiting to sell you inventory, they will get upset and report you.
- Get a private mailbox from your local UPS Store, and use that instead of your home address as your mailing address for packages and business correspondence.

- Unless you absolutely need them, don't buy copiers or other office machinery that generates a lot of noise. Use the ones at your local UPS Store or Kinkos instead.
- Ship all your items from your local UPS Store or post office. If the local kids can't play basketball on the street because they are too busy dodging UPS trucks going to and from your home, your neighbors will get upset and report you.
- Keep the noise level down at all times—don't run copiers, packing equipment, or other machinery late at night or early in the morning.
- If you have more than one part-time employee helping out with your eBay selling business, it's time to move the business out of the house and rent a "real" office.

Ideally, your home-based business should be invisible to your neighbors. I've been running several businesses out of my home for over ten years now, and most people living on my street don't even know I work out of the home. That's the way it should be.

Homeowner's Insurance: Will It Cover a Home-Based Business?

Q: ***"I am selling stuff on eBay out of my home. Will my homeowner's insurance policy cover my eBay inventory if the place burns down?"***

A: Generally, no. Your homeowner's policy generally covers only loss or damage to your home and its personal contents. It does not cover business-related assets, which are presumed (just to show how the insurance industry hasn't caught up with the times) not to be home related and thus are presumed to be covered under another policy.

Most homeowner's insurance policies offer a home office rider that would cover your office furniture, equipment, and eBay inventory in the event of casualty. Look into that, as it's almost always a better deal than seeking a separate business insurance policy for your home-based business.

Taking the Home Office Deduction

Q: ***"Is it true that taking the home office deduction will almost always trigger an audit?"***

A: No. Don't believe what other people may tell you or what you might read in some older, pre-2000 tax guides. Taking the home office deduction is not going to trigger an audit that will automatically expose you and your tax return to review by the IRS. Back in the 1980s and 1990s, the IRS did audit aggressively in this area, but Congress and the courts have done a lot since then to clarify the rules under which you can legitimately take the home office deduction. Furthermore, so many people are taking the home office deduction now that the IRS doesn't have time to chase them all down.

There is absolutely no reason why you shouldn't take the home office deduction if you are indeed conducting your eBay activities out of a bona fide home office.

Q: ***"It's very difficult to measure my home office space, because there are pieces of it in several rooms of my house. Can I still take the home office deduction?"***

A: Technically, yes, but if you are ever audited it's going to be difficult to calculate your home office space with everything spread out like that. The best home office is in a dedicated room of your house (such as a spare bedroom or the loft space above your garage) that is self-contained. That way it's a lot easier to measure. It's also a lot easier to keep personal stuff out of a dedicated home office than a corner of a kitchen, family room, or living room. You can use duct tape to mark off the business area of these rooms, but it doesn't look very attractive.

The steps involved when you take the home office deduction are discussed on pages 202–205 of my book *The eBay Seller's Tax and Legal Answer Book.*

Q: ***"Can you talk about the requirements for the décor of a home office? I've had a home office set up for the past several years. It is decorated to suit my taste in décor and collectibles and also has custom bookcases with books I enjoy. Must I completely remove everything not associated with eBay sales in order to claim it?"***

A: Not at all. You can have appropriate décor in your home office if it's something you would have in an outside office. So, for example, a bookcase with general business books (not eBay specific) is perfectly okay. A bookcase full of romance novels (unless, of course, you sell romance novels on eBay) probably wouldn't be.

If you sell Asian antiques, by all means put Japanese prints on the wall. Rock posters, on the other hand (unless they are anime-themed or in Japanese for a rock concert at the Budokan amphitheater in Tokyo), probably should go elsewhere.

Always keep in mind that when the IRS audits a home office, the first thing they look for is inappropriate furnishings and decorations. If you have any doubts about a specific item, it's probably safer to remove it than to take the risk of blowing your home office deduction.

Q: ***"Can I deduct storage space for my eBay inventory as part of my home office deduction?"***

A: If you use areas in your basement, garage, or attic as storage space for your inventory, you can add it to your home office space in order to take the deduction. You cannot deduct your entire basement, though, if you use only a portion of that space to store inventory. Use duct tape to make the boundaries of the business portion of your basement, attic, garage, or barn, so that if you are ever audited, the IRS agent can see clearly where your home office space ends and your personal space begins.

Q: ***"When I take the home office deduction, can I deduct all of my home office expenses?"***

A: No, but you can deduct most of them. Expenses for which you already take a deduction, such as the interest on your home mortgage, cannot be deducted a second time when you take the home office deduction.

Expenses for work done outside the home (such as lawn care or landscaping services) cannot be deducted when you take the home office deduction, since by definition a home office can only be inside a home—unless, of course, your home-based business is a lemonade stand.

Similarly, expenses that are deemed to be of a strictly personal nature cannot be deducted when you take the home office deduction. If you're a Hollywood actor, you probably can deduct the services of a masseuse or personal trainer who comes to your home and performs these services there. I wouldn't try deducting these for an eBay selling business, however, no matter how stressful it may be putting up all those listings.

Q: ***"Where can I find a list of deductions associated with a home office? I am curious whether expenses such as my trash service and my water bill are included. Also, if my Internet service is used 100 percent of the time for conducting business (my husband and I run two separate businesses that require Internet service), can I deduct the entire cost instead of the home office percentage?"***

A: Appendix E to this book is a useful checklist of things that a typical eBay seller can deduct; items marked with an asterisk (*) on this checklist may be taken as part of the home office deduction, to the extent of your home office percentage. This percentage (actually a fraction) is the ratio of the square footage of your home office to the total interior square footage of your home. So, for example, if you have a 5,000-square-foot home and you use 1,000 square feet of that space for a home office, your *home office percentage* is one-fifth, or 20 percent, and you can deduct 20 percent of all qualifying home office expenses.

IRS Publication 587, Business Use of a Home, is the source of all knowledge when it comes to the home office deduction (like all IRS publications and forms, it is available as a free download from the IRS website, www.irs.gov). According to this publication, the "home office fraction" of both your trash service and your water bill is deductible. If you can prove your Internet service is used exclusively for your eBay business, you should be able to deduct the entire cost on Schedule C, but be really careful here lest the IRS auditor find even one video game on your computer.

Q: ***"If I take the home office deduction, will I have to pay capital gain taxes on the business portion of my house when I sell it?"***

A: This was the law prior to 2003, and it may well be the law again someday when Congress has to raise cash in a hurry, but it's not the law today.

As long as you live in your home for at least two out of the five years before you sell it, the first $250,000 (for single taxpayers) or $500,000 (for married taxpayers filing jointly) of profit is not taxable. Taking the home office deduction does not affect or change that in any way.

You will, however, have to pay a capital gain tax (called a *depreciation recapture*) in the year you sell your home, equal to 25 percent of the total depreciation deductions you took on your home office since May 6, 1997—but only the depreciation deductions, not every other deduction you took for your home office.

And if you didn't depreciate your home for tax purposes (which is a complex decision requiring the assistance of your accountant or tax adviser), you won't have to pay even that.

Q: ***"Can you take a home office deduction if you rent rather than own your home?"***

A: If you rent a home or apartment, you can take the home office deduction for the home office percentage of your rent and other household expenses.

Since you do not own your home or apartment, however, you cannot depreciate it for tax purposes.

You are also required to give your landlord a Form 1099-MISC each year showing how much of your rental payments (not other expenses) you deducted. Your landlord will absolutely love you for doing this (not!), so be sure to give your landlord a heads-up before giving them a nasty surprise come tax season next year.

Q: ***"I use a portion of my neighbor's basement to store my eBay inventory. Can I take a home office deduction for that portion of her basement I use for storage?"***

A: No. You cannot take a home office deduction on any portion of another person's home. But there may be another way you can deduct it: Have your attorney draw up a lease for the space, have the owner of the other home signed as "landlord" (you would sign as "tenant"), and pay the other homeowner a reasonable rent for the space. That way, you could deduct the rent you pay the other homeowner for the use of her garage, attic, basement, or barn. Make sure you are paying a fair market rent.

Do not conduct any other business at the other homeowner's address, or else you open yourself up to an IRS claim that you are not conducting your eBay selling business "solely and exclusively" from your home office. Also, don't let your relationship with the other homeowner get too cozy, because if you do, there's a risk the other person might be considered your partner in the eBay business (see Chapter 20), which has significant legal and tax ramifications for both of you.

20 How Do I Deal with Employees/ Business Partners/Colleagues?

Are We Partners?

Q: ***"My spouse helps me out sometimes with my eBay sales, and I pay him some money. Ultimately, everything, of course, ends up in our joint checking account. Do I have to make him my partner for tax purposes?"***

A: Not if you don't want to, but that's what the IRS will assume unless you do some paperwork. Partners generally share in the profits and losses of a business. Contrary to what a lot of people think, you don't have to have a written partnership agreement to have a legal partnership—partnerships can be formed by a handshake agreement, or even by accident.

The problem here is that everything you're doing on eBay is commingled with your personal finances. Get a federal tax ID number for your eBay selling, register with your state tax authority for sales taxes, and then open a separate checking account for your business that is tied to your federal tax ID number.

If your spouse is working for you only occasionally and sets his own hours, you may be able to treat him as an *independent contractor* for tax purposes. Write checks from your business account to your joint banking account for the hourly or daily fees you pay him, and (if you pay him more than $600 total during the calendar year) send him a Form 1099 next January, just as you would do for any other contractor.

If your spouse is working only a few hours in your business, there's no advantage (tax or otherwise) in treating him as an employee for tax purposes. He has to sign IRS Form W-4 and Immigration Form I-9 (and show you proof that he is a citizen!), you have to withhold payroll taxes from his compensation, and you also have to send him a Form W-2 next January. This is too much work for a very small tax reward—you will save only about $50 in federal unemployment tax (FUTA).

If you do decide to make your spouse your partner for tax purposes, get a federal tax ID number for the partnership (you can't use your Social Security number anymore when you have a partnership) and start filing IRS Form 1065 each year.

Whichever way you decide to proceed, make sure it's in writing and crystal clear. You don't want to treat your spouse as an independent contractor, only to find out when he slaps you with divorce papers that he's thought of himself as your business partner all these years.

Q: ***"My buddy and I just started out selling on eBay and are doing quite well. But I just realized that everything—bank accounts, eBay user IDs, credit card merchant accounts—is in my name. We split the profits, but the IRS will think that it is all my income unless we form a partnership, right?"***

A: Not necessarily. If you have been splitting profits and losses from your eBay selling with your buddy, you are partners, no matter how your property is legally titled. Don't get me wrong—if you dissolve your partnership at any time, your buddy wouldn't be entitled to 50 percent of everything you own. That's the beauty of having everything titled in your name. It does mean, however, that you and your buddy should be filing IRS Form 1065 each year and otherwise holding yourself out as partners when you do business with people. Otherwise, if somebody sues you, you will have to take the full hit.

Talk to a lawyer about having a short, written partnership agreement drawn up that spells out clearly what the two of you are doing together and how much each of you is legally entitled to as a result of your partnership activities. You may think of your buddy as a 20 percent partner, but there's nothing right now to prevent him from claiming 50 percent of the partnership assets if he thinks he's the one doing all the work.

Then send him Form K-1 in January or February next year (no later than that, please, even though the IRS allows you until April 15 to send it), showing him how much the partnership earned and what his share of the profits and losses are. That way, the IRS at least won't be confused about your intentions.

If this is too much hassle and you would rather treat your buddy as an independent contractor for tax purposes, see the answer to the previous question.

Q: ***"I started selling on eBay last year in partnership with my cousin, but I'm doing all the work and I resent the fact that she's getting 50 percent of all my profits. How can I legally dissolve the partnership?"***

A: Dissolving a partnership is easy—just tell your partner you no longer want to work with her. You should file a Form 1065 with the IRS (and a similar return to your state tax authority, if your state has an income tax) for the period from January 1 to the date the partnership terminated, making sure to check the "final return" box on the form so the IRS knows this is the last Form 1065 they will receive from you.

The tough part comes later, when you have to figure out:

- Who gets to keep the partnership assets (such as your eBay inventory, your eBay user ID if it is held in a joint name, your business trade name, and the money in your PayPal account)
- Whether the two of you are still on the hook to creditors of the partnership (such as a credit card merchant account on which the partnership has a balance)

Before you break up your partnership, draw up a "separation checklist" detailing how you would like each of these matters to be resolved, and give it to your partner, along with an invitation to discuss it with her attorney and her tax advisers. This will open the door to a negotiated settlement that will resolve these issues so you can both get on with your lives with a minimum of fuss and bother. Make sure to include an "acceptance line" at the end for her signature, so if she agrees to your separation proposal, she can sign the document and return it to you, saving you hundreds of dollars in legal fees.

Employees Versus Independent Contractors

Q: ***"If I hire people to help me with my eBay business for a few hours each week, can I treat them as independent contractors for tax purposes?"***

A: Unless they are your business partners (see previous questions), everyone who works with you in your eBay business is either an *employee* or an *independent contractor* for tax purposes.

If people are your employees, you must withhold income and payroll taxes from the money you pay them, and they are entitled to all of the many rights afforded to employees by federal and state law. Give them IRS Form W-2 each January, showing the income and payroll taxes you withheld and the gross amount of their wages for the preceding calendar year.

If people are your independent contractors, you don't withhold income and payroll taxes from the money you pay them and they have none of the legal rights that employees have. If you pay them more than $600 total during the calendar year, send them IRS Form 1099 each January, showing the gross amount of their compensation for the preceding calendar year.

When people work for you part-time or only occasionally (such as during your holiday season "crunch time"), you would like to treat them as independent contractors so you don't have to deal with all the legal and tax paperwork. The trouble is, you often can't.

The law here is simple to state, but difficult to apply in practice: If you can "direct and control"people's activities while they are working with you, by telling them what to do, when to do it, where to do it, and how to do it, they are your employees, even if they work only a few hours each week (or just during the holidays). If you cannot "direct and control"people's activities—they get to determine their own hours and decide how, when, and where the work will be done—they are independent contractors.

It sounds simple, doesn't it? But the devil lives in the details. Here are some examples to show how tough this decision can be:

- You hire a student intern to help put up your eBay listings; he comes over to your home on Wednesday afternoons after class and works for three hours before going home for dinner. The student intern is a part-time employee and should not be treated as an independent contractor because he works a regular schedule and you provide him with all the tools and equipment necessary to do his job.
- You hire a neighbor to help you pack boxes and ship the items you sell on eBay "for ten hours a week." Each week she works different days, depending on her child's day-care schedule, but she has to work ten hours a week, and when she is working on your premises you assign her projects and otherwise control her working hours. This person is a part-time

employee and should not be treated as an independent contractor, even though there's no regular schedule, because you require a certain number of hours each week and (most important) control her time whenever she is available to work for you.

- You meet someone at a local networking group meeting who is temporarily out of work. You ask him to help you put listings on eBay for a few hours a week to give him some money until he finds other work. After a while, however, he's working sixty hours a week for you, you are his sole source of income, and he isn't looking for work elsewhere because he is comfortable with the money you are paying him. This person is an employee for tax purposes, since he doesn't work for anyone else and doesn't have a reasonable chance of working for someone else because of all the hours he's working for you.
- You hire an attorney to review a purchase contract. You tell him you need his comments by Friday of this week because that's when you are meeting with the vendor to review the contract, but in between now and Friday the attorney is free to schedule this job whenever he wants and he is not limited in the amount of time he can spend reviewing your contract (other than his personal ethics and his desire to keep you as a valued client). The attorney is an independent contractor for tax purposes.
- Your bathroom toilet has sprung a leak. You call a plumber, who comes to your house, bringing all his tools and equipment with him, and spends four hours repairing your toilet, even though he estimated it would be only a two-hour job. The plumber is an independent contractor for tax purposes because he is in control of his time, works for lots of other people, and uses his own tools and equipment.

See how tricky this gets? It isn't always easy to tell if someone is an employee or an independent contractor for tax purposes, and you have to get it right. The IRS audits this area of tax law very aggressively, and they focus their attention on small business owners. If you're not exactly sure if you are "controlling" someone's activities enough to make them an employee, talk to an attorney who specializes in labor and employment law and get his or her opinion. This is one area of the law where guesswork doesn't pay.

Q: ***"If someone works for me less than ten hours per week, is he an employee or an independent contractor for tax purposes?"***

A: There is no minimum number of hours that makes someone an independent contractor or an employee for tax purposes. Even someone who works only a few hours a week can be an employee if you control his activities during the time he is actually working for you.

Q: ***"If I have a written agreement with someone in which he agrees that he is an independent contractor for tax purposes, will the IRS be bound by that?"***

A: No. If your business is ever audited by the IRS, the auditor will look at all the facts and circumstances of the relationship to determine whether the individual is actually an employee. If they determine that he is, the IRS is free to disregard the written agreement and slap you with interest and penalties on all the payroll taxes you should have been paying on this individual's wages.

Q: ***"If someone working for me has her own corporation or limited liability company (LLC), can I sign a contract with her corporation or LLC rather than with her personally and treat her company as an independent contractor?"***

A: Generally, only natural persons (human beings) can be employees for tax purposes—legal entities such as corporations and LLCs cannot. But if the individual is the sole owner or "member" of the corporation or LLC and hasn't been paying close attention to the legal and tax paperwork that has to be done when you have a legal entity, there's a good chance that the IRS will pierce the corporate veil on audit and disregard the person's corporation or LLC on the grounds that it existed solely to help her (and you) avoid taxes. If it's a "real" corporation or LLC, with other owners and lines of business that don't involve you, you may have a stronger chance of claiming independent contractor status for the company (not the individual).

Hiring Employees

Q: ***"Posting listings on eBay is very time consuming. I would like to hire an employee to help me with that so I can focus on the more fun aspects of the business, like finding good inventory. When should I consider hiring my first employee?"***

A: Like any business decision, when hiring your first employee you should weigh the costs against the benefits. Hiring this person will free up your time so you can spend it doing more important things to build the business—sourcing the right products, optimizing your eBay Store for search engines, writing a weekly e-mail newsletter to your customers, and so forth.

But . . . will all that activity generate enough revenue to cover the additional costs (wages, benefits, equipment, overhead) that new employee will generate?

Here's a rule of thumb: An employee's average cost is generally two to three times the person's base salary (before you withhold taxes). If the employee's base salary is $30,000 a year pretax, you have to generate $60,000 to $90,000 in additional revenue to cover those costs. Is that feasible, based on your past experience with this type of merchandise? If you are selling bobble-head dolls on eBay for $10 each, you will have to sell lots and lots and *lots* more bobble-head dolls to reach those numbers.

Q: ***"How do I avoid discriminating when interviewing candidates for a job?"***

A: When hiring employees, you cannot discriminate on the basis of race, religion, sex, age, marital status, pregnancy, or national origin. In many states, you also cannot discriminate on the basis of sexual orientation.

When interviewing candidates for a job, you should be concerned only with that person's qualifications for the job. Avoid saying anything that signals that you are focusing on something other than the person's qualifications—even if your intentions are good, because we all know "the road to hell is paved with good intentions." Here are some questions that are *guaranteed* to get you into legal trouble:

- "Abdul, that's a beautiful turban you're wearing; you know, I've always wondered—how long does it take to wind that around your head in the morning?"
- "Congratulations, Mary, I can see your new baby is due any minute. Let me ask, how long a maternity leave do you think you'll need when the baby arrives?"
- "Luther, you're a perfect fit for this job, but you probably know we deal in a lot of Black Americana antiques. Since you're obviously African American, how will you feel about listing those items on eBay?"

- "I think it's just horrible that you lost both your arms during the Iraq war. I'm assuming you were honorably discharged, by the way. What was it like when you woke up in the field hospital the next day?"
- "I see your fiancé/husband is working for Company X here in town. You probably know they're planning to shut down their offices and move out of state pretty soon. How will that affect your ability to devote your full time and attention to this job?"

Talk to an attorney if you sense there are sensitive issues that may come to the surface when interviewing a particular candidate—common sense should be your guide here.

Q: ***"I recently posted an advertisement for a delivery truck driver. Several individuals responded to the ad, but when I interviewed them I noticed that one of the applicants—a Gulf War veteran—had a prosthetic arm. I believe strongly in hiring veterans, and I realize they've made many technical advances in prosthetic limbs, but I'm really worried about this individual's ability to do the job. I'm also worried that if I hire one of the other qualified individuals, this guy will sue me for discrimination. What can I do?"***

A: The federal Americans with Disabilities Act (ADA) absolutely prohibits discriminating against disabled persons. I congratulate you for knowing that the law applies even to small businesses. If a disabled person thinks you are violating the ADA and making it impossible for disabled or handicapped individuals to find jobs with your firm, he or she can certainly sue for discrimination. Yet clearly there are certain jobs people with certain disabilities will never be able to do. How do you avoid discrimination lawsuits without being forced to hire individuals who cannot perform the jobs they have applied for?

First, make sure you haven't already discriminated against this individual during your initial job interview. Whenever you interview disabled or handicapped individuals for jobs, you have to be careful that you don't inadvertently signal that you're focusing on their disabilities. So, for example, you would be totally out of line (and could well be sued) if you say something to this individual like "Hey, didn't you read my ad? I'm looking for a truck driver. How the heck can you drive a truck with only one arm?" Even though you have a legitimate concern about this individual's ability to do the job, by focusing your attention on the person's disability you make it very likely he will feel he is being discriminated against.

The correct way to deal with this situation is by saying something like this: "As you saw from our ad, one of the essential functions of this position is driving a truck. Are you aware of any circumstances that would restrict or prohibit you from performing that essential function?" I know, I know, it's tough to remember all that, and it does sound a little like legalese, but that's the way the law requires you to ask that question.

The next step is to determine if driving a truck is an "essential function" of the position you've advertised. Let's say you had a position that involved 95 percent clerical work and 5 percent driving a forklift in your warehouse. If a person with a prosthetic limb applies for this position, he or she clearly can perform the clerical functions (the essential part of the job), but his or her ability to drive the forklift is in question. The ADA in this instance would require you to "restructure" the job and eliminate the forklift-driving component as a "reasonable accommodation" of the applicant's disability. Based on your e-mail message, I am assuming that driving a truck is an essential function of the job you've advertised.

You are correct in pointing out that medical science has made tremendous advances in prosthetic limb technology in the past few years. Since this applicant is neither blind nor illiterate and presumably knows that he is applying for a position driving a truck, he obviously thinks his disability won't stand in the way of his being able to do the job. Why not have him prove his ability by performing a short driving test in one of your company's trucks? If you do:

- Be sure to test him under actual conditions. Don't just have him drive around your parking lot; have him carry out an actual delivery so you can see firsthand how he is likely to perform on the job.

- Be sure to "ride shotgun" with him so you can evaluate his performance, and have another individual present during the test so he or she can corroborate your evaluation.

- If you conclude that the applicant isn't qualified for the position, take detailed notes during the test documenting specific tasks he is unable to perform, and keep those notes in your employment records in the event he does sue you.

- Most important, be sure you require this test of *all* applicants, so it doesn't look like you're singling him out because of his disability.

If he flunks the test, consider whether you might have another open position he might qualify for, and if you do, encourage him to apply for that position. Hiring a vet is one of the most noble things any small business can do, and you should go a little out of your way to find room for him in your organization. Not only is this the patriotic thing to do, but I think you'll find, as many of my law clients have, that vets are incredibly loyal, grateful, disciplined, hardworking employees, and they can be a major asset to any small business. This guy did you (and a lot of other people) a big favor once by serving in the armed forces during wartime, and you owe him—big time.

Employee Rights and Labor Laws

Q: ***"I've just hired my first real employee. Where can I learn more about his rights and my legal responsibilities to him?"***

A: Even if you have only one or two employees, they have legal rights. Not only must you, as an employer, be aware of them, but you must make your employees aware of them as well. A brief summary of the most important ones appears in Chapter 12 of my book *The eBay Seller's Tax and Legal Answer Book,* but every state law is a little bit different, and different rules apply depending on the nature of your business, the type of employees you hire (warehouse versus clerical, for example), and the number of employees you have.

There are three things you need to do as soon as you hire your first employee:

1. Develop a relationship with a local attorney who specializes in labor and employment law, and put his or her telephone number on your telephone speed dial.
2. Have your attorney draft an employee manual describing your employee policies and procedures. Depending on where you live, an attorney should be able to do this for a fee in the $1,000 to $2,000 range as long as you don't request a lot of specific provisions.

3. Have a poster prepared for your office eating area or other community space that educates your employees about their rights and responsibilities under federal and state law. You can do this online at the HROne website (www.hrone.com). When the poster arrives, be sure to read it yourself before posting it.

Keep in mind that your employee manual is a contract—your employees are legally entitled to the rights and benefits you put in your manual. You can change the contents of your manual, but only by giving notice of the change to all your employees.

Payroll Taxes and Hiring Family Members

Q: *"How do I deal with payroll taxes when I hire my first employee?"*

A: You are required to withhold income taxes from each of your employees' paychecks. In addition, you are required to pay (and sometimes also deduct from your employees' wages) federal employment, or "payroll," taxes: Social Security (also known as FICA), federal unemployment tax (known as FUTA), and Medicare tax. The calculation of these three amounts is complicated, but it generally totals 15.3 percent of each employee's gross taxable wages (as defined by the IRS).

The simplest advice when it comes to calculating payroll taxes is: *Don't do it yourself!* The procedure is extremely complicated—make one mistake here and the IRS will be all over you like savage dogs on a piece of raw meat. If you have only one or two employees, have your accountant make these calculations and give her access to your business checking account so she can automatically debit it when payroll taxes are due to the IRS.

If you have more than two employees or anticipate having more within the next few months, hire a payroll service to do your payroll tax calculations for you. The service most frequently used by small business owners is Paychex (www.paychex.com), but there are plenty of others—search on the Web for "small business payroll service" and you will see the biggest and most reputable companies on the first page of the search results.

Q: ***"Are there any tax advantages to hiring family members to help me with my eBay business?"***

A: There is no tax benefit to hiring your spouse or parents. They are treated the same as other employees. If you employ your spouse, you can save about $56 a year in federal unemployment tax (FUTA), but that's about it.

You can, however, provide health insurance and other employee benefits to a spouse who works for you and take the full deduction (see Chapter 14). By hiring your spouse, you can also go on business trips together and deduct your spouse's meals and lodging along with your own.

Now, hiring your kids is another matter. If your children work in your business and each of them makes less than $5,000 a year, they don't pay income taxes (unless they have income from investments). If each of your children makes more than $5,000 a year, they pay taxes, but at a much lower rate than you do. If your child is under age eighteen, you don't have to withhold or pay Social Security or Medicare taxes on his or her income. If your child is under twenty-one, you don't have to pay federal unemployment tax (FUTA), either.

Make sure, though, that your children are truly employees and are actually working in the business. And make sure their compensation is reasonable—no ten-year-old should be making $200 an hour, no matter how smart he or she is.

Firing Employees

Q: ***"We hired an employee last year, but he's not working out. How can we fire him without getting sued?"***

A: Very, very carefully. These days, if you so much as look at an employee cross-eyed, the person goes looking for a lawyer. There really is no 100 percent foolproof way to make sure you won't get sued by a disgruntled employee, but here are some tips that will make it really tough for the person to prove a case against you:

- Make sure there are no surprises. Give employees a performance evaluation with specific criticism and give them the opportunity to improve before you fire them.

- Don't give employees a raise or a positive performance evaluation and then fire them two weeks later. Employees should never be shocked when you deliver the bad news.

- If the person you're firing is your company's only female, Asian, or African American employee, go to extra lengths to document and explain that the termination is performance related.

- Always fire people on a Monday, never a Friday, so they don't have the chance to "stew" over the weekend and come in to the office on Monday morning with a 12-gauge shotgun.

- Escort employees to the door immediately after firing them—don't let them hang around the office and poison your relationship with other employees. If they have to stop by their desk to pick up personal belongings, make sure someone is standing there watching them so they don't change all the passwords on the office computer.

- Call a meeting of your remaining employees, explain that "so-and-so will no longer be working with us" (don't give reasons!), and reassign the terminated employee's duties to other employees. This will help keep the rumor mill quiet.

- Offer fired employees an extra week's severance pay in exchange for having them sign a liability release. Be sure to have an attorney draft this (don't *ever* pull one of these off the Web!), as there are special provisions that have to be included if the terminated employee is age forty or older.

- Signal to fired employees that you will not give a negative evaluation if their future employer calls you and asks for a reference. Be as specific as possible about what you will and will not say.

- Don't challenge employees' applications for unemployment benefits. They usually get the benefits anyway, no matter what you tell the unemployment office, and the hearing or proceeding is usually tape-recorded so fired employees have excellent ammunition for a lawsuit against you if you say something stupid during the hearing.

For more information about firing employees, see Chapter 12 of my book *The eBay Seller's Tax and Legal Answer Book.*

Sending Out Form 1099

Q: ***"When do I have to give people a 1099 form if they help me out with my eBay selling business during the year?"***

A: If someone worked for you as an independent contractor and you paid that worker more than $600 during the year, you must send that worker an IRS Form 1099 no later than January 31 (postmark date) of the following year, and send copies to the IRS and your state tax authority by no later than February 28 or 29 of the following year, along with IRS Form 1096 (basically a cover letter for the 1099).

Technically, that means every independent contractor, including lawyers, accountants, other professionals, drop shippers, and people who give you stuff to sell on eBay, needs to get this form. But you can use some discretion here. The people who absolutely must get 1099s are people you do not think are intelligent, disciplined, or honest enough to report your payments as income on their tax returns. Sending someone a 1099 insulates you from liability if that someone decides to hide income from the IRS.

If you send 1099 forms out late, you have to pay a $50 penalty to the IRS for each overdue 1099. You also incur the wrath of your contractor, who probably has already filed a tax return and now has to amend it to attach your 1099.

Note: You cannot download 1096 and 1099 forms from the IRS website and send photocopies to people. This is one of the few cases where the IRS requires you to use the actual paper form. You can get them from your nearest IRS field office (look in the telephone book in the blue government pages), or order them online from the IRS website (www.irs.gov)—and don't wait until January 30 to do so.

Q: ***"Do I have to give 1099 forms to drop shippers and people who consign stuff for me to sell on eBay?"***

A: If the drop shipper was a corporation or a limited liability company (LLC) with more than one member, the answer is no. These people are deemed to be business professionals who should know their responsibility to pay taxes.

If the drop shipper or consignor (that's somebody who consigns stuff to you to sell on eBay) was an individual or partnership, and you paid them more than $600 total during the calendar year, you are required to send them a 1099 form by January 31 next year.

If the drop shipper or consignor was an LLC with only one owner (called a *member*), and you paid them more than $600 total during the calendar year, send them a 1099 form by January 31 next year, even though you are not technically required to do that. A single-member LLC is considered a *disregarded entity* for tax purposes—in other words, inseparable from the person who owns it—and the rules aren't 100 percent clear about what you should do in this situation if your contractor fails to pay taxes and the IRS disregards his LLC. It takes about fifteen minutes to fill out Form 1099. For the peace of mind it gives you, if nothing else, it is worth the effort.

Q: ***"I am a very small sole proprietor and have provided over $600 in services to twelve customers in 2006, but I have received only one 1099 form to date. Am I responsible for the customers who have not mailed me the 1099? Some of my customers have sent me W-9 forms, but I haven't responded because I don't want them to know my Social Security number. My accountant told me I might be penalized for not responding to a request for a W-9 form. I am ready to mail my tax returns, but I don't know if I should mail them in without the 1099 forms from my customers. What should I do?"***

A: You must, of course, report all income your customers paid you and pay taxes on it, whether or not they sent you a 1099 form, but you are not required to attach 1099s to your tax return if your customers forgot to send them to you. Just attach the ones you did receive to your Form 1040 and off you go. It is your customers who should be concerned that they didn't send you 1099s. If you fail to report income you received from them and are later audited by the IRS, they may get caught up in your audit.

The W-9 question is a bit trickier. Form W-9, which is a Request for Taxpayer ID Number, is usually sent to independent contractors and others who must receive a Form 1099 at the end of the year. If someone sends you a W-9 form, you must fill it out and return it within thirty days. Otherwise, your customer may be required to withhold 31 percent of the interest, dividends, and certain other payments they make to you. This is called *backup withholding*. Furthermore, you may be subject to a $50 penalty from their failing to provide a W-9 upon demand.

Your reluctance to give your Social Security number to your customers is understandable. To avoid that, get a federal tax identification number for your business and use that on any W-9 forms you have to sign. Better yet, form a corporation for your business—that way, your customers won't have to send you Form 1099s at all, making you both very happy.

21 I've Got This Other Business . . .

Selling on eBay as an Extension of an Existing Brick-and-Mortar Business

Q: ***"I have an incorporated brick-and-mortar retail store and only recently began selling on eBay. Does it make sense to have a separate legal entity set up for my eBay business? Should I keep separate accounting and bookkeeping records?"***

A: It depends. If you are selling the same type of merchandise on eBay that you sell in your brick-and-mortar store, there is no compelling reason to have a separate legal entity for your eBay business. As long as you make sure your buyers on eBay know that they are dealing with your corporation or limited liability company (LLC), and not you personally, you should be sufficiently protected against any legal liability arising from your eBay selling activities. For example, your eBay user ID should be registered to your corporation, not you personally, and your About Me page on eBay should clearly state your corporation's name. I would also include a picture of the brick-and-mortar store, as it is always comforting for buyers on eBay to see that you are a real business that has been around for a while.

It may make sense to keep separate accounting and bookkeeping records for your eBay business, as that will make it easier for you to figure out how successful your online selling activities are vis-à-vis your brick-and-mortar store. You may find out, for example, that certain items are selling much more briskly on eBay than in your brick-and-mortar store or that your profit margins for certain items on eBay are greater than they are elsewhere. It's difficult and time consuming to do that when all your records are lumped together and you have to break everything out separately. I have actually known people who have shut down their brick-and-mortar stores entirely once they have become successful selling online!

Running Several Different Businesses Simultaneously on eBay

Q: ***"I run several different businesses on eBay. Do I have to file a Schedule C for each one?"***

A: Assuming that you are the only person involved in each of these businesses, the short answer is no—you can lump them all together on a single Schedule C and use the same federal and state tax ID numbers for each business.

The only time you should seriously consider separate Schedule Cs (and separate tax ID numbers) is when the businesses' income and deduction profiles are sufficiently different that separation gives the IRS a more accurate picture of what you are doing.

Let me explain . . .

A lawyer who has her own solo practice generally does not have much in the way of travel, meals, and entertainment expenses to deduct on her tax return. Even if she travels extensively, her clients normally pick up the tab for her meals, entertainment, and so forth. If the lawyer claims too much in travel, meals, and entertainment expenses on her tax return, she exposes herself to audit.

A professional speaker, on the other hand, normally has a considerable amount of travel, meals, and entertainment expenses. He is constantly on the road, and often the organization that's sponsoring his talk doesn't reimburse all of his travel, meals, and lodging. Most professional speakers I know keep detailed records of their expenses for tax time.

So a solo lawyer who is also a professional speaker has a bit of a dilemma: If she lumps her two businesses together on a single Schedule C, she will show a significant amount of travel, meals, and entertainment deductions, which might raise a few eyebrows at the IRS. She probably would be better advised to get a separate federal tax ID number for her professional speaking business, file two separate Schedule Cs, and allocate all of the travel, meals, and entertainment deductions to the professional speaking Schedule C, not her law practice Schedule C.

If you are engaged in multiple businesses that have different profiles for income or deductions, then you're well advised to file separate Schedule Cs for them.

One last point: If you have businesses with separate federal tax ID numbers, you *must* file separate Schedule Cs for each of them. You cannot combine multiple tax IDs on a single Schedule C or disregard one of the ID numbers—even if one of your businesses made no money this year, you should file a Schedule C for that business (and that tax ID) consisting of zeroes on each line. Once you obtain a federal tax ID number, the IRS expects to see a tax return for that number each year.

Q: ***"I sell laptops on eBay, and my wife sells children's clothing. We have separate eBay user IDs but have been combining all our sales proceeds in the same checking account. Does it make sense to put these in the same business or eBay Store?"***

A: It's a good idea to have separate eBay user IDs when you sell radically different merchandise on eBay. People are a little nervous about buying children's clothing from "bikerguy123," or a laptop computer from "suziesfantasies," even if those sellers have excellent feedback. That doesn't mean, though, that you have to treat them for tax purposes as two separate businesses.

What you have here is an informal partnership with your wife to sell things on eBay. As far as I'm concerned, that's just one business, even though you have multiple user IDs or eBay Stores. You should file IRS Form 1065 (partnership tax return) each year—although some accountants believe that's not necessary for a husband-and-wife partnership—and the corresponding tax form required by your state tax authority (if your state has an income tax). You should also have a federal tax ID number for the business, as the IRS allows only sole proprietors and other single-person businesses to use their Social Security number as a tax ID.

Now, I think it makes perfect sense to have separate eBay Stores for your laptops and your wife's clothing—in fact, I think you would be crazy to put both lines into a single store, because it would confuse your buyers. If you are selling lines of merchandise that have *synergy*—meaning that people who buy one line normally buy the other so you can cross-sell them—then putting them in the same eBay Store (or perhaps linked stores) makes some sense. I don't see much synergy, though, between laptops and children's clothing. Those two stores are going to look very different and will optimize very differently for search engines, if they are designed properly.

Selling Partnership Assets on eBay

Q: ***"I have a computer repair business with my cousin Joe. Just recently I started selling computer parts on eBay, and I've been doing pretty well. Some of these parts come from the inventory of the repair business. I really don't want to share the money from eBay with Cousin Joe. What can I do?"***

A: There is a legal term for what you are doing right now: *theft*. Stop it immediately!

When you are in partnership with someone (as you are right now with your cousin Joe), every asset of the business is owned *jointly* by the two of you. In other words, you do not own 100 percent of anything, Cousin Joe doesn't own 100 percent of anything—each of you owns 50 percent (or whatever percentage split you and he agreed to when you started the business) of every asset of the partnership, right down to the pencils and paper clips. By taking inventory and selling it on eBay without your cousin Joe's knowledge or approval, you are stealing from the business. If Cousin Joe doesn't mind that you are doing this, then you should be sharing the revenue from your eBay selling fifty-fifty with Cousin Joe (or whatever percentage split you and he agreed to when you started the business).

Also, if a sale on eBay goes bad and you are actually sued by the buyer, your cousin Joe will also be sued, since partners have what we lawyers call *joint and several liability*—if one goes down, they *all* go down together. Just imagine explaining to Cousin Joe that he's going to lose his house because of a sideline business you've been running for years behind his back.

If you are making money selling on eBay, make it a partnership business and share the proceeds.

Selling on eBay for a Family Manufacturing Business

Q: ***"My family runs a manufacturing business in the Philippines. My wife and I, who are U.S. citizens, want to sell our family's products on eBay. Do we have to do this as part of the family business, or can it be separate?"***

A: It's usually a good idea for overseas manufacturers to set up a U.S. importing business as a separate legal entity. Since the importing business is subject to U.S. laws, taxes, and regulations, and your family's company in the Philippines presumably does not have a U.S. presence of any kind right now, creating a separate company insulates your family's business from legal and tax liability in the United States.

By setting the U.S. company up as a limited liability company (LLC) or regular C corporation, members of your family who live in the Philippines could become part owners (shareholders of a corporation or members of an LLC) of the company without incurring personal U.S. tax liability (the shareholders of a Subchapter S corporation can be only U.S. citizens or green card holders). The Philippines company could also make an investment in the U.S. business (i.e., purchase shares) in exchange for a percentage of the business's profits and losses. It could also make loans to the U.S. business. You may, however, have to withhold certain taxes on dividends and other distributions of income to business owners who are not resident in the United States (see IRS Publication 515 and Form 1042).

To simplify your accounting and bookkeeping, the U.S. business should be the entity that sells on eBay and should pay all federal and state taxes.

As for how the U.S. company imports goods from the Philippines company, this can be structured in one of two ways: as a *sales agency* or as a *distributorship*.

In an agency relationship, the U.S. company would sell the Philippines company's goods on eBay, keep a percentage of the winning bid amount as a *sales commission*, and remit the balance to the Philippines company, and the Philippines company would ship goods directly to the buyers on eBay (similar to a drop-shipping or consignment arrangement). Title to the goods passes directly from the Philippines company to the ultimate buyer.

In a distributor relationship, the Philippines company would ship the goods to the U.S. company, which would pay a wholesale price for the goods up front. The U.S. company would then warehouse the goods in the United States, sell them on eBay, and keep 100 percent of the proceeds for themselves (similar to a true wholesaler-retailer relationship). Title to the goods passes first from the Philippines company to the U.S. company, then from the U.S. company to the ultimate buyer.

Multiple Businesses on eBay, with Different Owners

Q: ***"I have a corporation that runs my eBay selling business. I've been approached by a leading Web designer in our area, and we're thinking of going into business together to design eBay Stores for people. Should I offer her shares in my corporation, and if things don't work out, how can I legally get rid of her?"***

A: Whenever you're thinking about bringing a partner into your business, keep this one thing in mind: If things don't work out with that partner, there is only one way you can legally get rid of him or her. That is to buy the person out, for whatever price he or she is willing to accept. You can't just tear up the person's stock certificates and pretend that nothing had ever happened.

It sounds as if you don't know this person really well. If that's right, then don't give her any shares in your corporation, because by doing that she is legally entitled to a percentage of *all* your eBay selling profits, not just the profits from your eBay Store design business. Unless she is willing to roll up her sleeves and help you create listings with Turbo Lister 2, she shouldn't be entitled to any piece of your eBay earnings.

I recommend that you form a separate limited liability company (LLC) for the eBay Store design business, so that business is kept separate from your existing corporation. Then offer her a small ownership percentage (not more than 25 percent) of the LLC, with the understanding that as the LLC business reaches certain agreed-upon revenue or profit levels (called *milestones*), she will be entitled to additional percentages until she is your 50 percent partner.

Such an arrangement (called an *earn-in*) would look something like the following in your LLC operating agreement:

> The parties agree that Mary will initially receive a 20 percent membership interest in the Company, provided that Mary will be entitled to an additional 10 percent membership interest when the Company has earned $100,000 in aggregate revenue with a gross margin of at least 30 percent, an additional 10 percent membership when the Company has earned $250,000 in aggregate revenue with a gross margin of at least 20 percent, and an additional 10 percent membership interest when the Company has earned $500,000 in aggregate

revenue with a gross margin of at least 10 percent; provided, however, that under no circumstances will Mary be entitled to receive more than a 50 percent membership interest in the Company.

Building a Holding Company Structure

Q: ***"My brother and I have been selling merchandise on eBay for the last few months and would like to establish a business formation. Once we have formalized our company, we plan on creating and utilizing our own website. Our website will have items for sale in addition to links to our active eBay auctions. Our auctions have consisted primarily of the resale of women's clothing and accessories (similar to an online consignment, but we are purchasing the items from individuals and then looking to flip them on eBay for a profit.) We hope to expand our sources for merchandise in the future.***

"We were thinking to establish a parent company, and we would like to have the ability to create subsidiaries that fall under the umbrella of the parent company. For example, we would like our website to have a different, jazzier name than that of the parent company. Our view is that down the line we might want separate entities that will focus on different things. In the future we might look into opening a small storefront or showroom specific to our product lines that will complement the website. Is this the best way to go about setting up our eBay business?"

A: This is called a *holding company* structure, and it is a very common way to organize a large-scale eBay selling business dealing with multiple product lines both on and off eBay.

You begin by forming a Subchapter S corporation or limited liability company (LLC) that is merely an umbrella—it owns shares in all the underlying companies that actually buy and sell on eBay, but the parent company itself does not engage in any real business. Then you set up *operating* companies (either LLCs or Subchapter S corporations if they are each 100 percent owned by the parent company) that engage in the actual buying and selling of goods on eBay, own the website, and engage in any related business activities.

Since forming corporations and LLCs is expensive, and the legal paperwork involved in operating multiple corporations can take up tons of management time that is better spent getting stuff sold on eBay, you may want to consider starting out with just a single corporation or LLC (the *parent*) and filing trade-name or "doing business as" (DBA) certificates (see Chapter 2) for each line of business you wish to engage in. Then, as the business grows and you can afford to deal with the paperwork this structure entails, you can form new corporations and LLCs, and have the parent company buy stock in each of these *subsidiaries* in exchange for the *assets* of one or more of your business lines.

Sound complicated? It is. Don't even think about building a corporate structure like this without the help of a good lawyer, a good accountant/tax adviser, and at least a few employees who can handle some of the grunt paperwork that needs to be done to keep track of everything.

Appendix A

Still Don't Have Your Answer? Business Resources for eBay Entrepreneurs

Books

To be a successful eBay seller, you need to build a modest library of reference books. Here are the twelve books on eBay and e-commerce I would take with me to a desert island. You should be able to score copies of all of them for less than $250 total. Many of these authors have written multiple books about eBay, so be sure to check out their other listings on Amazon.com or BarnesandNoble.com (or, for that matter, eBay!).

1. *eBay Business The Smart Way: Buying and Selling Internationally on the World's #1 Auction Site,* by Joseph T. Sinclair (AMACOM, 2004).
2. *The Seven Essential Steps to Successful eBay Marketing,* by Janelle Elms, Phil Dunn, and Amy Balsbaugh (McGraw-Hill Osborne, 2005).
3. *Search Engine Advertising: Buying Your Way to the Top to Increase Sales,* by Catherine Seda (New Riders Press, 2004).
4. *How to Win Sales and Influence Spiders: Boosting Your Business and Buzz on the Web,* by Catherine Seda (New Riders Press, 2007). I know—two books by the same author, but she's really good!
5. *eBay Millionaire or Bust: Hidden Strategies That Maximize Profits and Create Wealth,* by Corey Kossack (Entrepreneur Education Group, 2007).
6. *Easy Auction Photography: A Guide for Everyone Who Sells on the Internet,* by Cindy Shebley (self-published by the author, available at www.ghostlegproductions.com).

7. *eBay Timesaving Techniques for Dummies,* by Marsha Collier (For Dummies, 2004).
8. *eBay PowerSeller Secrets: Insider Tips from eBay's Most Successful Sellers,* by Debra and Brad Schepp (second edition, McGraw-Hill, 2007).
9. *How to Start and Run an eBay Consignment Business,* by Skip McGrath (McGraw-Hill, 2006).
10. *eBay Performance! Selling Success with Market Research and Product Sourcing,* by Robin Cowie and Jen Cano (BookSurge Publishing, 2007).
11. *Export/Import Procedures and Documentation,* by Thomas Johnson (AMACOM, 2002).
12. *The eBay Seller's Tax and Legal Answer Book: Everything You Need to Know to Keep the Government Off Your Back and Out of Your Wallet,* by Cliff Ennico (AMACOM, 2007).

Videos, DVDs, and E-Courses

Sometimes it isn't enough to read about something—you have to actually see it being done. Here are some great videos that will help you get your answers visually:

The eBay Store Success Video, by Janelle Elms. More than four hours of eBay Store tips and tactics. Available at http://stores.ebay.com/Auction-Profit-Education-Consulting.

The Complete eBay Marketing System, by Skip McGrath. Available at http://www.skipmcgrath.com/products/ebaypackage.shtml.

Add Video to eBay Auctions, by Cindy Shebley. Available at http://www.ezauctionphotos.com.

Classes/One-on-One Instruction

Sometimes even video isn't enough—you just have to *talk* to someone! There are a lot of people out there giving classes, but only a handful really know what they're talking about.

When looking for one-on-one instruction on running an eBay business, consider:

- *eBay Certified Education Specialists.* These people are usually (but not always) eBay PowerSellers who give adult education classes on eBay at local high schools, community colleges, and other such venues. To find one near you, go to http://www.poweru.net/ebay/student/searchIndex.asp and type in your city, state, and zip code. Be sure to ask the specialists what level of experience they have on eBay—you're looking for someone who doesn't just talk the talk but walks the walk as well.
- *eBay Certified Business Consultants.* These people have been trained by eBay not only in how to teach buying and selling on eBay but also in the basics of running an e-commerce business. To find one near you, go to http://www.poweru.net/ebay/student/bizCons.asp and type in your city, state, and zip code. The Certified Business Consultant program is relatively new, and there are only a handful of people around the country who have passed eBay's rigorous training requirements. Be prepared to travel some distance (or pay the consultant's travel and lodging expenses to visit your business). These people are probably the best resource for an existing brick-and-mortar retail business that's looking to add eBay as a distribution channel.
- *eBay University.* Every weekend a team of eBay experts, including Jim "Uncle Griff" Griffith and PayPal guru Jason Miner, travel the country giving all-day programs on the finer points of selling on eBay and introducing eBayers to their local Certified Education Specialists. To find out when these programs are held in your area, go to the eBay site, click on Help, then Learning Center, then Classroom Instruction.

Lawyers, Accountants, and Other Professionals

Some questions can be answered only by lawyers, accountants, tax professionals, insurance brokers, and other experts. When you are in business, you need a good lawyer and a good accountant, and you need to pay them well—there is no exception for eBay sellers. Nobody likes paying professional fees, just as nobody likes paying taxes, but it's a cost of doing business, and, hey, it's deductible!

There are several websites that offer to help you find lawyers and accountants in your zip code (such as www.findlaw.com), but don't use them to find help for an eBay business, because their search mechanisms aren't specific enough (you can find a "small business attorney" on findlaw.com, for example, but this person may never even have heard of eBay).

The best place to find lawyers and accountants for an eBay business is on the eBay discussion boards and groups. In fact, this is one of the best uses of the Community features on the eBay site. Click on the Community tab on the eBay home page, click on Groups, find the group for your area or region, and post a request for recommendations for "a good attorney and accountant in the following town (give them city, state, and zip code) who really understand what we do on eBay." If the same names crops up more than once, give that person a call. And don't be afraid to negotiate their fees the same way you would the fees for one of your suppliers!

Appendix B

Finding the Answers You Need on the eBay Website: A Step-by-Step Tutorial

The best place to get answers to your "how do I use eBay?" questions is on the eBay website itself. There is an absolute treasure trove of information on eBay's website for people selling on eBay—if you're willing to take the time to look for it.

Step 1: Get the Answer on eBay's Seller Central and Help Pages

Go to eBay's home page and look in the upper-right-hand corner. You will see five tabs, labeled Buy, Sell, My eBay, Community, and Help. Clicking on two of these tabs—Sell and Help—can help you access all of the seller-related information and content on the eBay website.

As you would expect, clicking on the Sell tab opens the door to hundreds of pages of information and advice on how to sell on eBay, including a step-by-step tutorial on how to set up and post an eBay listing.

Click on the Sell tab, scroll down to the very bottom of the page, and click on the Seller Central page. *Bookmark this page*—eBay has a nasty habit of moving this thing around, and you should know where it is at all times.

The Seller Central page is a site map to all of the seller-related information, advice, and resources on eBay. Click on the Resources tab, and you will see a directory of mini-tutorials on virtually all topics of interest to eBay sellers.

Now, go back to the Seller Central page, click on Getting Started, then scroll down to the bottom of the page and click on Merchant Center. You will see yet another directory of information and tutorials for people looking to build a real business on eBay.

Now go back to the eBay home page. Click on the Help tab in the upper-right-hand corner, then scroll down to the bottom of the page. You will see yet another directory, organized by topic, with links to information, advice, and answers to your specific questions.

Now, scroll back up to the top of the Help page and click on A–Z Index. Here you will find answers to the most common eBay questions (organized alphabetically by topic) as well as links to more specialized advice pages on the eBay website. For example, click on the letter "P," then scroll down to the word "Policy," and you will see an alphabetical list of virtually all of eBay's policies and rules for sellers. Make it a point to read one of these a day, and soon you will have the answers to the most common questions eBay sellers have about them.

Finally, if you still can't find the answer, you can click on the Contact Us link on the Help page and ask questions via e-mail, which will be answered by members of eBay's customer support team based in Salt Lake City, Utah.

Virtually 99.9 percent of all questions sellers have about doing business on eBay can be answered from the Seller Central and Help pages of the eBay site. Before going to the Community section and asking for help from other community members, it's always a good idea to spend at least one hour trying to find the information on eBay. Most of the time, you will find the answer you need in that time frame.

Step 2: Ask the Community

eBay is really two things: It's a Fortune 100 corporation based in San Jose, California, that operates a platform for people to sell things to and buy things from each other online, of course, but it's also a community of more than two hundred million people worldwide who are engaged in online buying and selling activities. With that many people, there ought to be *someone* out there who can answer your question!

Go to the eBay home page and click on the Community tab in the upper-right-hand corner. You will see a directory of Community resources on the eBay site.

First, scroll down to the Education section and click on the Workshops link. Here you will see online classes, called *webinars*, conducted by eBay and Pay-

Pal employees, eBay experts (including me), and eBay community members who have specialized knowledge of all things eBay. *Bookmark this page,* and check it out every couple of weeks or so. These workshops are interactive—you can ask questions of the workshop presenter "live" via e-mail—and you will learn a lot about the issues and problems that most frequently bedevil eBay sellers. Make it your goal to attend at least one eBay workshop a month—they're free, after all!

Now go back to the Community page, scroll down to the Education page again, and click on the Mentoring Group link. A number of prominent eBay sellers have set up mentoring groups to help eBayers who share a common interest, such as selling video games on eBay or dealing in rare books. Joining one of these groups gives you access to fast advice when you need it.

Finally, go back to the Community page and click on the Answer Center link. This is the peer-to-peer page, where eBay community members give advice, support, and the occasional hug to each other. Click on the PayPal link, for example, and you will see hundreds of pages of discussion threads (a posted question, followed by answer posts) relating to PayPal issues. Skim the first ten or fifteen pages of discussion threads—I almost guarantee you that your question has been asked by another community member before, and you will find the answer here. If you see the answer to your question here, *do not post a redundant question.* That just wastes everyone's time and gets the Answer Center regulars really ticked off at your naivete and thoughtlessness.

If your question has never been asked in the appropriate Answer Center thread, it means one of two possible things: Either your question is so unique or new that no one has asked it before (in which case you should be the first to post the question in the Answer Center) or your question is so obvious and dumb that everybody else is finding the answer easily on the eBay site without having to disturb the "sleeping Rottweilers" that lurk in the eBay Answer Center pages. Make no mistake—if you ask a dumb, obvious question in the Answer Center, these folks will tell you nicely but in no uncertain terms to stop wasting their time.

It is your responsibility as an eBay seller to know and learn about what you are doing on eBay. Devote an hour or two a day to studying the eBay Seller Central, Help, and Community Answer Center threads thoroughly, and pretty soon you won't have to ask questions anymore!

Step 3: Ask an Expert

Sometimes when you have a question, you just have to talk to a human being. There are a lot of people out there giving classes, but only a handful really know what they're talking about.

When looking for one-on-one instruction on running an eBay business, consider:

- *eBay Certified Education Specialists.* These people are usually (but not always) eBay PowerSellers who give adult education classes on eBay at local high schools, community colleges, and other such venues. To find one near you, go to the Seller Central page on eBay, scroll down to the bottom of the page, click on Merchant Solutions Center, scroll down to the bottom of that page, and click on Education Specialists. You will see a list of the top-ranked Certified Education Specialists around the country. Pick the one closest to you, click on the link, and you will be taken to the person's website, where you can find out where classes are being held, what they're all about on eBay, and so forth. Be sure to ask these specialists what level of experience they have on eBay—you're looking for someone who doesn't just talk the talk but walks the walk as well.
- *eBay Certified Business Consultants.* These people have been trained by eBay not only in how to teach buying and selling on eBay but also in the basics of running an e-commerce business. To find one near you, go to http://www.poweru.net/ebay/student/bizCons.asp and type in your city, state, and zip code. The Certified Business Consultant program is relatively new, and there are only a handful of people around the country who have passed eBay's rigorous training requirements. Be prepared to travel some distance (or pay the consultant's travel and lodging expenses to visit your business), but these people are probably the best resource for an existing brick-and-mortar retail business that's looking to add eBay as a distribution channel.
- *eBay University.* Every weekend a team of eBay experts, including Jim "Uncle Griff" Griffith and PayPal guru Jason Miner, travel the country giving all-day programs on the finer points of selling on eBay and intro-

ducing eBayers to their local Certified Education Specialists. To find out when these programs are held in your area, go to the eBay site, click on Help, then Learning Center, then Classroom Instruction.

- *eBay Radio/PayPal Radio.* Once a week Jim "Uncle Griff" Griffith holds forth on his Internet radio show, and he takes calls! Go to www.wsradio.com and click on eBay Radio for details. Also, PayPal expert Jason Miner (who is quoted several times in this book) has a show of his own: Go to www.wsradio.com and click on PayPal Radio for details.

Appendix C

Ten Things to Do Before You Ask a Question on eBay

One of the admitted goals of this book is to reduce the number of redundant postings on eBay's Community section pages. The eBay members who take the time and trouble to help other community members in the eBay Answer Center are truly beautiful human beings, and I really hate to see their time wasted answering the same questions over and over again. They deserve better.

Ideally, the only questions that should be posted on eBay are questions that truly haven't been asked by anyone before. Before you post a question on the eBay Answer Center or approach one of eBay's customer service representatives, you should at least make an effort to get the answer yourself. Here are ten things you should do before you ask a question on eBay; by following these steps, you will never ask the same question twice and you will be sure your question is a darn good one before you throw it blindly into the eBay community for discussion.

1. *Calm down.* Many of the postings in the eBay Answer Center are obviously written in the heat of extreme emotion or frustration, especially those dealing with "bad buyers" and eBay's (alleged) failure to police all its policies all the time. Count to ten before you vent on eBay. Try to consider things from the other (the buyer's, or eBay's) point of view, and ask yourself if your listing, behavior, or conduct on eBay has contributed to the problem. Nothing, and I mean *nothing,* is more embarrassing than to post a question on eBay, looking for sympathy and support, only to have fifteen people point out that the problem was entirely your fault and you have only yourself to blame (with your eBay user ID posted prominently on each response so that everyone can see what an idiot you are).

2. *Brush up on your English.* Many of the postings on eBay's Answer Center are riddled with misspelled words, typographical errors, and poor grammar—so many, in fact, that I have concluded that many of the people asking questions

there simply are not fluent enough in the English language to look up the answers themselves. While you do not have to be fluent in English to sell on eBay, it does help when you are using eBay's educational or community resources, which are primarily, if not exclusively, in English.

If you do not speak English fluently, have someone who does (your spouse, a business partner, or employee) help you find the answers you need on the eBay website before you post a question on the Answer Center that was answered in a previous discussion thread.

3. *Skim the chapter headings in this book.* Most business books are organized by subject matter heading. Since many eBay sellers do not know which heading their question falls under, I have attempted to make it easier for them to find the answers they need by asking general or big-picture questions in the chapter headings themselves. So, for example, all questions relating to eBay Stores can be found in the chapter titled "Should I Set Up an eBay Store?" (Chapter 15).

Questions within each chapter are organized from general to specific. Find the chapter heading that comes closest to the question you actually have, then skim through the questions in each chapter until you find the one closest to the one you want to ask.

4. *Look for the answer on eBay's Seller Central page.* Click the Sell tab on any eBay webpage and find the link to the Seller Central page on eBay. This is a site map to all the seller resources available on eBay's website, organized by topic. With just a few minutes of searching, you should be able to find the answer to your question.

5. *Check the alphabetical listing in eBay's Help section.* Click the Help tab on any eBay webpage, and find the link to the A–Z Index. With a little searching, you probably can find a link to a page that answers your question.

For example, are you thinking about doing something on eBay but you're worried that it might violate one of eBay's many user policies? Go to the A–Z Index, click on the letter "P," then scroll down to the word "Policy." Voila! Almost all of eBay's policies are listed here, in alphabetical order. Sit down with a pot of strong coffee and read every single one of them. Now you no longer have an excuse for being booted off eBay because you didn't know about their policies! As we lawyers have said for centuries, "Ignorance of the law is no excuse."

6. *Look for a community workshop.* Go to the following page: http://pages.ebay.com/community/workshopcalendar/current.html. Whenever eBay members are getting stuck in a particular area, eBay employees, other community

members, or experts (including me) are asked to host online webinars, or workshops, that walk people through the process step-by-step. Almost always, whenever eBay changes its user policies or updates one of its software tools, it hosts a workshop about the changes.

Skim the workshop listings and sign up for any workshops that relate to the question you have—they're free! Even if the host doesn't specifically answer your question during the workshop, you can ask your question in real time by e-mail during the workshop, and the host will answer it.

Missed a workshop that related to your question? Not to worry—click on one of the Archives links on the left-hand side of the page. Finished workshops (both the host's content and the back-and-forth discussion threads between the host and people who asked questions during the workshop) remain on the site for a long time. You can even e-mail the host of that workshop if you don't think your specific question was addressed.

Go back far enough in the workshop archives and I'm sure you will find a workshop that related to your question—just don't go back too far or the information might be out of date!

As a committed eBay seller, you should make it a point to participate in at least one eBay workshop each month—the more you do this, the fewer questions you will have.

7. *Read the PayPal User Agreement.* Most of the PayPal questions in eBay's community Answer Center are covered in PayPal's User Agreement. To find this, go to the PayPal home page, click on the Legal Agreements link at the bottom of the page, then click on User Agreement in the left-hand column.

Despite being a legal document, PayPal's User Agreement is written in plain English and is fairly easy to understand. Print it out, sit down with a pot of strong coffee, and read the User Agreement cover to cover. It won't take more than an hour or two, and I guarantee it will answer most of your PayPal-related questions.

For example, many PayPal users with a personal account are shocked when their accounts are frozen without warning. One of the most common reasons for this (spelled out in Section 4.1 of the User Agreement) is that their monthly account balance has exceeded $500. When that happens, PayPal wants you to upgrade your account to Business or Premier status (and pay higher fees for the upgrade) before they will allow you to receive funds in excess of $500 per month. Upgrade your account, and it will be unfrozen.

One of the most common questions regarding PayPal is "When do my eBay listings qualify for PayPal's Seller Protection Policy?" Read Section 11.3 of the User Agreement, and you will have your answer.

8. *Review the latest threads in eBay's community Answer Center.* Still haven't found your answer? Okay, now I think it's time to look at the eBay community Answer Center (click on the Community tab, then scroll down to Answer Center), but *don't post your question yet*! Skim the first ten or fifteen pages of the eBay Answer Center and see if someone else has asked a similar question. I am pretty sure you will find that someone has. I am amazed to see people asking questions that are (almost) word-for-word identical to a question posted just a few entries down on the same page! But don't waste a lot of time—if you don't see anything closely resembling your question in the first ten or fifteen pages, then it's time to post your question. If it's been asked before, someone will point you to the prior thread where you can get your answer.

9. *Develop a continuing education program.* There's a lot to learn about eBay, and you will never know everything there is to know. Find an hour or two every week to study the eBay website, participate in a workshop, read the latest threads in the eBay community Answer Center, and otherwise keep on top of things. Make it a part of your eBay routine.

Lawyers, doctors, and other professionals in many states are required by law to attend continuing education classes to stay on top of new techniques and developments in their fields. You're a professional, too, when you sell on eBay, and you have no less an obligation to educate yourself.

10. *Find Certified Education Specialists—and pay them for their time.* Believe it or not, there are eBay PowerSellers around the country who have been specifically trained by eBay to answer your most common questions. They are called eBay Certified Education Specialists, and you can find the one nearest you at http://www.poweru.net/ebay/student/searchIndex.asp.

Certified Education Specialists normally host classes for eBay members at local high schools, community colleges, and other adult education venues. Many will take the time to provide you with one-on-one consulting, but you should expect to pay them an hourly fee for personalized assistance.

When All Else Fails, You Can Ask Me, but Beware . . .

I'm always on the lookout for eBay-related questions that haven't been asked before. If you have followed the ten steps in this appendix and you still don't have your answer, feel free to send me an e-mail at crennico@gmail.com, and either I will answer your question or I will forward it to an eBay expert who will answer it. But be advised . . .

- My time (like yours) is extremely valuable. If your question is not truly unique, new, or different, or if I feel you haven't taken the time to find the answer on your own using the steps outlined in Appendix B, I will either ignore your e-mail or respond with a message saying "Seek and Ye Shall Find."
- You will not get your answer immediately—expect a delay of a few days to two weeks at the maximum before I can get an answer back to you.
- You agree that your question may appear in the next edition of this book (without your name or eBay user ID being mentioned, of course).

Appendix D

The Best Nonbusiness Books for eBay Sellers

Very often, the best books for entrepreneurs have little if anything to do with business per se.

Let me explain. . . .

When you're starting out in your own business, your first and biggest challenge is to get customers or clients. It's the biggest challenge because in business you have absolutely no control over customers and what they want. You can be the greatest business genius since J. P. Morgan, but if you're selling products and services no one wants to buy, you will find yourself in bankruptcy court along with all of the ignoramuses.

Getting customers and generating sales does not require a knowledge of business so much as it does an appreciation of human nature. Virtually all of my most successful small business clients spend a lot of time and effort crawling inside their customers' heads and learning what makes them tick. Show me an entrepreneur who understands how the human mind works and has a keen understanding of the forces shaping and changing American society and culture, and I will (almost always) show you a successful entrepreneur.

To understand your customers and spot market opportunities before your competition does, I strongly suggest that you leave the Business section of your bookstore behind and mosey on over to the Psychology and Sociology sections. Very often, the best books for your business can be found there.

Here are some excellent nonbusiness books that will help you build a successful business. They are also fun to read.

Amusing Ourselves to Death: Public Discourse in the Age of Show Business, by Neal Postman (Viking, 1985). Anybody who wants to understand how modern American society works needs to read every book written by Neal Postman. Originally published in 1985 (before the Internet!), this groundbreaking book describes the corrosive effects of television on American society. Postman's theme is the decline of the printed word and the ascendancy of the "tube," with its tendency to present everything—murder, mayhem, politics, even weather—as entertainment.

Life: The Movie: How Entertainment Conquered Reality, by Neal Gabler (Knopf, 1998). A leading Hollywood historian and biographer of Walt Disney, Gabler takes Postman's thesis a step further and argues that the omnipresence of media in our lives is causing us to lose our grip on reality. Instead of confronting life as it is, Gabler argues, we develop and act out "scripts" as if we were acting in a movie or theatrical production. Anyone who has ever waited in line at a Starbucks will understand completely what Gabler is talking about.

Rejuvenile: Kickball, Cartoons, Cupcakes, and the Reinvention of the American Grown-up, by Christopher Noxon (Crown, 2006). A funny but sobering account of how Baby Boomers and Generation Xers have cast aside traditional notions of maturity in favor of indulging their "inner children" well into middle age. (In a related vein, although with a more polemical bent, see *The Death of the Grown-Up: How America's Arrested Development Is Bringing Down Western Civilization,* by Diana West, St. Martin's Press, 2007.)

Bobos in Paradise: The New Upper Class and How They Got There, by David Brooks (Simon & Schuster, 2001). Observers of the Baby Boom generation have long noted two contradictory impulses: their ruthless drive to succeed in business and their adoption of the bohemian, "hippie" lifestyles and beliefs of the 1960s and 1970s counterculture. Brooks's book attempts to reconcile these two extremes by pointing out the ways in which Boomers are increasingly using capitalistic means to achieve socialistic ends.

The Paradox of Choice: Why More Is Less, by Barry Schwartz (Ecco, 2003). A persuasive argument that human beings can handle only so many choices at a given time and that a marketer's challenge is to find the optimum number of options for customers, without attempting to customize products and services for every single individual on earth. Required reading for anyone who owns an eBay Store.

I'm a Stranger Here Myself: Notes on Returning to America After Twenty Years Away, by Bill Bryson (Broadway, 1999). The dust jacket calls Bryson a "humorist," which I don't think is right, because he isn't really funny (*droll* would be a better word). But this collection of newspaper articles, written by an American who returned to the United States after a twenty-year stint abroad, contains some very sharp and subtle perceptions about how America changed during the 1980s and 1990s.

The e-Myth Revisited: Why Most Small Businesses Don't Work and What to Do About It, by Michael Gerber (HarperCollins, 1995). Probably the best book ever written on what it truly means to be an entrepreneur. Gerber's thesis—that most self-employed people are "technicians" who focus on day-to-day operations and "doing the job" at the expense of building a business with lasting value and "getting the job done"—is one that will resonate loudly with eBay sellers who are so busy listing items and packing boxes that they have no idea what business they're in or even how much they're making.

Democracy in America, by Alexis de Tocqueville. Observations of America by non-Americans, intended for an overseas market, are always worth reading. This is one of the oldest, and still the best. If you didn't read it in college, now's the time—we may look a lot different than we did in Tocqueville's time, but we're still basically the same people. Or, as the French say, "The more things change, the more they remain the same."

Happy reading!

Appendix E

Checklist: Some Expenses an eBay Seller (Usually) Can Deduct

NOTE: This list is for general guidance only and is not exhaustive. Some deductions are subject to rules and limits not covered in this checklist. If you have a home office, items marked with an asterisk (*) can be deducted only to the extent of your home office percentage (square feet of home office and related storage space divided by total square feet of home—see Chapter 19).

Accountant's fees

Advances to professionals (prepaid fees)

Advertising expenses

Alarm systems*

Answering service

Assessments for sewer repairs*

Association dues (if business related)

Attorneys' fees

Audits

Automobile expenses (subject to certain restrictions)

Automobile leases (but not 100 percent—see IRS Publication 463 for details)

Bad or bounced checks that buyers write you

Bad debts

Bank charges

Bankruptcy filings

Bartered goods

Billboard advertising

Bonuses to employees (not to yourself)

Bookkeeping fees

Books (if business related)

Building depreciation*

Business association dues

Business cards

Business gifts up to $25 in any one year

Business licenses and registrations

Business trips

Carrying charges

Casualty losses (if not covered by insurance)

Charitable contributions

Cleaning service*

Club dues (if business related)

Coffee service

Commissions to finders or brokers for referring sales

Compensation to employees (including family members, but not to yourself)

Computers

Conferences (such as eBay Live!)

Construction expenses*

Consulting fees you pay to others

Contract preparation fees

Copyrights

Courier service

Credit card chargebacks

Credit card fees and interest (if business related)

Customs fees, duties, and tariffs

Damages for breach of contract (including punitive damages), unless imposed by a government agency

Day care for employees' children (not your own)

Decorating expenses*

Delivery/freight charges on goods you sell

Deposits (if nonrefundable)

Depreciation on business equipment

Design costs (e.g., Web design)

Disability insurance for your employees (not yourself)

Dues to business groups

eBay insertion, option/enhancement, and final value fees

eBay Live! convention

Education expenses (but only if the class maintains or improves a skill required in your business)

Electricity and other utilities*

Employee wages and benefits

Employment agency fees

Employment/payroll taxes

Entertainment expenses (50 percent)

Equipment

Expenses incurred by employees that you reimburse

Extermination service*

Family members on payroll

Fees paid to consignors (reduce your income, but not technically deductible)

Fees paid to drop shippers (reduce your income, but not technically deductible)

Fees paid to independent contractors (such as accountants and bookkeepers)

FICA (Social Security) taxes paid for employees

Finance charges for things you purchase with a credit card

Flowers given as gifts to employees, clients, etc.

Freight costs on goods you sell

Fringe benefits to employees

Fuel (unless you are using the mileage deduction)

Furniture

FUTA (federal unemployment tax) paid for employees

Garbage service*

Greeting cards to business clients, employees, etc.

Grooming expenses (if traveling on business)

Group health insurance for your employees (not for yourself)

Guard dog (Rottweiler yes, Pomeranian no)

Handicapped access compliance costs*

Health insurance for employees

Health insurance for yourself, spouses, and dependents (unless you are eligible for insurance through your day job employer)

Heating expenses

Home improvements*

Homeowner's association fees*

Import fees

Insurance premiums for business insurance (liability, business interruption, property/casualty)

Interest on business loans

Interest on personal loans if the proceeds were used in your business

Internet access fees

Inventory taxes

Janitorial service

Kickbacks (if legal)

Landscaping/lawn maintenance expenses (except for home office)

Leases of automobiles (with special limits and rules)

Leases of office or retail space

Legal fees

Life insurance on employees

Lobbying expenses if less than $2,000 (with some exceptions)

Lodging (when traveling on business)

Long-term care insurance for employees

Long-term care insurance for yourself, spouse, and dependents (with some limits)

Magazines and newsletters (if business related)

Mailing list rentals and purchases

Market research expenses

Meals while traveling on business (50 percent)

Meals with customers and suppliers (50 percent)

Medical emergency supplies (i.e., first aid kit)

Medicare tax paid for employees

Membership fees (if business related)

Messenger service

Mileage allowance

Moving expenses*

Music system (with some limits)

Net operating losses

Newsletters and newspapers

Office equipment

Office party (if open to all employees)

Office plants

Office supplies

Parking costs

PayPal fees

Payroll expenses (other than for yourself)

Payroll taxes

Pension plans

Personal property taxes

PESA (Professional eBay Seller's Alliance) membership dues

Postage

Post office box or private mailbox (e.g., UPS Store)

Prepaid expenses

Prizes to customers and suppliers

Property taxes*

Rebates you pay to others (if legal)

Referral fees you pay to others (if legal)

Refunds on returned goods (but goods are added back to inventory)

Repairs of business property

Retirement plan contributions for employees

Safe deposit boxes

Safety equipment

Salaries to employees (not to yourself)

Section 179 deduction for equipment

Service contracts and extended warranties

Sewer charges

Shoplifting losses

Signs

Social Security tax (employer's portion only)

Software (depreciate over three years)

SquareTrade fees

Start-up costs (amortize over five years)

State taxes

Stationery used for business

Stereo system (with some limits)

Stolen equipment (to the extent not depreciated)

Stolen inventory (as part of cost of goods sold)

Storage costs (i.e., rent of a storage unit)

Taxes (other than federal income and self-employment taxes)

Telephone services, fees, and taxes

Tips (50 percent, if part of an otherwise deductible business meal)

Toll charges for vehicles

Trademarks (amortize over fifteen-year period)

Trade show admission fees

Transportation and travel expenses (other than commuting to and from work)

Trucks used for business

TurboTax Online Premier for eBay Sellers, fees for using

Uncashed checks

Unemployment insurance payments

Unemployment taxes (including state disability funds)

Use taxes

Utilities*

Vehicle expenses (with many restrictions and limits)

Wages paid to employees

Warehouse costs

Water utilities

Website design and hosting

Worthless inventory (as part of cost of goods sold)

Yellow Pages ads and listings

Appendix F

Checklist: Some Expenses an eBay Seller (Usually) Cannot Deduct

NOTE: This list is for general guidance only and is not exhaustive. Some rules regarding nondeductible expenses are subject to exceptions not covered in this checklist.

Allowance for bad debts (as opposed to bad debts themselves)

Antiques (unless sold as inventory)

Artwork (unless sold as inventory)

Athletic club dues (unless on-premises and open to all employees)

Bounced checks you write to someone else

Boxes (are part of inventory)

Bribes and illegal kickbacks

Bubble wrap (is part of inventory)

Campaign contributions (political)

Cartons (are part of inventory)

Clothing (unless a uniform worn by all employees)

Commuting expenses

Containers (are part of inventory)

Contributions to capital of a business

Day care for your own children

Deposits (if refundable)

Disability insurance (for yourself)

Discounts given to customers (these reduce your income, but are not deductions)

Estimated tax payments

Expenses of spouse in attending convention or conference (unless he/she is an employee)

Fines and penalties for breaking the law

Freight charges for inventory/assets you purchase

Gardening and lawn care expenses for a home office

Goods you hold on consignment for others (are not inventory)

Grooming expenses (except when traveling on business)

Group health insurance for yourself

Hobby expenses

Illegal expenses (e.g., illegal kickbacks)

Income taxes

Interest on back taxes

Investment expenses

Kickbacks (if illegal)

Landscaping/lawn maintenance expenses for home office

Laundry expenses (except uniforms worn by employees)

Life insurance on yourself

Meals at work

Owner's compensation

Packaging materials (are part of inventory)

Parking tickets

Penalties and fines for breaking the law

Plastic packing peanuts (are part of inventory)

Political contributions

Reserves for bad debts

Sales and use taxes (are added to inventory)

Self-employment taxes (although can deduct part of it on your personal Form 1040)

Self-insurance

Shipping supplies (are added to inventory)

Tax penalties

Appendix G

Demystifying the Business Organization, or How to Select the Right Legal Entity for Your eBay Selling Business

I. Introduction
   A. There are five "flavors" of business organization currently allowed under the laws of most states: the sole proprietorship, the general partnership, the limited partnership, the regular (or C) corporation, the S corporation (or Subchapter S corporation), and the limited liability company (or LLC). Most states also allow limited liability partnerships (or LLPs).
   B. There is no one perfect way to organize your business; each "flavor" involves certain trade-offs, and only you can weigh the pros and cons to determine which one is right for you.

II. The Sole Proprietorship
   A. This is what you are right now—a solitary human being engaged in a trade or business.
   B. *What's good about a sole proprietorship?*
      1. You don't need a lawyer to set up a sole proprietorship; there are no start-up costs.
      2. The only required piece of legal paperwork is a trade name or fictitious name certificate—and this only if you are doing business using a name other than your own name (you file this in the city or town clerk's office in each town or city in which you maintain an office).
      3. Taxes are easy, too: You fill out Schedule C on your Form 1040 and pay taxes at your individual rate.
   C. *What's bad about a sole proprietorship?*
      1. You have unlimited personal liability for every business mistake you make—you breach a contract, you lose your house; you get into a traffic

accident (that's not covered by insurance), you lose your house; you bake cookies that make people sick, you lose your house.

2. You can limit this risk by buying an umbrella liability policy, but this can get expensive, depending on the nature of your business.

III. The General Partnership

A. A general partnership is formed when two or more sole proprietors agree to pool their resources and—this is the key—share profits and losses from the business (i.e., if two or more lawyers share office space and refer clients to each other but render separate bills for their services and keep what the client pays them, this is not a partnership; if they render a joint bill for their services and split the profits fifty-fifty, that's a partnership).

B. *What's good about a general partnership?*

1. It's easy to form and there are no start-up costs; you don't need a written partnership agreement (legally) to form a general partnership—you can do it with a handshake (of course, if you do so, there will be a lot of unresolved questions that may have to be resolved in the courts, which is why most people have a written partnership agreement even if the law does not specifically require one).

2. Taxes are easy, too: The partnership files an information return on Form 1065 but pays no taxes—each partner pays taxes on his/her pro rata share of the partnership's profits at his/her individual tax rate. If the sole partners of a partnership are a husband and wife, you may not have to file Form 1065—instead you would file Schedule "C" on your Form 1040 each year. Ask your accountant about this, however—some accountants will recommend you file Form 1065 anyway.

C. *What's bad about a general partnership?*

1. You have unlimited personal liability, the same as a sole proprietorship, but with a twist: If A and B are partners, and B runs someone over with his car while on partnership business, both A and B lose their houses, even though A had nothing to do with the accident. Lawyers call this *joint and several* liability.

2. Partnerships have what tax lawyers call a *phantom income* problem, in that the partners have to pay taxes on their pro rata shares of the partnership's profits, even though the partnership did not pay them cash to pay the taxes with.

IV. The Limited Partnership

A. A limited partnership is a partnership with two tiers, or classes, of partners: *general partners,* who have unlimited personal liability for the things they do (or don't do) while on partnership business, and *limited partners,* who are liable only for the money they contribute (or pledge to contribute) to the partnership.

B. Because relatively few operating businesses—businesses that provide products or services—use the limited partnership form, this outline won't go into the details (the limited partnership is, however, an excellent vehicle for certain passive investment types of business, such as real estate investment or oil and gas exploration).

C. Basically the "what's good" and "what's bad" aspects of limited partnerships are the same as they are for general partnerships, with the differences that (1) only the general partners have unlimited personal liability, (2) limited partners cannot participate in the management or operation of the limited partnership's business without becoming a general partner (and therefore "going naked" for anything bad that happens), and (3) limited partnerships are more complex than general partnerships and require more paperwork and legal expense. Lawyers like limited partnerships.

V. The Regular, or C, Corporation

A. A corporation, unlike a partnership, is a taxable entity—when you form a corporation it is as if you have had a baby, with the difference that the baby pays taxes from the day it's born.

B. It's called a C corporation because it is taxed under Subchapter C of the Internal Revenue Code of 1986 (you had to ask).

C. *What's good about a C corporation?*

1. You have limited liability—generally, the owners of a C corporation (called *shareholders* or *stockholders*) are liable only for the amounts they contribute (or agree to contribute) as capital to the corporation, but they are still liable for their own negligence or stupidity.

Example 1: A and B are shareholders of ABC Corporation. A runs over someone with his car while on the corporation's business. The injured party may sue the corporation and win a judgment up to the amount of the corporation's assets (because that's all it has). The injured party may sue A in his/her individual capacity and take A's house away. But the injured party cannot sue B in any way unless it can be shown that B contributed actively in some way to his/her injury (for example, by serving A too much liquor, which caused A to be intoxicated at the wheel).

Example 2: A and B are shareholders of ABC Corporation. ABC Corporation enters into a contract with a supplier to buy ten thousand widgets, and then discovers that it doesn't have enough money to pay for the widgets. ABC Corporation breaches the contract, and the supplier sues. The supplier may sue the corporation and win a judgment up to the amount of the corporation's assets, but the supplier cannot sue either A or B, even if A or B actually signed the contract as an officer or employee of ABC Corporation.

D. *What's bad about a C corporation?*

1. They are expensive to form—legal expenses and filing fees are usually between $1,000 and $1,500 to form a corporation in most states.
2. They are expensive to keep alive—if a corporation fails to pay taxes for *x* consecutive years or fails to file a report (and pay a fee) every *y* years with the secretary of state's office, the attorney general comes along and dissolves the corporation (and your limited liability along with it). To add insult to injury, you are not informed that this has been done, so you continue blissfully in business, thinking you have a corporation when you really don't.
3. If you don't use the corporation and treat it with respect, you lose the corporation; people suing you for something your corporation did will always try to argue they didn't know they were dealing with a corporation—if you conducted business in your own name, writing checks from your own checking account and accepting money in your own name that should have gone to the corporation, you can't argue it was really the corporation that should be sued and not you personally. Lawyers call this "piercing the corporate veil."
4. It requires lots of paperwork. When you have a corporation, you don't do anything; the corporation does everything. This means that for a corporation to do anything, the shareholders (that's you) have to prepare written documents (called *resolutions* or *minutes*) authorizing the directors of the corporation (again, that's you) to do the thing, and the directors have to prepare written documents authorizing the officers of the corporation (again, that's you) to do the thing. Resolutions are a pain in

the neck, but if you don't do them, you will be tempting the courts to say that you didn't treat your corporation with the proper respect so that creditors are allowed to get at your personal assets.

5. Taxes—because corporations are taxable entities, they pay taxes (albeit at a lower rate than you do yourself, in most cases); this means that any income a corporation earns is taxed twice.

   Example: XYZ Corporation has two stockholders, A and B, and makes $100 in net income for a particular year. The corporation pays 15 percent to Uncle Sam as federal income tax and books the remaining $85 as net after-tax earnings. XYZ Corporation then resolves (remember those minutes?) to pay A and B the $85 in the form of a dividend and distributes $42.50 each to A and B. Both A and B have to report that $42.50 as income on their respective 1040 forms for the year and pay taxes on that $42.50 at their individual rate. The result? If A and B are in the top tax bracket, that $100 in corporate income has dwindled to about $26 in each of A's and B's hands after federal income taxes. Add state and local taxes to this calculation, and the tax bite becomes much larger.

VI. The S Corporation

A. An S corporation is the same as a regular, or C, corporation, with one important difference: It is not taxed by the federal government. This means that the S corporation is taxed just like a general partnership, but with the powerful advantage that stockholders in an S corporation have limited liability.

B. Some states and municipalities (such as New York City), however, do not recognize S corporations. This means that S corporations with offices in such states are taxed twice at the state level.

C. *What's good about an S corporation?* The same things that are good about a regular, or C, corporation.

D. *What's bad about an S corporation?* The same things that are bad about a regular, or C, corporation (except the tax part), with a couple of additions:

   1. Because S corporations are taxed like partnerships, S corporations have the phantom income problem (if you've forgotten what this was, look under III.C., "What's bad about general partnerships," in this outline).
   2. S corporations have lots of icky little rules that you have to comply with if you don't want to be taxed as a regular, or C, corporation. (Note: If the

IRS takes away your S corporation status, you don't—repeat don't—lose your limited liability; the worst thing that happens is that you're taxed as a regular, or C, corporation.) For example, you can't have anything but natural human beings as stockholders in an S corporation (forget parent-subsidiary arrangements), you can't have more than one hundred stockholders, all shareholders must be U.S. citizens or green card holders, and so forth.

3. S corporations file different forms with the IRS than regular, or C, corporations do, and they have to report certain items of income differently. It is virtually impossible to operate as an S corporation without a darned good accountant. Both accountants and lawyers like S corporations.

VII. The Limited Liability Company

A. The limited liability company, or LLC, has become the most popular alternative for small business formations since the IRS approved it in 1988. Virtually all states allow LLCs in some form.

B. What is an LLC? Well, it's basically an S corporation without all the icky little rules that make S corporations unattractive for a lot of folks.

C. *What's good about LLCs?*

1. Owners of an LLC (called *members*) have limited liability—if A and B are members of an LLC and B runs someone over with his car while on LLC business, B may lose his house, but A will not lose her house unless A actively contributed to the injury.
2. Like partnerships, LLCs are simple to operate—there is no need to prepare resolutions or minutes to authorize people to do things (although banks and some other folks may still require you to do resolutions because they haven't gotten the idea yet); they just do them.
3. The costs of starting up an LLC are likely to be much less than those of forming a C corporation or an S corporation.
4. LLCs are taxed like partnerships, so there is no double taxation of an LLC's income.
5. If you are doing a lot of overseas business, the LLC format may give you an edge over your competition. Most foreign business organizations (such as the German GmbH and the Italian S.r.l.) are a lot closer in structure to an LLC than they are to a partnership or corporation; with an LLC you can give your managers the same titles as their European or

Asian counterparts (Europeans especially cannot understand that in America, you can be a director of a corporation and have absolutely no power to bind the corporation; in Europe, business organizations are managed by their directors, not by officers or mere employees).

D. *What's bad about LLCs?*

1. There is really not a lot that's bad about LLCs—although they are not perfect, LLCs are the closest thing to a perfect business organization the law has come up with to date.
2. Because LLCs are taxed like partnerships, they have the phantom income problem (if you've forgotten what this was, look under III.C., "What's bad about general partnerships," in this outline).
3. There are restrictions on what you can and cannot do if an LLC has employees—for example, you may not be able to claim 100 percent deductibility for health insurance premiums.
4. It may be difficult for existing businesses to convert to LLCs. Corporations and their shareholders incur double taxation upon liquidation, while general and limited partnerships formed to acquire or hold title to real estate (as many are) may incur transfer taxes and other fees upon converting to an LLC.
5. If your business is high-tech or seeks outside capital within the first twelve to eighteen months of operations, be aware that many investors (wrongly) associate LLCs with "small business, mom-and-pop, no growth potential." While this perception is unfair, it is widespread, and you may want to consider becoming a C corporation instead (preferably in a high-visibility state like Delaware).
6. The LLC structure is not recommended for businesses that have a physical location in New York. When New York adopted its LLC statute in 1994, it included a burdensome "publication" requirement that drives up the costs of forming a New York LLC. While this requirement has been challenged in court, it may be a while before there's a resolution. In the meantime, it may actually be less expensive to form a corporation or S corporation in New York than an LLC! Also, keep in mind that LLCs located in New York City are subject to that city's unincorporated business tax.
7. A growing number of states are imposing special taxes or "minimum taxes" on LLCs and other unincorporated business organizations. For

example, Connecticut requires both domestic and foreign LLCs to pay an annual tax of $250, whether or not they make money.

VIII. So Why Should I Even Consider a Corporation?

The LLC is wildly popular right now, but the corporation is far from dead. You should consider a corporation instead of an LLC when:

A. *You are paranoid about losing your house to a business creditor.* Just like a corporation's shareholders, LLC members enjoy limited liability for the LLC's debts, obligations, acts, and omissions. Because LLCs are so new, however, this protection has not been tested in the courts to the same extent that it has for corporations. In extremely horrendous cases, it is possible that courts might be tempted to pierce the veil and subject LLC members to personal liability. So if you are engaged in a high-risk business activity (such as child care), you may want to consider a corporation, just to be safe.

2. *You expect to have a lot of employees very soon.* While an LLC can have employees just like a corporation, there are limits to the types of deductible benefit plans and other perks you can set up for your employees. For example, under current law, an LLC with more than one member cannot set up a 401(k) plan. Corporations, on the other hand, can deduct just about all employee-related expenses.

3. *You expect to have a lot of health-related issues in the near future.* Unlike corporate officers and employees, LLC members cannot deduct amounts they are reimbursed for medical and health-related expenses.

4. *You plan to seek venture capital very soon.* When sophisticated or professional investors see the "LLC" designation after a company name, they tend to think "small time, mom-and-pop, will never grow big." This is a false view, as there is nothing in the law to prevent an LLC from growing big or even eventually going public. The bias against LLCs, however irrational, is strongly felt within the investment community. Accordingly, a new business that plans to seek venture capital or private equity funding (*angel money*) within the first one to two years of its existence should be set up as a corporation, preferably in a state like Delaware that offers a number of advantages to venture capital–backed companies.

5. *You hate paying quarterly estimated taxes.* LLC members, like all other self-employed people, are required to estimate and pay their federal and state income, withholding, Social Security, Medicare, and other taxes in quarterly

installments. If you are worried that you will not be disciplined enough to make these payments when they become due, you may want to consider forming a Subchapter S corporation and making yourself an employee of the corporation. That way, although you won't save much on taxes, you can receive a regular paycheck and have taxes taken out of each paycheck, just like the good old days, and you won't have to worry about not having enough cash in the bank to make a large quarterly estimated tax payment.

6. *You hate paying Social Security and Medicare taxes.* LLC members, like all other self-employed people, must pay self-employment tax consisting of income, Social Security, Medicare, and other taxes. By forming an S corporation and making yourself an officer or employee of the corporation, you may be able to separate your compensation into two pieces: your salary as an officer (which will be subject to income, Social Security, Medicare, and other taxes) and the remaining share of profits (which will be subject only to income taxes). For example, if your Subchapter S corporation has net income of $200,000 this year, you may be able to treat $120,000 as salary and $80,000 as *passive* income. Although you will have to pay Social Security and Medicare taxes (about 15.8 percent) on the $120,000 salary portion, you will pay only income taxes (not Social Security or Medicare taxes) on the $80,000 passive portion. This is very tricky, however, and your accountant should tell you the best way to do this to avoid triggering an IRS audit.

IX. Limited Liability Partnerships (LLPs)

A. Limited liability partnerships, or LLPs, are allowed in a growing number of states; while theoretically any business can operate as an LLP, this form of organization is best suited to lawyers, doctors, accountants, and other professional practices, and to existing general partnerships that wish to achieve limited liability status with a minimum of legal expense.

B. An LLP is a general partnership in which the partners have limited liability for the acts and omissions of the other LLP partners; an LLP partner is always liable for his or her own negligence or willful misconduct.

C. An LLP partner also enjoys limited liability for contracts he or she signs on behalf of the LLP.

D. An existing general partnership that converts to an LLP can continue to use its existing partnership agreement, usually without significant modification. This is an advantage for older partnerships that may have lengthy, detailed partnership agreements that the partners do not wish to renegotiate at the present time.

E. In practice, LLPs are best suited to professional practices, particularly those with offices in two or more states (such as the so-called Big Five accounting firms). In some states, professionals are not allowed to conduct business in corporate or LLC form. By reorganizing as an LLP in each state where it does business, a multistate professional practice complies with local laws, ensures consistent accounting and tax treatment in all states where it does business, and provides at least some limited liability protection for its partners.

IX. Conclusion

A. As we said at the beginning, there is no perfect way to organize your business activities. Each of the "flavors" discussed in this outline has pros and cons, and most lawyers will want to spend some time learning about your business plans before recommending that you consider one or another.

B. Generally, the less you are concerned about limiting your liability, the less legal complexity and hassle you will be forced to live with. The more you are concerned about limiting your liability, the more complexity and hassle you will live with, and will have to learn to live with.

C. A good lawyer is someone who doesn't just form the corporation and then leave you to figure out the rest; a good lawyer is a good teacher, who helps you figure out how to do the paperwork, keep the records, and otherwise avoid making the dumb mistakes that can get you into trouble.

Index